The Puzzles of Childhood

Manning Clark was born in Sydney in 1915. He was educated at Victorian State schools and at Melbourne Grammar School, and then at the Universities of Melbourne, Oxford and Bonn. He taught at schools in England and Australia, and at the Universities of Melbourne, the Australian National University, Duke University and at Harvard. He first taught Australian history at Melbourne in 1946; this was to be his ruling passion until he retired from the Australian National University at the end of 1974.

Other books by Manning Clark:

A History of Australia (6 vols, 1962–87)
Meeting Soviet Man (1960)
A Short History of Australia (1963) (revised illustrated edition 1986)
In Search of Henry Lawson (1978)
Occasional Writings and Speeches (1980)
Collected Short Stories (1986)

Manning Clark

The Puzzles of Childhood

Penguin Books

Penguin Books Australia Ltd
487 Maroondah Highway, P.O. Box 257
Ringwood, Victoria 3134, Australia
Penguin Books Ltd
Harmondsworth, Middlesex, England
Viking Penguin Inc.
40 West 23rd Street, New York, NY 10010, USA
Penguin Books Canada Limited
2801 John Street, Markham, Ontario, Canada L3R 1B4
Penguin Books (N.Z.) Ltd
182-190 Wairau Road, Auckland 10, New Zealand

First published 1989 by Viking
Reprinted 1989
Published in Penguin, 1990
10 9 8 7 6 5 4 3 2 1

Typeset in 11/13 Berkeley Old Style by Midland Typesetters, Maryborough, Vic.
Made and printed in Australia by Australian Print Group, Maryborough, Vic.

CIP

Clark, Manning, 1915-
The puzzles of childhood.
ISBN 0 14 013937 0.
1. Clark, Manning, 1915- . 2 Historians - Australia
Biography. I. Title.
994.007202

For Dymphna

Contents

We shall not cease from exploration
And the end of all our exploring
Will be to arrive where we started
And know the place for the first time.

T. S. ELIOT, 'Little Gidding'.

Preface

This book records what lives on in my memory. It is not based on research into the history of either my mother's or my father's family. It makes some use of the material collected for *A History of Australia*. It may help to explain my choice of themes for that history. Who knows? It is my memory of what happened, my memory being my way of moving out of the darkness into the light. The names of the people cited in the text are not fictitious. Other people may have different memories of the same events. It is about all those things which I never forget.

I would like to thank Susan Ryan for encouraging me to start. I have always enjoyed working with her. I would also like to thank Ros Russell for her help, and Pat Dobrez, Alison Clark, Don Baker, David Malouf, Bill Gammage, Ken Inglis and Humphrey McQueen for their advice. I must also thank Jack Randell for help in Kempsey.

Manning Clark
Canberra
3 March 1989

My Father

My memories of childhood are like a still-life painting: there is no movement. I live always with such pictures in my mind. One is of my father, the other of my mother. Some time early in 1919, I do not remember the day, the week or the month, I am sitting on the back lawn of our house in Park Road, Burwood, New South Wales. I look up and I see a man smiling at me. It is my father. He has just returned from the war. I do not remember how I felt on first seeing him, or what happened immediately after I saw him. I remember he smiled. It was not until I was nearly forty that I had any idea of what he had to live through in his life. It took over sixty years before I would view him with the eye of pity and the eye of love. By then I wanted to speak to him and say I now understood what had happened. By then it was too late: his body was rotting in the grave in Box Hill cemetery. I had failed to be aware of how much he had suffered.

Another scene haunts me. I am again sitting on the lawn in the back yard at Burwood ('Why are you always by yourself, Mann dear?', I still hear my mother ask). There is a huge iron bird in the sky. My mother tells me it is an aeroplane piloted by Keith and Ross Smith. They have flown all the way from England to Australia. It is December 1919, and I am four and a half years old. I make a remark to my mother. I do not remember what I said, but I remember what *she* said: 'Mann, dear, you are a very special boy. There's nothing you can't do, if you want to do it.' I remember that remark now, because all my life there was to be a gap between my mother's estimate of my capacity and character and the estimate of others. My mother knew the innocent me. My mother was a believer. Others saw something quite different.

I recall one other still-life scene from the days when we lived in Park Road, Burwood. My brother and I are sitting under the billiard table, which my mother's parents had given to my father and mother as a wedding present. When not in use the table was covered with a cloth which reached down to the carpet on all four sides. Under the table was our indoor cubby house. My brother and I were clinking glasses together. My mother lifted one part of the table cover, and asked, 'What on earth do you boys think you are doing?' My brother said not a word. I said, 'We're doing what Dad and Uncle Herman do when you're not here.' I had betrayed my father. I recall now my mother's face, wearing one of those expressions I wished then and wish now I had never seen, the expression of a woman who had been let down. I see her now in what I came to know as her unhappy pose, the chin cupped in the left hand, the mouth half-open, as though it were about to say one of those things which were to trouble me so much in life: 'There are things in my life, Mann dear, I hope you will never know anything about.' (She does not say that then, that was to come later.) I remember the expression on my father's face, the expression perhaps of fear. I did not know then that this still-life scene, my first role as both a betrayer and a betrayed, was my introduction to one of the puzzles of childhood: why was my mother always so worried, why was my father often so angry?

My father was born on 21 August 1881 at 86 Hudson Road, Plumstead, London. My father was a romantic. He always told me he was born at Shooters' Hill. In my childhood I heard much about my mother's family: I heard very little about my father's family. Although he was only two when he and his father, his mother and his baby sister Alice migrated to Australia, he always spoke of Shooters' Hill as though that were the one place where he had been happy. In childhood I never understood why my father needed this fantasy world of Shooters' Hill, the place where his heart was turning ever. I had no idea then why he comforted or deluded himself with the memory of a time of innocence. Those were the years of the gigantic cover-ups, the years when a man nursed his guilt in silence. All I knew as a child was the fright and the puzzle of living with a man who spoke with such loving kindness, who wanted to be kind to everyone, but who exploded into rages.

His father was a blacksmith, who was proud of not belonging to the unskilled working class. He belonged to the respectable working class, the class which feared God and honoured the King, the class which accepted the world as it was and did not entertain any hopes of anything better. He was an acceptor: he was a deferrer. All his life he called those above him on the social ladder Mr or Mrs or Sir. He never called them Governor or Guv. He was no cheeky Cockney boy or larrikin. He had his own dream about the glorious past of his own family, just as my mother's family had their dream of a glorious past. He told his family he was descended from one of the Spanish naval officers who had swum ashore after the defeat of the Spanish Armada in 1588. He sat in a chair and surveyed the scene in a working-class parlour in Sydney with the haughtiness of a Spanish hidalgo.

He cultivated the dignity of the skilled worker. He wore a suit every Sunday of his adult life. He accepted St Paul's principle that the man was the head, and the woman the heart of the family. He was a prude in front of women – believing their ears should not be affronted by coarse language. I never heard him tell dirty stories when the women-folk were not there, or snigger when men discussed 'country matters'. I had the impression that one did not take such liberties in the presence of my grandfather. Yet, like my father, he enjoyed a joke about the gentry, those who, he once told me without either malice or bitterness, 'belonged to your mother's class'.

His wife, née Jane Ann Logan, was Protestant Irish from Tipperary. 'My dear old mother, boy, was Irish', my father used to say. He did not tell me very much about her: she played the piano; she taught in schools. She had inherited from her family the prudery of the Protestant Irish. I remember she always wore black dresses, sat in dark rooms, on one wall of which there was always a painting of the Crucifixion, again in sombre colours, the expression on the face of the Saviour being not of triumph over death but of resignation. Christ, she used to say in the voice of a woman who did not expect much from human endeavour, came into the world to save sinners. As a boy I got the impression she did not believe human beings could do much to help themselves. She believed in asking the Saviour for help.

She had four children, my father followed by three daughters. So my father grew up in the company of four adorers. Perhaps that was why in later years, when I began to think about the tragi-comedy of my father's life, I put into my wallet a photo of him in clerical dress, the only man in a room with eight women. I also put into

3

the wallet a photo of my mother as a child, and one of my mother at the age of twenty-five before life changed her beauty of face and figure.

In the late 1870s and early 1880s there was a depression in the Arsenal district of London, and the future of skilled tradesmen looked bleak. My grandfather decided to migrate to Australia. It has been said that people may change the sky above them, but not their soul, when they cross the seas. My grandfather, always a law unto himself, changed his trade; he became a builder after they arrived in Sydney in 1883. He made one other change. He became a house-owner. He bought a house in Brown Street, St Peters, and became a *petit-bourgeois* property-owner, a man with a stake in the land. His family was respectable. They did not waste their substance or their savings in the bars of St Peters. They went to the Church of St Peter, Cook's River, each Sunday. That was a strand in the web of fate. My mother's great-uncle, James Samuel Hassall, had once been a curate at St Peter's not long after its design by Edmund Blacket and its consecration by William Grant Broughton. My father knew nothing about the Marsdens, the Hassalls or the Hopes when, as a small boy, he was enchanted by the Reverend James Napoleon Manning, the Vicar of the Church of St Peter, Cook's River – a spell-binder in those days when men with such gifts found an outlet for their talents in the pulpit rather than on the stage, in the classroom, the lecture theatre, or the political forum. Fate was beginning to entwine my father with my mother's world.

There were other things in life than being entranced by the Reverend Mr Manning. There was fishing in Cook's River with a bent pin for a hook, and string for a line. There he could dream on the banks of that river, or under the bridge on the Great South Road, about a life away from all the skimping and scraping his 'dear old mother' had to practise. He was being lured towards a life free of the sneers and ridicule to which he was exposed in the streets of St Peters. Being a Reverend, Mr Manning would shield him from the mockers who called him a sissy, and those women who made the painful remarks about him being a 'mother's boy' and 'mummy's little darling'.

As a boy in St Peter's church my father was entranced when Mr Manning told the congregation that in the world they must expect tribulation and sorrow. He was not quite sure he understood such words, but he hoped Mr Manning meant release from all the things he (my father) found so painful. Christ was offering an escape from the bullies, the ones he could not charm – the ones who did not recognise what was in him, those gifts his mother detected in him, which made her Charlie a very special person. This was no training in or preparation for the ordeals to come. It was an inducement to look always for the escape hole, to seek protection in buffoonery, and consolation in the woman's world as the world in which talents were inflated and character not up for examination. That was the 'cubby' his mother provided for him.

From hints he dropped to me just before his death I gathered he discovered to his pain that a man was not safe even in the woman's world. Men said the wounding things, women 'drew character sketches'. What he did not foresee was that a man searching for consolation might transgress against the lore of the tribe to which he belonged. The Christ Mr Manning preached about taught his followers to forgive transgressors at least seventy times seven. The straiteners of Australian suburbia, he was to find, never forgave and never forgot.

He was like that himself. He never forgave, and he never forgot. So it was not surprising that his favourite verse from the Epistles of St Paul was 'Alexander the coppersmith did me much evil: the Lord reward him according to his works.' But in professing to believe St Paul's precept he was nourishing a delusion about himself. One of the many puzzles about my father was how well he knew himself. My father never acted as though he believed it was God's prerogative to distribute rewards for wrongdoing, or for causing pain to other human beings, yet he was fond of the words '"Vengeance is mine" saith the Lord, "I will repay."'

He himself spent much of his time dreaming over what he would say to the men and women who hurt him. Any insult, any wounding words would mean an almost sleepless night, tossing in the bed, one brilliance following another, until his whole mind and body were enslaved to the fevers of revenge, and my mother would ask 'Why are you so restless tonight, Charlie?' And my father would reply, 'I'm thinking about the sermon for next Sunday.' My father, for a reason I did not understand in childhood, dared not risk letting my mother see what manner of man he was. That would only invite yet another character sketch, more wounds, more tossing in the bed with the brain coming up with words to soothe the pains in the heart, words he knew he would never use except in anger – and if he did, that

5

would only make the situation worse. All that was in the future, his behaviour as a child only foreshadowed his fate as a man.

He was looking for a place where he would not be hurt. He also wanted to get on. Fame was the thing. He could not be expected to know as a child that anyone who sought a refuge was disqualifying himself from getting on: revenge fantasisers died of their own poisons. As a child he did not know that anyone who dwelt inwardly on the dark side of the heart would never find a cure for his own infirmity. He did not know that there was no forgiveness for a man who had spent his life indulging in the fantasies of revenge. Revenge was a mortal sin. The Catholics acknowledged that. The Protestants, to their cost, had concentrated on other sins, especially the sins of the flesh, the sins no man could help committing.

Humour was an anodyne. Perhaps that was why he used to say so often, 'At least we can all have a good laugh.' He laughed a lot in childhood, and all his life he laughed about the foibles and the follies of other people. As a child he had an unerring eye for the weak spot in the armour of other children. He remembered all his life comic scenes from childhood. He was always a brilliant story-teller.

'When I was a child, boy,' he would tell me later, 'the dentists' waiting rooms were filled with drunks. That was in the days before injections to deaden pain. The clever customers among the dentists, boy, always had their surgeries near a hotel – the places where you could buy a few glasses of "sarsaparilla" [as he pronounced it] for two or three pence – enough, boy, to make goodnight a certainty.' 'I wish you wouldn't talk like that to Manning, Charlie', my mother would say. 'He's not like the other children.' And my father, who never liked being interrupted, would reply, 'God spare me days, woman, I ought to be able to decide for myself what I will say to the boy.' He would continue, 'As I was saying, boy, the surgeries were full of drunks.' When he paused my mother would drop the remark that they were not all like that. Where she had grown up as a child the men in dentists' waiting rooms behaved like gentlemen. There it was again. My father and mother came from different classes.

Mr Manning taught him something else about Christ: Christ had the power to draw all manner of men unto him. So, if a man became like Christ, people would adore him, people would acclaim him. He would be the centre of attraction. He would have a fame the money-changers knew nothing about, a fame in the hearts of men and women. He would be loved – that was the one big thing. By becoming a servant of Christ a man might escape the sneerers and the mockers. Working for Christ, saving souls for Christ, would be something like that which his mother was doing in her school in St Peters: he and she would be working together to teach men, women and children that human beings did not return to the dust from which they came; human beings had the life of the world to come. By man had come death: Christ had overcome death. Christ had overcome the two fears of my father – the fear of death and the fear of other people, not of all other people, because he was a lover of many, a reacher-out, an embracer. My father feared those who were hard of heart, those who derided him, those who said the wounding words if he came near.

What if Christ did not rise from the dead? What if even He, that most perfect being, son of the Father, the one without sin, what if He had not overcome the sharpness of death and opened a Kingdom of Heaven to all believers? I do not know if he was tormented by doubt when he was a child, whether he feared that if Christ did not rise from the dead, if not even He could overcome death, then human beings would tear at each other like wild beasts. With God and Christ there was order. Without God and Christ there was chaos. All I know is that when I was a child he said to me, 'Look, boy, I am as sure of it [the resurrection] as I am of anything living.' But I never knew then, and I do not know now whether he was saying this to stifle a doubt which tormented him all his life. 'When I turned thirty-two, boy, you were not born. For that birthday my dear old mother gave me *The Poetical Works of Alfred Lord Tennyson*. My mother adored me, boy. She wrote in the book her prayer floated to heaven that "His blessings may fall upon you, my son". She knew a thing or two, boy. She knew I could not abide the thought that all of us "end but in being our own corpse coffins". We won't be "swallowed in vastness". I know it, boy. You mark my words. You'll find out one day, boy.' I never did find out. And I wonder now if *he* ever found out.

My father lost in childhood another Great Expectation. As a boy he had listened to the talk in working-class St Peters about a great future for humanity. Labour was the hope of the world. Evil conditions had made people evil – good conditions would make men good, yes, and women too. ('You've got to include the women, boy, or there'll be hell to pay. You mark my words, boy.' I did not know what he was talking about then; I do now.) My father was always an enthusiast, always searching for a world in which he would be safe. The idealists in the new Labour Movement held out such a promise. By the time my father was ten, George Black was telling the New South Wales Legislative Assembly that Labour members of Parliament had entered the House to 'make and unmake social conditions'.

My father listened to the George Blacks of St Peters, because, as he was to find out, he was like them. The Reverend Mr Manning gave him a vision of God's throne: the George Blacks of St Peters gave him a vision of harmony in the here and now. There was no need to wait for the world to come. It could all happen now. He did not know then that the George Blacks were the men who could not stop, that those who indulged in emotional extravaganzas often found satisfaction in the arms of women. The great preachers, the great orators, needed lots of 'horizontal refreshment'. Enthusiasts were often sensualists, men for the wine-cup and a woman's body. Enthusiasts for the future of humanity did not practise what they preached. 'When I was young, boy,' my father told me, 'the treasurer of the local branch of the Labour Party tickled the peter for the party funds and imshied off to San Francisco. I have never forgotten it, boy.'

That was what Henry Lawson would have identified as 'the whole bloody trouble' in his life. My father was a divided man. He was attracted to all those who were enlargers of life. He was always uncomfortable in the presence of the straiteners and the frowners, being often their victim, being often the one they selected for their own darker satisfactions. He was never at ease with the self-appointed improvers of humanity. Yet paradoxically he was to join a profession, and be a minister of the Church of England in a diocese which was evangelical in doctrine and puritanical in morals. My father was attracted to the one who had walked beside the waters of Galilee, plucking the ears of the corn, the one who asked his followers to consider the lilies of the field. My father was also attracted to the Christ who spoke harshly to those who rejected him, 'Woe unto thee, Cho-razin! Woe unto thee, Beth-sa-i-da!'

Christ was a fisherman: my father fished all his life. He went fishing with me on the day he had his final stroke. Christ advised his fellow fishermen to launch out into the deep. All his life my father spoke with rapture, with an almost spiritual exaltation of the joys of catching a deep-sea leather-johnny, or a deep-sea bluenose. He was still talking about bluenoses with the same light in the eye on the last day he fished. But there was the rub. He remained all his life a coast-hugger. He fished from the rocks, dropping his line straight over, never casting out into the deep, hoping the big ones he coveted would swim into the kelp attached to the rocks from which he cast his line. That, he found, was like love: it should have happened all the time, but for him it happened, as he would say, 'only once in a blue moon'. He never gave up hoping or trying. He was fishing from the rocks the day the darkness descended.

Fishing was a temporary respite from the world. In the world there could not be a resolution to the divisions within himself. As a child he was attracted by Christ's promises. He always loved the promise that Christ had come so that human beings could have life and have it more abundantly. He loved the talk about life as a banquet, and about the least of the little ones. He liked the words about loving everyone. Christ was a life affirmer, a man with reverence for life, a man who wanted all of us to look at each other with tenderness, with eyes of still laughter. He wanted to reach out to all human beings. But there again was the rub: many of the men and the women, especially the women, in the church at St Peters were straiteners and life-deniers. In the church at St Peters he heard talk about human beings as 'miserable sinners'. The words of the hymns had little, if anything, to do with the picture of Christ he had in his mind:

> Foul I to the fountain fly,
> Wash me SAVIOUR, or I die.

There were all those petitions to Almighty God to save us all from our great folly – all this 'Lord, I am not worthy . . .' He was not aware of the contradiction during the years of innocence, when he bathed in his mother's love and fished in Cook's River, and listened to the clergyman each Sunday morning telling him about Christ. What he did not notice then was that the men and women with whom he was ill at ease, the frowners, the ones who put on black looks when he came near, had a lore of their own. All transgressors against that lore would be punished unmercifully. Christ may have urged all those who truly turned to Him to forgive sinners seventy times seven, but these people never forgave and they never forgot. They recited every Sunday the words of the one prayer Christ had taught them to use, '. . . and forgive us our trespasses, as we forgive them that trespass against us'. He joined in saying those words, not knowing then what was to happen to him. It never occurred to him that he, too, would never forgive those that trespassed against him.

The Reverend Mr Manning detected the talent. But where could my father go after the primary school at St Peters? Mr Manning knew my father had musical talents, his mother having taught him to read music and to play the piano. My grandfather played the violin, his rendition of the 'Londonderry Air' and Liszt's 'Träumerei' being his response to the larrikins of St Peters. So Mr Manning suggested my father should apply for admission to the Choir School of St Andrew's Cathedral in Sydney, a school founded by Bishop Barker to the greater glory of God and to introduce Sydneysiders to the civilising and refining influences of English church music. In 1892, at the age of eleven, my father became a pupil of the school and a member of the choir of St Andrew's Cathedral.

He joined in singing the responses, the Benedictus, the Te Deum, the Magnificat, the Nunc Dimittis, the Psalms, the hymns and the anthems. The music and the words which it adorned strengthened the hopes planted in his mind during the services at St Peter's. Once again he heard of a world where a man was safe. He was wafted away into another world. There were the words of the Nunc Dimittis, sung unaccompanied by all the choir-boys: 'Lord, now lettest Thou thy servant depart in peace, according to Thy word.' Then, to a crescendo on the organ, and the men's voices rising in volume with the organ, there were those comforting words, those words about that other world: 'For mine eyes have seen Thy salvation, which Thou hast prepared: before the face of all people.' Then there were the responses to the prayers: 'For Thou alone makest us to live in safety.' There was the constant reassurance in the Psalms that God was on the side of his people, expressed with such comfort in the words: 'The Lord of Hosts is with us. The God of Jacob is our refuge.' The followers of Christ were on the side of the winners. It was like a football game in which your side was bound to win, having at least two (and possibly three, if the Holy Ghost were counted) unbeatable players.

My father wanted to remain part of that world. One way to do that was to study for holy orders in the Church of England. That meant studying for a Diploma in Theology at Moore College, Sydney. He was admitted to the College on 6 April 1904. He sat for the Oxford and Cambridge Preliminary Examination in October 1906, and failed in Ecclesiastical Latin. He passed the Moore College post exám in that subject, and received the Moore College certificate in theology. Archbishop Saumarez Smith ordained him a deacon in December 1906, and a priest on 22 December 1907. His mother was delighted, his father proud. His three sisters, Alice, Pearl and Ruby, thought their brother Charlie had won a place in a better world than the world in and around St Peter's. Their Charlie was on the way up.

They had no idea of the conflicts inside my father's mind. To them he was the one who knew the answers. He always used the language of certainty when he spoke to them. 'Alice [or Pearl or Ruby]' – though he always said later Alice was his favourite sister – I'm as sure of it as I am sure of anything living.' They believed him. Their Charlie knew. But inwardly my father was already tormented by doubts – not doubts about the truth of the Christian religion, or the claims of the Church of England to be a true member of the Church Christ had inaugurated. At least he always protested he was as sure of both of those propositions as he was of anything living. He often upset my mother by seeming to defer to Catholic bishops. No, the trouble was that at Moore College he found he had to keep quiet about things that meant a lot to him. He had to live a double life: as a conformer to the teaching and way of life of an evangelical theological college, and the inner life of a man who sensed even then that much in their behaviour could not be reconciled with Christ's offer of enjoying life more abundantly.

There was alcohol. The Warden of the College, the Reverend Mr Jones, and other members of the teaching staff cited all those spoil-sport remarks in the Old Testament about the evils of alcohol. The contents of the wine-cup bit like an adder. My father took his stand then, and always, on Christ's first miracle at Cana in Galilee. Christ had given the drinkers more. Christ wanted men and women to be happy. But the men in power, the men in black, said 'No'. My father had to pretend to agree: he had to practise the cover-up. He decided not to fight but to evade, to wear the mask of the conformer, and keep the heart of the *bon viveur*.

He was not an addict, never one of those men who could not stop. He had no 'strange infirmity', no desperate swallowing of whisky, wine or beer to make bearable the otherwise unbearable. For him alcohol was an aid to cheerfulness, a means of cultivating kindliness and feelings of goodwill towards all people. It was his toast to all men (including women) of goodwill, his recipe for peace on earth. But those frowners at Moore College did not see it that way. Perhaps

11

they knew he was not really one of them. My father could never be at ease with the men in black. He could never, never enjoy their approval. All he could hope for was that they did not find out what was going on in his heart. Vain hope. THEY always know. THEY are not fools.

There was another question which came between my father and those in high places in the Diocese of Sydney. They accepted the Pauline–Calvinist–Augustine doctrine of the division between the body and the soul. The body was evil, a corrupter; the lusts of the flesh were sinful. The Catechism made this quite plain. The Apostle Paul had written it into the doctrines of the Church: no fornicator, liar or drunkard could enter the Kingdom of Heaven. So, be on your guard – man's adversary, the devil, prowled around seeking whom he might devour. Christians must resist the sinful lusts of the flesh; Christians must abstain from unlawful sex, just as they must abstain from all intoxicating fluids. My father did not agree. He had read the New Testament, and could find no remark by Christ which censured those who enjoyed the pleasures of the body. True, there was the condemnation of adultery. But Christ, as my father read him, seemed to be on the side of lovers. Christ forgave the woman caught in the act of adultery because she had loved much. Christ enjoyed the company of those through whom the gale of life blew very high.

My father already had in his mind a picture of a life different from the life of the miserables of Moore College. During his College years he read a pamphlet by Annie Besant, an early advocate of birth control. It had a profound influence on his life. He kept it always in a special box containing most of the secrets of his life. His eyes were opened. God, he believed, wanted human beings to enjoy their bodies. The Old Testament acknowledged one of the wonders of the world was 'the wonder of a man with a maid'. No one else in Moore College seemed to share his view. It was like drinking alcohol. On both questions he found it prudent to be an underground man, not to let others know what was in his mind. He believed there must be someone, somewhere, who would understand, someone to whom he could risk showing his view, showing what was going on in his heart. He was learning the hard way that there were very few people to whom he could speak. That was painful, because he was, by nature, a gregarious man. He was a charmer. To be a charmer a man must show what was going on inside him. The mask might slip, and the punishers could then wield the whip. He began to wonder whether there was anyone he could trust, anyone to whom he could confide what was going on inside him. There must be someone, somewhere.

From the stories he told me later about his life in Moore College I gather he made no move to meet people at the University. St Paul's College, the Anglican College, was next door to Moore College. It might as well have been on another planet. The classrooms of the University of Sydney were within walking distance, but my father never entered them. Professor Arnold Wood was in the flowering time of his life; J. Le Gay Brereton would have had much to say to my father; Christopher Brennan was beginning to give those talks which delighted all those who came near. But my father never came near. At Moore College he read the English poets. He loved especially Charles Wolfe's 'The Burial of Sir John Moore – After Corunna', indeed all poems about death. It was as though he feared death might rob a man of his faith. Perhaps that was why one of his recurring incantations was his profession of certainty about Christ's resurrection from the dead: 'That's my favourite subject, boy', he used to say to me, but he always seemed reluctant to explore it in detail.

He read Shakespeare. He loved the words in *Richard III* about treachery. 'Listen to this, boy. Clarence has "passed a miserable night". He has had "fearful dreams", tormented by the knowledge of what he has done . . . You wait, boy, till you reach the age when you cannot live with what you have done . . . when you fear there could never be forgiveness for your past. Then, boy, you will know "ugly sights" in your dreams.' 'I wish you wouldn't speak to Manning like that, Charlie. He's not like the other two. He's a brooder. He's a worrier', my mother said. But my father never heeded my mother's requests. He wanted me to be forearmed. 'Clarence, boy, knew all about the tempest in the soul. Listen to this, boy. This is Clarence in hell. You'll know all about hell one day, boy.'

> 'Clarence is come – false, fleeting, perjured Clarence,
> That stabbed me in the field by Tewkesbury.
> Seize on him, Furies, take him unto torment!'
> With that, methoughts, a legion of foul fiends
> Environed me, and howled in mine ears
> Such hideous cries that with the very noise
> I, trembling, waked, and for a season after
> Could not believe but that I was in hell,
> Such terrible impression made my dream.

I did not know then why my father was so animated when he recited the words: it was as though the words were coming up from somewhere deep inside him. I did not know then that he was using Shakespeare to communicate his own experience of life.

At Moore College he also fell in love with the works of Dickens. He devoured all the emotional extravaganzas in Dickens. 'You wait till you grow up, boy, and read how Sykes killed Nancy.' 'Charlie,' my mother said, 'I wish you wouldn't dwell on the horrors when you're talking to Manning. He already has enough nightmares as it is.' 'And Mr Dorritt, boy, the man who knew all about failure . . . And Mr Micawber, boy, the man who always believed something was going to turn up . . . Listen to this, boy.' He would read one of his favourite speeches by Micawber. 'Charlie,' my mother said, 'I wish you wouldn't read all those passages to Manning where Dickens is laughing at human weakness. All human beings are part of God's creation.' I did not know what she was talking about. I do now.

At Moore College, too, my father discovered in Dickens the other theme which he always wore in his heart of hearts. He discovered the man of compassion, the man who was compassionate to the least of the little ones. My father discovered Tiny Tim and Bob Cratchit, and all the men, women and children, like himself from the working classes, who had compassion for each other. 'Listen to this, boy. It's Bob Cratchit talking. I can never read it boy, without weeping. Anyone who can read the Tiny Tim scene without weeping must have a heart of stone.' Treachery and sentimentality were his two subjects. But he dared not let anyone at Moore College know what moved him to tears. He remembered the words Christ often used: 'See that you tell no man about this.' Don't let anyone know what is going on in your mind. The life-deniers of Moore College took tears as proof of weakness, of being unsteady, unreliable. So did the men in high places in St Andrew's Cathedral. There they did not even have a cross on the altar. It was as though the Christian religion were not about suffering, not about sin and repentance, but about the punishment of transgressors.

At Moore College he also read Longfellow. My father's life was always full of contradictions and paradoxes. There was the paradox of a man of his temperament, his passions, his warmth of heart, studying in such a chilly atmosphere. The lecturers in Moore College believed all enthusiasts had fallen prey to their adversary, the devil. They were the advocates of 'godly quiet'. But my father never was

14

quiet, never could be quiet. He devoured Longfellow's religion of humanity. As a boy of thirteen he was given *The Poetical Works of Henry Wadsworth Longfellow* as a prize for arithmetic. He was not only a man of imagination, a man of passion, he was also a meticulous man. 'I'm a beggar for time, boy', he·used to say. His father always carried a watch in the fob pocket of his waistcoat, and took it out at 12.30 pm every Saturday and Sunday, the time when he expected his dinner on the table. My father was a slave to punctuality. Being punctual was one of his ways of drawing attention to himself. Yet he had all the longings, the hopes, the desires of the dreamer. Longfellow fed those hopes. There was the 'Psalm of Life':

> *Tell me not in mournful numbers,*
> *'Life is but an empty dream!'*
> *For the soul is dead that slumbers,*
> *And things are not what they seem.*
>
> *Life is real! Life is earnest!*
> *And the grave is not its goal;*
> *'Dust thou art, to dust returnest',*
> *Was not spoken of the soul.*

That was my father's great hope – that those who were 'up and doing', those who nourished loving-kindness in their hearts, those who learned 'to labour and to wait' would reap a rich harvest in the life of the world to come. The trouble was his heart was not always filled with loving-kindness. He was not capable of loving those who did him great evil, of blessing those who persecuted him, let alone of forgiving those who had trespassed against him. Tears came to his eyes when he sang the responses during Evensong in St Andrew's Cathedral: 'Give peace in our time, O Lord.' That was what he so desperately searched for all his life – safety; safety from abuse, safety from the character sketch. Love for the whole of God's creation flowed over him: he wanted to embrace everyone, yes, and even forgive everyone. But if any member of the choir, any clergyman, or any woman, criticised him in the vestry after the service – either by making a joke about his appearance or dwelling on some weakness in his character, such as his vanity or his insatiable thirst for applause and praise, for approval (if my father had re-written the Lord's Prayer he would have added the petition 'Give us this day our daily clap'), or any unkind questioning of his sincerity, or his reliability – any one of these remarks would trigger off a sleepless night during which his fevered brain tossed up all sorts of brilliant things he could say next time he met the one who had hurt him. But the trouble with settling scores, he found, was that his last state was often worse than his first. In taking revenge he let his enemies see that the young man in clerical garb was a wolf in sheep's clothing, that the would-be lover of all mankind was himself often consumed with the opposite of love. I doubt whether my father ever knew why he, who had such a warm, loving heart, should be shunned by the people whose approval he coveted all his life.

Perhaps that was why music meant so much to him. It was a balm for hurt minds, hurt hearts. My father played the piano and the organ. Ever since his years in the choir school at St Andrew's Cathedral he had found the organ to be the answer to some of his great hungers. But there too was the rub. He wanted to play Bach's 'Passacaglia in C Minor'. It expressed much of what he felt about life. Years later he had a small organ of his own. 'Listen to this chord, boy,' he would say to me in the years before I found I too needed Bach, needed the same comforter as my father; 'now listen to its resolution.' In childhood that was lost on me, though the memory remains – indeed is so strong in the late autumn of life that I too find comfort and reassurance in Bach. But again nature had been unkind to my father as it was to be unkind to me. He could not himself extract from the organ the might, the majesty and the power of Bach.

Between the desire and the capacity there was a gap. That was just as anger-making as wounding words, just as stern a master in teaching him what manner of man he was. There was the faith of his mother, there was the flattery of those less gifted than he. But there was always that never-ending fear that the recognition he craved was forever out of reach. He was not consumed by the envy of the mediocre: he had to live with the more painful knowledge that he could be brilliant in the company of the mediocre, but was out of his depth if he drifted into the company of the very gifted. He had to settle for the clapping of the men and women (especially the women) who attended church gatherings. In the pulpit he was a spell-binder. After the service he wanted praise, enthusiasm, eulogies, not criticism from the logic-choppers, certainly not any comments from those smart-alecs and know-alls who mocked at his contradictions, or the liberties he took with the laws of logic. 'Never answer them, boy, just give them a smile', he would advise me later.

He believed there must be someone somewhere to whom he could speak. He could speak to a few of his fellow theologues about cricket and football, he could talk to a few about fishing; but there were so many things he did not dare to speak about. The 'Arch' (as he always called an Archbishop, retaining all his life the cheeky deference of the St Peters' working class to those in high places) was pleased with him. The Dean of the Cathedral, the canons and the precentor all prophesied he would go far in the Church. He had all the talents: he was handsome, he was charming, very understanding and gentle with those who were in any way afflicted or distressed in mind, body or estate. He could sing, he could preach, he could teach, he could play cricket. 'Have I ever shown you, boy, how I used to play a late-cut when I played for the Petersham second eleven? Or did I ever show you how Victor Trumper played a leg glance? Watch this flourish of the bat, boy, at the end of the stroke as the ball is about to strike the pickets.'

There was still the search for someone to talk to. He was twenty-six. His mother was always hinting it was time for him to be married. His younger sister Alice already had three children. His sisters chaffed him as a real ladies' man. 'Everyone loves our Charlie', or so they said. But nothing ever happened. Perhaps he was too much a mother's boy. They had no idea of the ferment in his soul, or of the fervour in his search. Early in 1908 Bishop Saumarez Smith offered him the position of curate at St John's, Ashfield. There he met Catherine Amelia Stuart Hope.

Like him, she was a pilgrim for the means of grace. Like him, she believed there was a Kingdom of Heaven for all believers. But there was a difference. My father, Charlie Clark, believed Christ had opened the Kingdom of Heaven to all believers. Katie Hope believed God the Father had opened that Kingdom. Charlie Clark spoke a lot about Christ. Christ was a fisherman. Christ forgave the woman who had loved much. Christ understood that the great sinners were the great lovers. Christ drove the money-changers out of the temple. Christ was not drawn to the 'Marthas' of this world, the ones who were 'much cumbered', the slaves of all the suburban kitchens of Australia, the ones who confounded virtue with the capacity to bake scones, or scrub floors, or rotate the mangle, or wash dishes. Christ praised Mary, the one who nourished the important thing in her heart. Christ loved women. Mary Magdalene was beside him during

17

the agony on the cross: Mary Magdalene, a lover, was one of the few who saw the risen Christ.

Katie Hope called Christ her Saviour, but she never expanded on that, she being no enthusiast for the Christ who had walked by and on the waters of Galilee. She never thought of Christ as a helper, or as the one who understood sinners and those who desperately needed to be forgiven. That was the point. She was a good woman, she was virtuous, she was no sinner. If she needed help she looked to God. She always spoke of the Father: 'I'm going to ask my Father to help me.' She never spoke of Christ in that way. My father knew the Dionysian frenzy, he was a fiery furnace of a man. My mother was an Apollonian, one of the cherubs to whom had been vouchsafed a vision of God's throne.

There must have been a moment when they recognised each other, a moment of awareness, possibly even a moment when they thought their meeting revealed an 'elective affinity'. That was one of the other puzzles of childhood. I did not hear then how my parents met. I do not know even now when they met. I do not know whether there was immediate recognition, or growing awareness. All I know is they met at St John's, Ashfield, early in 1908. On 7 December 1910 they were married by the Reverend Dr S. Yarnold in St John's Church.

My Mother

My mother was a fine flower of patrician and genteel Sydney: my father was a child of the London dockyard and the respectable working-class areas of St Peters. That was one of many differences between them. My mother was a woman of beauty, both of body and soul – not the beauty which stirs the madness in men's blood, but the beauty which the world might soil. Nature had been kind to her. She had a commanding presence; she was gifted. She had acquired all the skills of a woman born into patrician Sydney: she played the piano, she knitted, she sewed, she cooked jam, she baked a roast of beef or mutton with the same inner confidence with which she played a movement in a Beethoven sonata, she played tennis in the decades when ladies served under-arm, wore long white tennis dresses and tucked their handkerchief neatly into a sleeve of their costume. The girdle, if firmly gathered around the waist, could outline the contours of the upper part of the body – but my mother was never one to advertise her body. She believed all she possessed was God's gift to her, that a day would come when she would be required to give an account of her stewardship before the throne of Almighty God. She believed in God, her heavenly Father: she believed in Charles Hope, her earthly father. She loved and feared them both. She had been told that the beginning of wisdom was to love and fear God: she felt the same about her own father. Perhaps part of my father's attraction was the name of Charlie.

Her father, Charles Hope, was the one of whom she was proud. He was the great-grandson of the Reverend Samuel Marsden. In 1846 his father, Dr Robert Hope, had married Catherine Hassall, the daughter of Anne Hassall (*née* Marsden). Anne Hassall was the first-born child of the Reverend Samuel and Eliza Marsden. She was born in a cabin on board the *William*, off the east coast of Van Diemen's Land (now Tasmania) on 2 March 1794. Marsden believed God had chosen him, unworthy though he was of the least of the divine favours, to carry the gospel of His Son to distant lands.

Marsden had his faith. Marsden regularly petitioned God to rescue him from all the follies and sins which flesh was heir to: 'Have pity on us, Lord,' he asked, 'for our great folly' – adding that God alone could make human beings live in safety. On 2 March 1794, as the *William* was being buffeted by the swell rolling up from the Antarctic, Eliza Marsden began to be unwell. That evening the waters from a huge wave washed over their new-born child, Anne Marsden. Marsden was so moved by the miracle of a new life that he wanted to thank someone. He could not thank a human being, he having no faith in man. He dried the child, and then thanked Almighty God for the 'great deliverance' he had brought 'to me and mine'. Marsden had faith in God. He believed in prayer: God would answer. He was my mother's model, my mother's guide on how to behave in all the crises of life.

She, too, prayed to her Father. She, too, had her faith. 'I'm going to ask the Father, again', she would say. She believed He would help: she believed He would save sinners. All her ancestors believed in asking the Father to help them. Anne Marsden, one of the daughters of Samuel Marsden, had 'an interest', as she put it, in God, so that one day she might be 'accounted worthy to join that glorious society above'. God was her insurance policy for the award she coveted, seeing her loved ones 'through all eternity'. Thomas Hassall, the husband of Anne Marsden, asked God to provide the answer to all the big questions. There is a family story that the Reverend Thomas Hassall sought the advice of his father-in-law, Samuel Marsden, on whether or not to accept a call to missionary work on the island of Tahiti, where he had lived as a child after arriving as a babe-in-arms on the mission ship *Duff* in 1796. Marsden told him his predecessor had had his head removed by the natives. Marsden suggested they should ask God for guidance, so these two men dressed in black fell to their knees in St John's vicarage at Parramatta, and besought their God to give them an answer. They were not long on their knees. When they rose Thomas Hassall told his father-in-law God had chosen him to be the vicar of Cobbitty, a parish stretching from Camden to the Darling and the Murray Rivers. Marsden, in my gloss on the story, then thanked his God in the words he had been taught to use: 'Thou art just, O Lord, for Thy ways are revealed!'

All through his life Thomas Hassall continued to ask God for the answers. Each morning and each night he offered up his 'heartfelt acknowledgements' to Almighty God for all the great benefits he had received at His hands. His daughter Catherine, who married Dr Robert Hope in 1846, carried on the tradition of her ancestors. When her baby died in November 1851 she asked God to assure her her baby would be received in Heaven, even though it had been baptised by her husband and not by a clergyman. She believed if she had to trust in her own goodness, neither she nor her baby would get there. That was the whole point in the tradition bequeathed to my mother by her clerical and landed gentry ancestors. God alone could save them from madness and folly. They were weak: God was strong.

My mother did not seem to notice that she had inherited curses as well as blessings from the Marsdens, the Hassalls and the Hopes. Marsden hungered all his life for the blessing of God, and the approval of men in high places. God blessed him with an abundance of worldly goods. The other hunger was never satisfied. There was something about the man which persuaded them not to trust him with high office. In 1824 Lord Bathurst, the secretary of state for the colonies, instructed Wilmot Horton not to 'give any additional trust or authority to Mr Marsden, who I consider a very turbulent Priest, with something more of malignancy in his character than will allow him ever to be quiet, or let other persons be so'. This spitefulness and malice towards those who ill-used him, this taking revenge against those who were displeasing in his sight cheated him of the admiration for which he hungered. The man who made voyages across the Tasman Sea in small sailing boats to bring to the Maoris of the north island of New Zealand the glad tidings of salvation did not enjoy the esteem of his own people. The man who asked God each Sunday to enable him to live in love and charity with all men was never quiet. He possibly never enjoyed that peace of God which passes all understanding.

Marsden believed man was incurably vile. Man could do nothing about such vileness. God could. The vile could be kept in check only by severity of punishment, fear of punishment, and fear of being sent to Hell. The vile could be flogged into submission to the laws of God and the laws of man. A chaplain in New South Wales was one of God's moral policemen; he had the divine command to punish wickedness and vice. For a brief period he was a magistrate, and during that time he sentenced the guilty to the maximum number of lashes for the offence of which they had been found guilty. The victims never forgot: 'God have mercy on our faults, because his reverence has none.' In later years he became a legend as the 'flogging parson'. He saw himself as a severe man: his contemporaries saw him as a cruel man. He was cast in a role, and nothing he ever did, no acts of goodness, kindness, mercy, compassion or forgiveness, would ever change the image. They laughed at him as a hypocrite. The Pharisees among Australian academics still mock him and dismiss him as the 'flogging parson'. Besides, he knew one thing about himself. He could never forgive those who had trespassed against him, even though he asked God each day to forgive him, just as he had forgiven his trespassers. He knew that was untrue, and that too made him 'unquiet'.

My mother knew nothing of the dark side of Marsden's heart, or if she did she never said so in my presence. From the moment I was aware of other people, and able to understand what they were saying, my mother spoke of her Australian ancestors with the words and gestures of a hagiographer. In every generation of her family since 1794 someone was called Marsden. The brother born after her was called Marsden. They had been very close, but he had died before he reached twenty-one. That was a shadow across my mother's path – a shadow which never vanished, to me one of those dreams referred to in 'O God, Our Help in Ages Past'. My mother never questioned why God had taken away her favourite brother. From what she said years later I gathered she wanted to blame herself, and she was puzzled why God should want to punish her. She did not know what she had done to deserve such vengeance from God. But there was worse to come.

In her own oral history of the heroes of her family, as told to me during the twenty-five years when we all too infrequently opened our hearts to each other, she was very selective. She spoke of the Marsdens, the Hassalls, the Oxleys, the Hopes, the Gormans, the Maberly-Smiths and the Hope-Marshalls, with the fervour of a neophyte speaking about salvation. Anne Marsden, who married Thomas Hassall in 1822, was never mentioned. I realise now that if she had been, my mother would have called her 'very peculiar', that being my mother's term for all those who could not pass her eye-of-the-needle test for her fellow human beings. She was lyrical about Thomas Hassall, the 'galloping parson'. 'When you grow up,

Mann dear,' she would say, 'you'll be told he was the vicar of the largest parish over which a clergyman has ever travelled.' I found out later my mother was right – I also found that Thomas Hassall, unlike Samuel Marsden, was greatly loved. No flogger he, no dark side to his heart. Belief and love came naturally to him. He never tormented himself with doubts about whether he would ever be forgiven, whether there was anyone who could forgive him – he had no need of forgiveness. On his death-bed he expressed no longing to be forgiven. He did not ask the members of his family to forgive him, or tell them he was confident God would forgive him. He knew Christ had opened the kingdom of heaven to all believers – he was about to enter that kingdom.

My mother's portrait of her father's father, Dr Robert Culbertson Hope, contained both fact and fiction. He was a man of achievements. My mother dwelt fondly on these. He was born at Lynnburn, Morebattle, Scotland, on 12 May 1812. He took his degree in medicine at the University of Edinburgh on 16 May 1833. In 1837 he and his brothers, George and James, decided to migrate to New South Wales, and on 19 April 1838 he set sail for Sydney on the *Lady Kennaway* from Leith, arriving on 12 August 1838. He practised medicine in Campbelltown from 1838 to 1846. On 12 August 1846 he married Catherine Hassall, one of the daughters of the Reverend Thomas Hassall. George and James overlanded to the Port Phillip District, and took up a squatting run on the Moorabool River near Geelong. George married Mary Ann Hassall on 12 February 1852. George persuaded Robert to join him in partnership, and George settled at Darriwill, Robert nearby at Lynnburn. James fell a victim to what was later known as the 'family complaint' – he became a gentleman drunk.

My mother's account of these events was highly selective. On the younger brother James she had few words to say, and those were very puzzling to me as a boy: 'Your great-uncle James, Mann dear, had a very sad end.' As I grew older she expanded on that a little: 'Your great-uncle James, Mann dear, was so excited when your great-grandfather returned to Melbourne after a trip abroad that he fell off the verandah of the hotel in which he was staying at Williamstown and never recovered.' Years later other members of my mother's family told me, to the accompaniment of that distinctive Hope laugh, 'James suffered from the family complaint.' When James fell out of the window he was in the alcoholic stupor in which he had lived almost ever since he arrived in Australia. James was to be pitied. My mother elevated him from a failure into a victim of family devotion.

My mother was not a liar. Disappointments in her life drove her to paint a picture of her ancestors as heroes and achievers. In real life Dr Robert Hope was Chairman of Committees in the Legislative Council of Victoria in 1864, and again from 1870 until his death in 1878. In real life Dr Robert Hope fell a victim to the Botany Bay disease of melancholia and irascibility. My mother drew a veil over those last years.

She spoke of her own father in the language of idolatry. Here she was on firmer ground. He was born at Lynnburn on 8 March 1855, and educated by tutors and at the Geelong College. In 1870 his father sent him to England to learn the wool trade. He sailed round Cape Horn, the trip taking 110 days. He was then employed by Sanderson, Murray and Co. as a wool sorter at Galashiels in Scotland. He was told the hours of work were 'from sax to sax'. When he asked if he came after breakfast would that do, he was told, 'The hours are frae sax to sax, and if ye dinna like to keep them ye can leave them altogether.' He stayed. He had both the will and the strength to endure. He had the virtues of the upright man, the man whose word was his bond, the man who did not cheat at the card table, the counting-house, or on the golf course.

After making a six weeks' tour of inspection of the woollen mills on the Continent he returned to the antipodes in 1873 to take up the position of assistant wool buyer for John Roberts and Co. in Dunedin, New Zealand. On 7 March 1878 he married Mary Hooper Kettle in Knox Church, Dunedin; the celebrant was the Reverend Dr Stuart. Mary Kettle was the daughter of Charles Kettle, the surveyor who had drawn the plan for the city of Dunedin. On 11 December 1878 my mother was born in Dundas Street, Dunedin. She was christened Catherine (after her father's mother) Amelia (the name of the ship in which Mary Kettle's father arrived in Dunedin) Stuart (after the Presbyterian clergyman). The family moved to Sydney in 1881 to enable her father to enter into partnership with John Sanderson and Company. In 1884 Charles Hope joined the firm of Harrison, Jones and Devlin Ltd, as assistant manager. When that company merged with Goldsbrough, Mort and Co. Ltd, he was again appointed assistant manager, a position he held until his death in May 1932. His colleagues in the wool trade held him in high esteem.

At the graveside they said he was 'white all through' and 'honest to the core'.

In childhood I accepted my mother's history of her own family. When I found out later the gap between her version and the truth I was puzzled why my mother, the soul of goodness, needed a life-lie about her past. I wondered for years why this should be so. Now I believe I know. But now my father and my mother, who probably hoped there would be someone who would understand what they had been through, are dead. I doubt whether anyone was ever allowed to come near my mother. She had been so deeply hurt by certain events that she could not speak to anyone. She could only toss up those painful hints out of the depths of her despair, the words I could never get out of my mind, and still cannot get out of my mind: 'There are things in my life, Mann dear, I hope you'll never know anything about.'

I do now. The knowledge has brought me, late in life, a little peace, a calm after the storm in which I lived for such a long time. I do not know why my mother should have been called on to endure such an ordeal. I do not know why things turned out for her the way they did. There was nothing in her life before the age of twenty-eight which foreshadowed what was to come. In the great lottery of life it looked as though she had drawn many prizes. What I remember was the never-ending litany about her family: 'Your great-great-great-grandfather, Mann, brought Christianity to New Zealand.' 'Your great-great-grandfather, Thomas Hassall, was vicar of the largest parish in Australia.' 'Your great-grandfather, Mann dear, was President of the Legislative Council of Victoria.' 'Your grandfather, Mann dear, is the general manager of Goldsbrough Mort.' During the recitation of the litany my father said not a word. That was one of his rare displays of the will to endure.

She never told me that one of her brothers did yoga exercises in the nude. She never told me that in every generation of her family from Sam Marsden to her own father and his sons there was always the maverick, the half-saint and half-devil, who must be in command, who could only work with 'Yes' men. There was always the one who had the power to attract all manner of men and women unto him, but if they dared to come near they were checked, they were rebuffed. There was always the one who thought he could not be reconciled with his enemies, the one who raged against his critics, yet was capable of the most generous gestures to any enemy who had suffered some loss, or was stricken by a mortal illness. She told me about the wheat, but not about the tares in my inheritance. We have been told there must be both tares and wheat if there is to be a harvest.

At Strathfield my mother's family lived a life of order and decorum. My grandfather, Charles Hope, took the train to the city, worked, lunched, worked, returned by train to Strathfield, ate his dinner, read the paper, and retired. In the weekend he played golf on Saturday, one of his favourite partners being Colonel Arnott of Arnott's Biscuits. My grandmother supervised the work of the maids and the cook; ordered provisions from the butchers, the bakers, the grocers, and the Chinese greengrocers, all of whom called each week; sewed, knitted, crocheted; played the harp; and at night sometimes risked a game of huff-patience with her husband, he not always being polite to members of what he knew to be the 'inferior sex'. She had ten children: my mother, Marsden, Sydney, Thomas, John, Florence, Miriam, Edith, Roberta and Gladys.

The death of Florence cast a shadow over my mother's life. She seemed to find her death inexplicable. An expression of inconsolable grief spread over her face when she spoke about it. 'Florence died, Mann dear.' She would sigh, she would sob, her whole body would shake, tears pouring out of her eyes and down her cheeks as she said 'Perhaps God punished me for being so wicked, Mann dear.' I did not understand then what she was talking about. I wanted her to stop blubbing, because her moments of despair, her breakdown moments, frightened me. The spectre of annihilation was never far from me. I lay awake for hours in the dark after such scenes, till my mother's face would emerge out of the darkness. She would stand beside the bed, her dark hair untied and reaching almost to the small of her back, the hair brushed back off her forehead, uncovering the shapely if forbidding brow, and wearing the nightdress which covered her body from her neck to her ankles. My mother's body was never visible. It was as though her body did not exist, as though she were all spirit. In the dark she always looked spectral, like someone from the spirit world. She tried to calm me down, to drive away my fears, but she had an odd way of doing that. She would say, 'I don't know what's going to happen to you one day, Mann dear, if you don't go to sleep.' And she would stroke my cheek, and kiss me, and tell me she was going to pray again to her Father in heaven. But nothing she said or did ever calmed the uproar in my soul.

I was puzzled by her unhappiness. Nothing I heard later about her own childhood and adolescence provided an answer to the puzzle. At school she was singled out as a woman of promise. She came from the social class which protected her from being the butt of vulgar jokes or wounding words about her family. She attended the Presbyterian Ladies' College at Croydon, a finishing school for the daughters of the patricians of the suburbs. She belonged: she never knew the torments of the outsider. She had talents in all the subjects in which she could exercise her imagination. At Christmas 1895, in her final year at the school, she being then seventeen, she won the first prize for English, history and geography. For her prize she chose a two-volume leather-bound edition of *Macaulay's History of England*. She played the piano. She played lawn tennis, and had a reputation for putting a strong spin on the ball. The family life was equally rewarding. Her brothers and sisters adored her: she was something special. There was always an aura about her, she having the air of authority, always bearing herself with such majesty that most people paused before they risked coming too near.

Of the years between the Presbyterian Ladies' College and St John's, Ashfield, I heard nothing from her while she was alive. They were a ten-year blank, posing questions to which I do not know the answer. There was the decision to work at St John's. That would not have been done to please her father, he being a man of few words on the subject of religion, all of which were unfavourable. He always dismissed Christianity as something which had been finally shoved into the dustbin of human history during the nineteenth century. Her mother rarely left the house, certainly never to attend a religious service. Her older brothers, Syd and Tom, were no God-botherers, Syd at an early age preferring the communion rail of the Wool Exchange Hotel to the communion table at either the Anglican or Presbyterian church. Tom was already showing signs of being what was then called 'mental'. The younger brother, John, was only fifteen when my mother started to teach Sunday School at St John's, and rumour had it that he was just a little bit odd, what with all his jokes against the snivelling low churchmen of Sydney, and his enthusiasm for the ritual and the gorgeous vestments of the Anglo-Catholics.

My mother never needed any intercessory aids to worship. She always spoke straight to God, her heavenly Father, the one who had even fewer words than her earthly father. Yet in 1906, in the year when she turned twenty-eight, she volunteered to teach in the Sunday School at St John's, Ashfield. Her father and her mother were nominal Presbyterians. She had been baptised in Knox Church, Dunedin. Her grandfather, Robert Hope, was a Presbyterian. Why, if not an apostasy, at least a change of denominations? Why offer her talents, her prestige, in the little world of genteel suburbanites, to the service of the life-deniers of Sydney? Like many other patrician families in Sydney the members of her family were creedless Puritans: the faith of the Puritans had gone; the morality remained. How did she acquire a faith?

She never spoke about it: she never uncovered her heart to me on those questions. I wonder now whether she ever told anyone. She could not tell her father, he being a scoffer at all knee-benders and grovellers before the Throne of Grace. She could not tell her mother because she, Mann dear, had the maddening habit of sighing an 'Oh, goodness' whenever she risked telling her anything serious. Her mother was the great conversation-stopper of the family, an incurable Martha, my mother being a Mary of the suburbs. I had the impression my mother had always been a believer, but why this should be so I never understood. My father's attachment to the Church of England was easy to understand, fated though it was to bring him great pain. The Church offered him an escape hatch from the suffocation of working-class St Peters. He believed he was moving out of the darkness into the light. Christ offered him a cure for all the wounds the world inflicted on his sensitive soul: Christ held out the promise of a miracle cure. But my mother did not need any such crutch. She was not possessed by any demons; she bore no grudges; she suffered from no slights; she was never the victim of the bully boys or the bully girls. People did not behave to my mother in that way. She held out no promise to such temperaments that they would find the satisfactions of the tormentor by mocking her. She did not carry in her memory any scenes of her humiliation: she did not understand the motive of revenge, the source of such madness, or the agonies of those, like my father, who spent sleepless nights savouring the insults and punishments they would inflict on their tormentors, on those who despitefully used them.

She did not understand those who had malice, envy, jealousy or spite in their hearts. The avengers puzzled her, she staring at them always with a look of astonishment and incredulity on her face. Yet she left the malicious, the mockers and the haters in no doubt that she saw into the heart of their darkness. Her natural goodness, her inclination to believe what people said, not to doubt men when they promised never to do something again, only stirred up the madness in the blood of those born with such a hell in their hearts. Yet they were always drawn to her, found themselves telling her what went on inside them, perhaps hoping she might redeem them, clean their dirty slate, and restore them to the innocence they had treasured in childhood. She was to discover that confessors, seekers after understanding, mercy and forgiveness, rarely if ever mended their ways. I remember always the shock I experienced on hearing her say in the room next door to where I was supposed to be asleep, 'How can I ever again believe a word you say?' These words were said not in anger, but out of those depths known to women who have been foolish enough to entertain expectations about their mission to those who have erred and strayed. At the time I was dumbfounded: I did not understand.

The source of my mother's religious beliefs still eludes me. I can understand that when the genteel poverty of life in a vicarage replaced the grandeur of her years in the mansions of the patricians she should compensate herself with the myth of a golden age in her past. But that does not explain her surrender to and dependence on her heavenly Father. 'Mann dear,' she would say, 'I'm going to ask my Father in Heaven again and *He* won't let me down.' The dependence on the heavenly Father began before she met my father. It is possible there was some connection between the food with which she fed her spiritual hungers and the need to romanticise the past of her family. It may be that she was attracted to Ashfield because her great-aunt Eliza Marsden Hassall was the principal of a school in the parish for the training of missionaries.

My mother was not a self-effacer, not a mystic seeking union with the creator of the universe. My mother was not one to declaim with passion the words, 'For our souls will never find peace until they are reunited in Thee.' Her God was on high, up there, far away from the human uproar. She never quoted the words, 'The Kingdom of God is within you.' She believed in missions, because she believed in the superiority of her religion over all other religions, just as she believed in the superiority of a British Protestant civilisation over all other civilisations. She believed it was the duty of all Christians in the English-speaking world to save the souls of the Chinese, the Japanese, the Indians, the Aborigines (she was a great believer in both the Australian Board of Missions and the Church Missionary Society) and all the other 'little people', as she called them. She never spoke with an air of condescension. She was never Lady Catherine De Burgh to my father's Reverend Mr Collins. She saw herself as a person who had received a great gift from God. As she saw it, it was her moral duty so to strive, so to fight with all her might that the 'heathen in his blindness' did not 'bow down to wood and stone'.

One of my poignant memories of my mother is the expression on her face as she sang the words of Charles Heber:

> Waft, waft, ye winds, His story,
> And you, ye waters, roll,
> Till, like a sea of glory,
> It spreads from pole to pole.

I can still see now the wild ecstasy in her eyes. The eyes were the lamp of her soul. They told those observing her of her hope that there was someone who would understand if she took the risk of allowing all her longings, all her passions, to gush out of her. The pain of seeing my mother in those moments when she was asking for what could never be, when she was enticed by a mirage, something which was not there, will never go away. There are also even more painful memories of her face, radiant with hope, as she sang in her beautiful voice, uncovering the passion in her heart:

> Jesu, Lover of my soul,
> Let me to Thy Bosom fly,
> While the gathering waters roll,
> While the tempest still is high:
> . . .
> Other refuge have I none;
> Hangs my helpless soul on Thee;
> Leave, ah! leave me not alone,
> Still support and comfort me.

In childhood I did not understand why this meant so much to her.

I am even beginning to understand the tragic grandeur of that moment when she first spoke to my father in 1908. I still have difficulty in imagining that moment when these two human beings were swept into the 'fret and fever of love'. Perhaps the tragedy was, in part, that the satisfaction of their passion for each other at that time in the history of Australia could be fulfilled only by the taking of vows, under which one of them, not my mother, would chafe in the years to come.

My mother, I believe, was left with God and her own family. That is why she sang so fervently: 'Leave, ah! leave me not alone,/Still support and comfort me'. I remember standing near her, my lips open in astonishment at my mother's passion. Later there were to be years of anger that my mother should entertain such hopes for something that could never be. I know now why that was so. I am tormented by my failure to respond to the hungers of her loving heart. I remember also the look on her face when she sang the words of the hymn 'Rock of Ages, cleft for me': 'Wash me, Saviour, or I die.' Again I was puzzled: why should my mother want to be washed? She was always so clean, always so good. Again, later there were the years of being angry with my mother for stooping to the infamy of self-accusation, to beseeching someone who was not there to wash her sins away. To me she always was and always will be the one without sin. I was young and foolish. I knew nothing about that pain of hers which would never go away. I failed her, just as I failed my father.

My father knew all about temptation. He lived with it all his life. The weak were attracted to him. Drunkards, fornicators, liars, thieves, even murderers, sought him out and confessed everything to him. He wanted them to be forgiven: he held out to them the hope that Christ would forgive everyone – that Christ would forgive even murderers. He wanted human beings to forgive each other. The weak sensed he neither judged nor condemned them, not because he was without sin, or the pure one, but because he was like the transgressors himself. My father was searching for someone to whom he could tell everything, someone to whom he could reveal what manner of man he was. Perhaps he was persuaded my mother would understand and forgive.

My mother presented another temptation to my father. She might be his deliverer from the world of St Peters: she might be the next rung on the ladder on which years earlier he had begun to climb out of the working classes. St Andrew's Choir School was the first rung, Moore College the second, and my mother and her family the third. My father was already on the way up. Marriage with my mother held out the promise of accelerating his climb. I have no idea of how far he thought he could go. He always behaved as though the high positions in the Church were quite out of reach.

I do not know much about his courtship of my mother. Some letters survive. They tell a story of a man going through the painful experience of being taught the truth about himself by a woman. My father began his courtship as a lover: he was the charmer, the enchanter, the leader. He was accepted. He believed the birthday of his life had come, that at long last he had met the person who was 'all in all' to him. He read love poetry; he read the Song of Songs; he read the sonnets of Shakespeare; he wept. But quite quickly he found himself like a prisoner in the dock, answering charges. There always had been omens of future suffering. His mother was jealous, she never being able to share her darling Charlie with anyone, let alone another woman, especially a woman of the grace and beauty and gifts of my mother. His father was divided, the hidalgo in him enjoying the entrée card his son presented him to the drawing-rooms of Sydney patricians. But life had convinced him that class was even more powerful than love or sensual passion. My mother's sisters were sceptical, even downright rude to my father, behaving as though he belonged to some species inferior to the one to which they belonged by birth.

They began to show their hand, they began to let my father know what was in their minds just as my mother was writing and speaking those early character sketches of my father, which would take him on the long journey of self-discovery. I do not know if my father had any intimations at the time of what lay ahead, any of those warnings nature plants in us to indicate danger lies ahead. It all began with what looked like a trifle. My father loved watching Rugby; he loved the crowd at a cricket test match between England and Australia; he loved a beer at the game, and a bucket of prawns afterwards with his brother-in-law Herman Heesch, husband of his sister Alice. My father loved the variety theatre. He told wonderful stories of a night at the Tivoli in Sydney. 'I tell you, boy, a comedian only had a minute in which to capture his audience. If the audience did not like him, they told him in no uncertain manner: "Out, out, out", and they would not stop until they had driven him off the stage.' My father found that funny. My mother found it what she called 'right down cruel'.

From the letters exchanged between them I gather she let my father know she thought Rugby crowds were 'vulgar larrikins', and anyone who enjoyed seeing another human being humiliated must be 'quite peculiar'. I gather the tiff about Rugby barrackers was soon over – or seemed to be. I say this because my mother, with her usual generosity, her passionate conviction that it was her duty to understand the whole of God's creation, persuaded herself it was her moral duty to be magnanimous to those who got their pleasures in that way. She wrote a letter to my father in which she expressed the hope that he would go to the next football match. She could see he needed such an outlet. She seemed to hope that would be the end of the matter.

She made a fatal mistake. My mother, like most human beings, was a bundle of contradictions. She believed all human beings were equal in the sight of God: she was a member of a family who accepted the 'great chain of being' from God, through the angels, human beings with all their grades, down to the brute creation and even lower. My mother's letter oozed condescension, the tone of a member of the superior classes addressing a member of the inferior classes. My mother, as I said before, was not a Catherine De Burgh, and my father could never be a Reverend Mr Collins. But the teachings of religion were not as strong as her inheritance from her ancestors.

She asked my father to forgive her for lecturing him on his fondness for variety and Rugby. She assumed that would end the matter. What she did not know then, and my father possibly did not know either, was that my father never forgave anyone – or rather that he never forgot – and what is not forgotten is often not forgiven. My father never forgot. He brooded over even the mildest rebuke; he remembered all his life every slight, every insult, every wound. My mother was not to know then that in an exchange to which she attached little importance she had assumed the role of the one abounding in virtue, and planted in my father's mind the idea that she detected a lack of virtue in him. That was over a triviality.

My father loved two alcoholic drinks: beer and whisky. Nature had been very kind to him. He drank beer to slake his thirst, and never to excess. He poured a generous quantity of whisky into a tumbler (my father was generous with everything except forgiveness), drank it in one swallow, and did not hold out his glass for more. My mother was afraid of alcohol. She knew, though she never let on she knew, all about the 'family complaint'. In every generation of her family in Australia at least one of the male members had fallen victim to it. My mother believed gentlemen only drank wine at the dinner table out of stemmed glasses filled by a table maid. My mother believed there was something not quite right in men drinking together. She believed only the weak, the low and the common got drunk. If members of her own class were often drunk then there must be some flaw in their character. She never let her mind linger over the question: why did God make a 'peculiar' gentleman? Someone had planted in my mother's mind the delusion that gentlemen were not weak in ways in which other men were weak. That was one of the delusions she lived with all her life. My mother wanted my father to be a gentleman, just as later she wanted her three children to be gentlemen and a gentlewoman. She was presuming to draw up the rules for my father. Her class had been drawing up the rules both here and in England and Scotland for centuries. My father had a choice: either to sit for the examination my mother was setting for him, and pass, or not change his own way of life. He chose the latter.

My father had a secret he dared not share with my mother. He was being driven to feel guilty about one of the greatest pleasures of his life. His life with his brother-in-law, Herman Heesch, was under threat. Not even smoking was safe. I have never seen anyone enjoy smoking a cigarette as much as my father. As he inhaled, both cheeks collapsed into a saucer-shape, his eyes glowed with pleasure. He sucked for so long that I used to think as a child of the smoke passing down through lungs, stomach and legs, right to his toe-nails. Then he exhaled, after which his nostrils quivered as though he had just scented some exquisite perfume. My mother also had opinions on smoking. Gentlemen did not smoke cigarettes: they smoked a pipe, and, provided that no ladies were present, they smoked a cigar with their brandy or while they read the paper.

It was early days yet. My father was nowhere near that state of desperation when he would use the words of the prophet as an account of what he had lived through: 'for in Thy sight shall no man living be justified'. The tragedy was my mother was not a punisher; she did not want to be the medium through whom suffering came to anyone. She did not want to be the cause of any man's wretchedness, let alone cause any man to discover his own swinishness. She never foresaw the hell they would both live through. Hell, she believed, was for sinners after death. She and her Charlie were not sinners. She did not know then that Hell is for those who can neither love nor be loved. Her God would not allow her to taste damnation.

My father's choice meant becoming an expert in the art of deception, of promising one thing, and doing another. That always puts any relationship between a man and a woman under an intolerable strain. There is the fear of discovery. After discovery there is the plea for forgiveness, followed by the renewal of promises. The beloved becomes a judge: the lover is on trial. The beloved is the model of rectitude: the lover is trapped in the cycle of transgression and forgiveness. Judges are transformed from love objects slowly into hate objects. My mother had a natural goodness, but not my father. Why some should be good, and others tormented all their lives by the divisions within themselves, is a mystery. Unwittingly, with all the maddening innocence of the good person, my mother was taking on the role those other self-appointed judges – those bishops, priests and deacons – had taken in my father's life. She was slipping into the role of those whose approval my father had so desperately coveted. My father did not realise that that approval would never be given, that for them tormenting a man with my father's temperament was a sport they could never resist. My mother was not a tormentor, a straitener, a life-denier, or a heart-dimmer. She was an enlarger of life. My mother never received darker satisfactions from her role as judge by the rules she and her class had drafted. She was puzzled: she tried to understand. Her Charlie could not be possessed by a devil. Her Charlie could not be a Merlin, half innocent, half devil. All would be well.

My mother had her 'certainties'. She was the inheritor of the faith of the men and women who believed God had planted in them the 'heroic ingredients': she was British, she was Protestant. She had read Macaulay and James Anthony Froude. She therefore believed without question the Whig view of Australian history, that wherever the British took their civilisation, wherever there were British political institutions and the Protestant religion, there was always a higher degree of material well-being, a greater degree of liberty, of toleration and the rule of law, than in Catholic or non-European societies. That was in the air she breathed in Strathfield, Burwood, the Presbyterian Ladies' College, and St John's, Ashfield.

My mother believed in God: He was the eternal loving Father, the Father in heaven, just as her own father was her father on earth. The English, the Scots and their descendants in Australia were the people of 'heroic ingredients' – but not the Irish. My father's mother was Irish; her family had migrated from Tipperary to London. There was another source of friction. My father adored his mother, and was proud of her Irish ancestry. 'My dear old mother, boy,' he used to say, 'was Irish.' That was the trouble. She, too, had the same goodness as my mother. Yet my mother, prisoner as she was of the British myth, never knew heart's ease with her. For her my father's mother was one of those who could never be *comme il faut* in my mother's world. My mother tried to understand, tried to draw close. Her religion taught her all were equal in the sight of God, but in the struggle between what her faith required of her, and her upbringing, the faith sometimes lost.

She knew what she believed. Her faith was so strong she was not open to other worlds, other possibilities. She believed in God the Father. My father had his passions, his loves, his enthusiasms. He loved the language of the Book of Common Prayer. He loved the cadences in the sentences: 'Ye that . . . are in love and charity with your neighbours and intend to lead a new life, following the commandments of God . . . draw near with faith and take this Holy Sacrament to your comfort . . . meekly kneeling upon your knees.' He loved the poetry. He loved the words in the Psalms, such as: 'Make me a clean heart, O God: and renew a right spirit within me' and 'The sacrifice of God is a troubled spirit: a broken and contrite heart, O God, shalt Thou not despise.' They were all about the things he wanted most in life. They put into words what he wanted: love, mercy, forgiveness, understanding, compassion. They were a catalogue of his secret longings, a promise that what he most desperately wanted was his for the asking, for the praying, his for the singing. My father knew what he wanted. I doubt whether he ever knew what he believed.

My father was a superb actor. From the turn of the century to the beginning of the First World War the pulpit was a stage for solo performances, morning prayer and evensong a grand opera with the minister singing the lead tenor or baritone part. There was no applause. In the churches there were no such demonstrations. There were other channels open to members of the congregation. There were the eyes of adoration. Who could tell whether women whose eyes mirrored some inner ecstasy were aroused by the love of God, or by love of a Byronic young man robed in white, as a symbol of a mystical union between Christ and his Church? The Anglican services provided a weekly emotional bath for all those who wanted what could never be – all those who could not live without a great delusion. My father loved the words; my father loved the music, part of his life since childhood years in St Peters; my father loved the adoration.

My father never examined closely what he believed. He was bored by all the arguments of the philosophers against the existence of God. 'Don't listen to them, boy', he used to say to me. 'They win all the arguments, but they lose their friends.' Another time he said to me, 'You take my tip, boy. When the atheists reel off their arguments just look them in the eye, boy, and say, "When you can make a worm, I'll listen to you." That'll shut them up, boy. They've got no answer to that.' My father was a ritualist: my father loved display, vestments, all the extravagances of the heart. He was brought up in the evangelical tradition of the Church of England, among those who believed in no intercessors between themselves and God. They were opposed to all ostentation. They were the dry souls of the Christian Church. They spoke of religion as though it were a theorem in geometry. They were suspicious of enthusiasm, suspicious of any devices to excite the passions. Theirs was a cosy religion, a religion which encouraged them to flock to their churches each Sunday to thank their God they were not as other people, they were not sinners, liars, fornicators, drunkards or adulterers. My father felt no bond with that kind of religion. My father wanted to shout to all those men and women who were all head and no heart, 'God, be merciful to me, a sinner.' My father was searching for a religion which would answer the needs of his heart. Life had already taught him to say to himself, 'There is no sin, there is no crime, there is only hunger.' There must be a church which had kept alive the image of Christ: there must be a church for kindred spirits.

So while he was courting my mother at St John's, Ashfield, he was sampling other churches. He went to a High Mass in Christ Church, St Laurence, at the top of George Street in Sydney. The celebrant was clothed in vestments of many colours, the deacon less gorgeously arrayed, yet much more interesting to the eye than the chaste dull black cassocks and the undecorated surplices worn by the clergy in the other churches of the diocese of Sydney. The service was like an opera, with the celebrant the choreographer of a ballet, the organist the musical conductor, with soloists and a full choir. My father was strangely moved. But, after the service, over tea and biscuits in the rectory, he noticed women were the great absentees, and the men often lapsed into high-pitched giggles. It was as though what for him was life, the wonder of a man and a woman, did not exist in the world of the High Churchmen. So he looked else-where – or planned to.

Rumours of what he was up to came back to my mother in garbled form. She was dismayed. She challenged him in one of her letters. 'People', she wrote, 'tell me you are thinking of becoming a Catholic.' So my father had yet another 'please explain' from my mother. Once again she professed her loving thoughts. She was not accusing him of anything, she knowing by then how hurt he could be by any criticism of his character or his morals. But my mother could not understand why he needed to 'err and stray' from God's ways like a lost sheep. She stood on entrenched ground; my father was never to know the peace of standing on such ground. My mother was never visited by doubts, she never needed to say to herself, 'Help thou my unbelief'. My father always uttered those words with a fervour which measured the longing in his soul for certainty, anything which would quieten the uproar inside him. My mother wanted him to deny that he was sniffing around the churches of Sydney, looking not so much for salvation as for confidence and serenity, looking for all those things in life on which the life-deniers amongst the Anglicans frowned, opening their lips a fraction to say their chilling 'No' or their disapproving 'Better not', before closing their mouths tight again. The ones who should have spoken rarely said a word. Yet, to deny the search was to be false to himself, to have yet another secret which he dared not share with my mother, and to risk her discovering that he did not believe in anything, that if the display part of him were stripped away she might find there was nothing there. Although this was not clear to him during those stormy years in Ashfield, she might find a person he did not dare to show to anyone. She might discover the man who was magnificently alive, the man on whom nature played a trick, giving him a taste for both Madonnas and Dionysians. My father at that time had not heeded Solon's advice to all human beings, 'Know thyself'.

Perhaps if he had he might have asked whether my mother was a Madonna who would never or perhaps could never abandon herself to any Dionysian frenzy. My father had already read Annie Besant. My father was ready to read Freud's *Three Essays on the Theory of Sexuality*. He was ready to be liberated from all the restraints, all the stultifying myths about the body as the source of evil, all the encrustations imposed by the Church, by the spoil-sports and creeps in clerical garb, those encrustations which had even concealed what Christ had said. My father loved the Song of Solomon. He loved these words: 'I am black but comely, O ye daughters of Jerusalem.' My father wanted to believe what he was told in the Bible, that if a man left his home and cleaved to the woman he loved then they two would become one flesh. He was fearful of the other possibility, certainly no stranger to the solemn pronouncement by the Preacher in Ecclesiastes: 'There is one alone, there cannot be a second.' The Word, he believed, was made flesh; man could be redeemed by the flesh; man could be healed by the flesh; man could know the peace of God which passeth all understanding through the flesh. Man was incomplete; man sought for that other half which alone could make him whole. There must be someone, somewhere, who would and could rescue a man, draw a man out of his 'lonely skin'. My mother, he hoped and believed, would give him that peace which the world could not give. She was 'mine dearest', his 'dearest, darling Katie'.

What did it matter if her sisters treated him as an outsider, if her father was granite-like, her brothers amused at Katie's folly of giving up the luxuries of a patrician's home for genteel poverty in a vicarage, and her mother wheezed and only managed to say, 'Oh, goodness', when told one of his stories about his early days in St Peters, and his own mother still looked pained if Katie tried to come too near, and his own father kept on throwing out those jeremiads about class barriers, and his three sisters wore a puzzled expression on their faces whenever Katie's name was mentioned? Nothing he did ever made either her family or his family unbend in the company of the other. Not even music could work the great marvel: no one was jolly; no one chuckled; no one laughed loudly. All social occasions were a strain. It was not what was said, it was what was left unsaid. But my father was an incurable romantic. He believed with Christ that if a man had faith he could move mountains. He was enslaved by a great passion: he was on the eve of fulfilment. He believed their eyes would be opened, and they would become as gods. They were setting out on a journey in which spite, malice, envy, jealousy, class loyalties, past superstitions and ignorance might bang and batter on the windows of their carriage, but would never disturb their peace or weaken the bond between them.

He never asked himself whether my mother believed the flesh had any role to play in redemption or salvation. The courtship conventions of his day stood between them both and such a discovery. There were so many subjects which should have been discussed, but the lore of their two tribes – my father's tribe and my mother's tribe – forbade them to raise the barrier on that frontier. My mother believed the flesh was evil, believed the lusts of the flesh corrupted the soul. She was not afraid of being sent to Hell. I never heard her mention Hell as a place for sinners, and the wicked. My father always knew about Hell – the Hell in the heart. I never heard him threaten sinners, those who could not stop, though he knew God's laws commanded them to stop. He knew the flesh was for many stronger than the fear of Hell. But he never warned those who could not stop that they would go to Hell. He never reminded them there was no escape from, or amelioration of, the torments of Hell. He never drew the attention of sinners to the prophet's warning that there were no fans in Hell. I think he liked to believe, as I also like to believe, that God is more forgiving than men, certainly more forgiving than women, indeed, that God ought to forgive everyone.

My mother never spoke of purity, or cleanliness, as being related to Godliness. She accepted the great chain of being: there was God, who was perfect; then there were the angels who had no serious problems because they knew nothing of the lusts of the flesh; then there were men and women, whom God had made lower than the angels, but superior to the brutes, it being God the Father's wish that men and women should model themselves on the angels, that is, with sex severely left out save for the purposes of procreation, that being the reason why God had ordained marriage; then there were the brutes, the chief evidence of their brutishness being their lack of control over their sexual behaviour, and their cruelty to the weak. Marriage was for procreation, the mutual comforting of each other, and for the avoidance of sin. My mother entertained no heady ideas about a walk in the Paradise Gardens, where she and her Charlie would become one flesh, or through her body her Charlie would know the glory. My mother had no such expectations – but my father did.

They were married at St John's Church, Ashfield, on 7 December 1910, four days before my mother turned thirty-two; my father was twenty-nine. Alfred Yarnold was the officiating minister, A. Amery was the best man, Roberta ('Bobbie'), my mother's sister, was the bridesmaid. So in St John's Church one of the women destined to cause my father great distress stood near him as he vowed from henceforth to forsake all others, yet my father was not troubled by any foreboding on that day. He already had a secret life he did not share with anyone. The Hope family was generous: the reception was held in a marquee erected for the occasion on the spacious back lawn at Langlo in Burwood Road, Burwood. Speeches were made. Toasts were drunk. My mother's sisters exchanged winks when one of my father's sisters seemed not to know that 'house' began with the letter 'h'. My father was too happy to notice such things. He and his Katie were to catch the night train to Condobolin, where they were to spend their honeymoon on the estate of Norman, George and Eric Hope at Birrarck. My father was travelling away from St Peters. The woman who was to marry my mother's brother Syd told me years later that as the bridal couple left the festive scene she wondered then whether Katie and Charlie would ever or could ever be 'properly married' - but at that time people kept such thoughts to themselves; they lived in great darkness.

While my father and my mother were starting their journey from the darkness into the light, Sigmund Freud was writing his *Three Essays on the Theory of Sexuality*, and the German Kaiser was sabre-rattling about an incident at Agadir. Out at Condobolin under that vast sky my father was finding my mother's cousin Norman was quite a character. 'He was eighteen stone, boy,' he would tell me later, 'but he could jump a tennis net with the greatest of ease.'

On their return to Sydney they lived in Park Road, Burwood. My brother Russell was born there on 3 December 1912. He was christened Thomas (after his grandfather Clark) Russell (after a clerical friend of my father's) Hope (after my mother's family). The mighty opposites were printed on his forehead at baptism just as they were to be on mine, and later on my sister's. That year my father resigned his curacy at St John's, Ashfield, to take up the position of clerk in holy orders and assistant minister at St Andrew's Cathedral in Sydney. So the would-be enlarger of life became a servant in the citadel of the life-deniers of Sydney. In 1913 he became Anglican chaplain to the State Penitentiaries at Darlinghurst and Long Bay, and the State Reformatory for Women. At the State Reformatory for Women he collaborated with the Reverend Dr Manning. He was praised for his 'regular and sympathetic labours in the gaol, more especially in the case of a prisoner condemned to death'. In his first report to the Governor of Darlinghurst Penitentiary he wrote that the 'thoughtful attention of the men' attending divine service 'has made my work a pleasure'.

It was the flowering time of his life. He never forgot the experience. His best stories were about his years as a gaol chaplain. He was fascinated by the bizarre in human behaviour.

'Some of the most interesting characters in the gaol, boy,' he would tell me later, 'were the confidence tricksters, known for short as the con-men. There was one old geezer in the gaol who had sold foot-warmers in railway compartments to old ladies for a fiver each. He would ask a wealthy woman whether she found the foot-warmer comforting, and when she said yes, she did, he would ask her whether she would like to buy it from him for only five pounds. And when the train arrived at Central Station she would ask a porter to carry the foot-warmer to her carriage as she had bought it. In the meantime, boy, the con-man had imshied. But the police always knew where to pick him up.' My father's stories were all about human gullibility, human stupidity.

There was another story, I remember, about a con-man who boarded an overseas liner in Sydney, befriended the wealthy women in first class, told them their money would not be worth as much in England as in Australia, and asked them whether they would like him to change it for gold coins in Melbourne. 'Of course, boy, he imshied, but the police soon picked him up. And I'll tell you another thing about the violent men in gaols, boy. Music calmed them down. Yes, boy, we had one wild fellow in Long Bay who was only quiet when he played scales on the piano. Mind you, boy, there is something good in everyone. I have seen condemned men weep when I offered them a little love.'

All his life after the Darlinghurst experience he kept the prayer book he had used in his ministrations to prisoner P. G. Wright, who was under sentence of death from 23 July to 17 August 1913. 'On the morning we heard the reprieve, boy, I held a special celebration of holy communion in the gaol for Wright. I tell you, you could hear a pin drop any time during the service. There is a great deal of genuine reverence amongst the down and outs.'

It was also a time when my father became aware that between him and the men in power in the Church of England in Sydney there was a great gulf set. If my father had been God he would have forgiven everyone – everyone except those who had hurt him, or let him down. My father was a seventy-times-seven man. He believed there was something good in everyone: he believed in the redeeming power of love. He was not a vindictive man, or a punishing man. The idea of an eye for an eye and a tooth for a tooth was revolting to him. He believed those words of Christ: 'love your enemies . . . bless them that persecute you' – or thought he did. He wanted everyone to like him. For him there was always the temptation to believe that by being nice to people they would think well of him, that by doing favours he could buy their goodwill, even their love. It was a shock to him to find that what he believed to be his strongest point – his capacity to win the approval of all the ones whom God seemed to have forgotten – was adjudged by his superiors in the Church to be a weakness. My father's passion to be loved and admired was so strong, so wilful, that he would pursue it even if that meant violating the laws of God, as he understood them.

My father did not believe in capital punishment. So he petitioned for the reprieve of all the condemned men, no matter how heinous or odious their crimes were in the eyes of men. He forgave them: he saw good in them. God would forgive them: God would see the goodness in them. Archbishop John Charles Wright, a worthy representative of Jehovah in Philistine Sydney, weighed his young chaplain in the balance and found him wanting in moral fibre. Perhaps Archbishop Wright was wiser in things of this world than my father acknowledged. Perhaps Wright knew that those who were obsessed with weakness in others, those who were 'soft' on publicans and sinners were themselves very likely to err and stray from God's ways like lost sheep. But my father never made any move to escape from the tight little world in which he found himself. He did not make the intellectual leap into another world, a world which would liberate him from his accusers and his judges. He soldiered on, hoping the Archbishop, the Archdeacon, the other clergy, his wife and her family would one day acclaim him. He allowed himself to be judged by a court which had already passed judgement. So my father became a hero among the outcasts, the odd, the mentally weak, all those who could not stop. They loved him, and they would go on loving him until the day he died. They gave him their approval: they hugged him, wept with him, and swore they would never forget him, that there should be more like him. Women adored him, because he understood their hunger to be loved. But the ones whose approval he so desperately coveted began to frown, and wear black looks whenever he came into their presence.

My mother tried to understand. She had not the same desire to be loved and admired. She did not believe love and respect could ever be won by indulging a weakness. By birth and education she accepted without question that there must be laws for the punish- ment of wickedness and vice. She did not understand why my father wept when he showed her the prayer book they gave him to commemorate the reprieve of the prisoner Wright. To her these men and women were what she called 'peculiar', their love or their approval meaning nothing to her. So what my father was most proud of meant little if anything to my mother. It was not possible for her to say what she did not mean. It would have meant much to my father if she could have said the words of praise, but that was not to be. It would have meant much to my father if she could have praised him to her own family for his work in the gaol. Again she was silent. My father had to settle for the approval of his mother, his sisters, and the weak ones he had helped. He took comfort from the words, 'Oh ye of little heart'. There must be someone who would understand, someone who would be aware of the generosity of his heart, and not dismiss his strength as some flaw in his being.

There was another cause of disquiet. War had broken out in Europe in August 1914. Australia had offered to help the Empire 'to the last man and the last shilling'. My mother feared the end of the world was at hand. She was then expecting her second child, and hoping it would be a girl. She was standing on Burwood Railway Station when she heard of the outbreak of war. That night she prayed God would take the child in her womb away from her: she did not want to bring any more children into such a wicked world. She hoped she would never have any more children. That wish, I imagine, must have caused terrible pain to my father, because he believed marriage was ordained by God so that a man may leave his home, cleave to the woman he loved and 'they twain shall become one flesh'. My father had had high hopes, and now it was all slipping away from him. Archbishop Wright, an Englishman, did not think my father was getting things straight. The walk in the Paradise Gardens had scarcely begun before it threatened to end. And what then?

Neither of my mother's prayers was answered. There was a child: it was a boy. He was born in her bedroom in Park Road, Burwood, on 3 March 1915. My father again chose the principal name – Manning (after another Reverend Mr Manning, one of the senior chaplains to the Sydney gaols). He shared my father's faith in the mission to 'the least of the little ones'. Perhaps, who knows, he too was a 'secret sharer', a man who knew all about the shadow. My mother chose the other two names – Charles (after her father) Hope (after her family name). So once again, as with my brother, a Hope and a Clark were joined in some uneasy association. My mother told me years later about the difficult birth, the size of the head requiring the use of instruments. Once again, as with my brother, she was not able to feed the baby. Again she asked God not to let her bear another child.

Perhaps that, too, contributed later to the uproar in my soul. But again, who can tell? If there are moles in our being at birth, if we inherit the ghosts of the past, it is the beginning of wisdom to remove the moles, and confront the ghosts. Alas, I was tempted to blame others, and to search outside myself for rescue. It took me many years before I put together the story of my own past. Knowledge brought wisdom and understanding, and a renewal of love for both my father and my mother. I wanted to tell them that now I understood, and to thank them for the great benefits I had received at their hands. By then it was too late: they were dead. All I could do was visit their graves in the Box Hill cemetery, and leave a flower from the one who never forgot. But I could not speak to them. Life, and death, kept us apart.

The Boy from Burwood

After my birth my mother again asked her Father in Heaven not to give her another child. Again her prayer was not answered, for by the last quarter of 1915 she was pregnant again. God's will must be obeyed. Each morning, each night, she knelt beside the double bed in Park Road, praying to her Father in Heaven, 'Thy will be done'. She meant it. She never scanned God: she accepted, even though she did not understand. On 25 June 1916 she bore a daughter. My father persuaded her to call her after his own 'dear old mother', Jane. My mother agreed. She asked that she also be known as Hope. And Hope she was to be.

After the birth my mother prayed even more fervently that this child would be the last. While she was down on her knees in Park Road, the Australian Prime Minister, 'Billy' Hughes, was promising General Haig that Australia would find ways and means of replacing the expected losses in the forthcoming push against the Germans on the Somme, and pledging his Labor government to a policy contrary to a plank in Labor's platform. Australia was about to be bitterly divided by the conscription debate. My father again did not dare to take sides – his mother was Irish; he belonged to the working classes of Sydney; his favourite sister, Alice, was married to a German. The Sydney diocese was making conscription a test of a man's character, and each Sunday the Archbishop of Sydney thanked Almighty God for being on the side of the Allies. My mother's family was for King and Empire. My father was bewildered; my father said not a word.

My childhood began at a time when the discerning were beginning to talk of two Australias – the Australia of the comfortable classes, to which my mother's family belonged, and the Australia of the working classes, to which my father belonged. Henry Lawson had written of the comfortable classes as supporters of the 'Old Dead Tree', and identified them as members of the 'cuff and collar push', but Henry Lawson was now a drunken wreck; few spoke for the 'Young Tree Green'. Shaw Neilson advised his brother not to fall for the recruiter's clap-trap. My father did not take sides. My father again took refuge in jokes, in the funny side of life: 'You would have liked it in those days, boy', he would say to me later. 'The only sure way to get out of military service was to have all your teeth out. Well, boy, you would have liked this. One of my mates had his teeth out, and when he came before the doctors in the local drill hall, one of them rejected him for having flat feet.' He dwelt on life's little cruelties, especially the cruel turns of fortune, with the delight of a cat with a wounded bird under its paw. He was very clever at concealing whether he ever used the claws when others were not looking.

I was not old enough to observe him at that time. The memories of childhood are like regaining consciousness after a major oper-ation. There are many pictures and there are many blanks. It is like sitting in a picture theatre in the days of the silent movies on one of those nights when the projector develops a fault. At one moment there is a picture on the screen, at the next there is darkness. Scenes from childhood keep flashing on to my mind's picture screen. There are moments of light, moments of total recall, moments of total darkness, memories of past terrors, past anxieties, ghosts that live on in the mind, ghosts from which I was only liberated so late in life that even that victory mocks my idea of the fitness of things.

I remember the terrors of childhood, I remember the scenes of shame. I remember the nightmare which haunted me always, the nightmare of an ever-present possibility of annihilation, of ceasing to be. Perhaps that is why, even now, nearly seventy years later, I can still see in my mind a nurse trying to calm me down, my mother desperately trying to soothe me, to coax me out of my convulsions of terror, promising me 'Mann dear, you won't know anything about it: you'll be asleep, you won't feel anything . . . I'll be with you all the time.' Then later finding this was not true: even my mother had let me down, my mother had told me a lie. I remember writhing on my back on a hospital table covered with a white cloth, and a man with one of those faces which will always unsettle me telling the nurses, 'He won't be screaming for much longer', as he covers my mouth with an evil-smelling, soft spongy cloth, and I scream in terror as I struggle in vain to remain conscious. The world is peopled with deceivers and deceived. Even my mother cannot be trusted. Adults tell lies: they tell me about a world free of pain. In the world I know there is blood, there is nausea, there is fear.

My mother tells me God's world is full of wonders, full of loveliness. My mother tells me everyone loves me, that I am her 'Pud'. My mother tells me I have a very large head, and 'there must be lots of brains in that head of yours, Mann dear.' My mother tells me one day I will be a famous man, 'only Mann dear, you must promise me faithfully you will always keep yourself clean, and clean your teeth with salt and water.' I do not like cleaning my teeth with salt and water, so I tell her, 'Yes, Mum, I have cleaned my teeth.' So I too tell lies. And my mother tells me, 'Mann dear, God does not like boys who tell lies.' Again I am afraid, because claiming to have cleaned my teeth when I have not is not my first lie. Nor will it be my last.

My mother is worried. She cannot understand why it has taken me so long to learn to walk properly; I am nearly four – 'Perhaps, Mann dear, your head is too big for your body.' My mother arranges for her two unmarried sisters, Edith and Gladys, to teach me to walk on the lawn at Langlo, the home of her father and mother – the house of many wonders for my mother. My father is sceptical. 'Manning is not like Russ. He learned to walk before he was two. Manning would fall over on a billiard table.' Everyone laughs – except me, because I do not take well to ridicule or humiliations or mockery. The maiden aunts take on the task: 'We'll teach him to walk, Katie.' My mother seems to fear that maybe I will never walk – for she, too, is one of the haunted.

My maiden aunts, Gladys and Edith, are two jolly souls – I see them now in their wide-brimmed floppy hats, their white dresses with the hem of the skirts almost touching the manicured lawn. I notice there is something odd about Aunt Edith's lip, something odd about the way she talks. I have asked my mother in the faltering, groping way a child asks about anything odd in the world, but my mother has always evaded the question, and told me, 'You'll learn all about that later on, Mann dear. Wait till you're much older.' My aunts are holding me by the hands. I break away and toddle over to a clump of lilies. 'Be careful, Mann dear', my mother calls in a voice close to hysteria. But I am fascinated; no use to speak to me once I have decided to do something. I want to see what makes the lily so beautiful. A bee stings my cheek. I yell, and rush towards my mother. My two aunts laugh.

When my mother tells my father later on that I have been stung by a bee while dipping my face into the cup of a lily my father also chuckles, and looks pleased and says, 'My word, that's rich.' And I think now he added something like 'Never be intoxicated by beauty, boy' (but who can ever be certain about a memory, the memory being just as deceitful as the heart, but probably not so wicked; memory glorifies the past, memory sugar-coats the horrors, the shaming moments), to which my mother added, 'I wish you wouldn't talk to Manning like that, Charlie. He's an easy victim to such ideas.'

I did not understand then why for my father his stories of men and women being discomfited were like strong drink to a drunkard: they nourished his vices. I did not understand then why he needed such nourishment. Life twisted the innocent choir boy from St Peters into a mocker – a man who loved most of all stories in which the mighty were taken down from their seats. My father liked stories about the hypocrisy of deans, archdeacons, bishops and arch-bishops, especially archbishops. To his undying pain my father had discovered things were not as they seemed to be in the Church of England. But there was something inside him which stopped him from becoming a rebel, or taking a stand. While craving for the satisfactions of the mocker, he was desperate for the approval of the ones he ridiculed. I did not understand that at the time. Later I realised why jokes at the expense of other people, stories of the misfortunes of people, were the breath of life for him.

There were many humiliations, many rebukes, many reproofs. My brother never seemed to be affected by them, or remember them for long. For me it was different: they never went away, they stayed with me forever. I remember even now my grandmother Hope speaking to me at Langlo. She always wheezed when she spoke. She seemed embarrassed. She told me how they all liked me very much. That made me wonder what was coming. But, she went on, there was just one thing they all wished I would not do. 'Yes, Manning dear, we all wish you would lift the lavatory seat before you pass water, because otherwise you leave a mark on the wood.' She wheezed again.

That was the trouble in life. In the middle of all this gentility, of meals served by maids in black dresses, white starched cuffs and collar and a white cap, the gleam on the sugar crystals in the silver bowl, the gold cuff-links in the shirt of my grandfather, the neatly folded copy of the *Sydney Morning Herald* reposing on a polished table, there were always these alarming intimations of something amiss. The adults whispered to each other about Tom, my mother's younger brother, who had been to the war. 'Don't take any notice of what he says to you, Manning', my father would say, 'He's a bit odd.' The adults whispered to each other about Syd, another brother of my mother, asking anxiously, 'Is he all right?'; my mother looked scared, as though she were about to be told something she did not want to hear, the light draining quickly out of her eyes. But the moment did not last for long. Order and decorum were restored.

There were other moments of terror. My brother and I start fighting on the drawing-room floor. My grandfather, always an object of terror, loses his composure, seizes me roughly, tucks me under his arm, and shouts that he will teach me a lesson I will never forget. His eyes are full of hatred, his whole body shaking with anger. My mother pleads with him, 'Please, father, do not thrash Manning. He will never recover from it: he will never forget.' My grandfather drops me on the carpet, lowers over me and says, 'I'll let you off this time, but don't let it happen again.' But I can never be at ease with him again. I lived in awe of him. I wondered when he was going to erupt again. I wondered why I should always get the blame, why I was always the victim, why I was the one singled out for punishment, why they seemed to delight in my terror.

The world is not what it seems to be. There is the make-believe of the drawing room, the smiles, the kisses, the hugs; there is the razor-strap, there is the hatred in my grandfather's eyes, there are my mother's sisters giggling with each other about my father. My mother tells me, 'God loves all of us, He loves everyone, Mann dear', but I already wonder whether perhaps this other Father she talks about, this Father in Heaven is like her own father, a man with a razor strap who whips little boys when they are naughty.

I have already heard the words about living in love and fellowship with each other, I have already heard the protestations of maiden aunts of how 'We all adore you, Manning dear. We think you're gorgeous.' Each night my mother clings to me: sometimes I think she is crying, and I wonder why. I look up at her from my bed, and see tear-drops on her cheeks, and she says to me, 'I worry sometimes, Mann dear, what's going to happen to you. You're not like the others.' I do not know what she is talking about, and only wish she would stop talking straight away, and blow out the lamp or the candle, the light which illuminates her troubled eyes. Then I can lie there and fantasise, and wonder what it is all about, as my brother Russell falls straight asleep, he not being cursed with a troubled soul.

Already I am fighting against the way of life my mother strives to impose on me. I am letting her down. I am disappointing her. I bite my finger-nails. She asks me to promise to stop. I promise. But the biting continues. I try to deny it. There is no point in lying. She grabs my fingers, and holds the guilty evidence before my eyes. She says, 'I don't know what's going to happen to you, Mann dear, if you go on like that.' She rubs bitter aloes onto my finger-nails, and hopes that will deter me. But nothing will ever stop me doing what I am driven to do, even if the results are painful. There are rages.

My mother wants me to stop playing with my 'toolie'. She gives no reason for this: she does not tell me it will not be good for me, or that God, that other Father in Heaven, will not be pleased. She just tells me to stop. But again I do not stop. So she binds my hands behind my back. She looks very displeased with me. There does not seem to be any way in which I can please my mother. I begin to escape into a world of my own. Yet each night my mother smothers me with kisses, and says she hopes that one day everything will be all right, and she prays for me every night. And I wonder why she has to pray for me, and not for Russell or Hope, and what was so odd about me, why I needed to be singled out in those nightly talks she has with her Father. I do not understand that my mother then had good reasons for her anxiety. Later, looking back, I realised she had entertained great fears and great expectations – she by then needing to believe in the future rather than the present – that the success of her second son might be some consolation. At the time, of course, I had no idea there was something amiss in my mother's life, that for her things had started to go wrong and she was at a loss to explain why this should be so, what it was in her life which had caused her to suffer in this way.

All I knew at the time was a life in which one moment of terror succeeded another. I remember a scene in the back garden at Park Road. I have one half of a broken bottle in my hand. My mother sees me fondling the jagged edges of the glass, testing them for sharpness, fascinated, absorbed. My mother is terrified at what I might do. She screams at me, 'Give me the glass immediately.' But no one can ever tell me what to do. I throw the glass over the fence, but as I do so the sharp edges split my right thumb open. Blood

51

spurts out on to the grass. My mother rushes me inside, and she stops the flow of blood. Later a doctor stitches the skin together again. The scar remains to this day as a reminder of my folly, that madness, that rush of blood to the head when anyone tells me what to do – or what is good, or what is right.

My mother held strong views about the body as well as about the soul. She believed we three children should use the 'potty' at least once a day. The body must be flushed clean. There was no problem about 'wee-wee', except making certain you did not pee in your pants or wet the bed. But 'arse' as she taught us to call faeces, well that was not quite so simple. My mother had three aids to lubrication for bowel failures – first, Epsom salts; second, sitting on a potty in which steam from hot water excited the anal passage; and third, the enema. Each night there was an inquisition, with my mother as grand inquisitor, and executioner. Each night the examination began with the question, 'Did you go to the potty today?' There was no desperate need for evasion or resort to a lie. One day's lapse meant only a dose of that nasty-tasting Epsom salts. I learnt quite early in life that there were far worse things than a dose of Epsom salts. The next night was inquisition night. There was the question, 'Have you been to the potty today?' A lie brought a temporary reprieve, but its own swift punishment – a mother's judgement on her son's character. 'Don't lie to me' was worse than an enema. Because that was the insoluble problem – how to avoid the enema without telling a lie. Every second night there was either the character sketch or the enema, or both. The enema was not painful: it was humiliating. I should really be grateful for the enema days. They gave me the material for the first and only musical I ever wrote. I did not get past the first couplet, and of course, like a good Australian, I borrowed the music. Here are the words:

> If the enema will not act
> Use more soap and water.

Perhaps that was the first of many futile attempts to settle scores with the world: a doggerel art was all I could ever rise to, then and possibly later on, when I was still foolishly settling scores, I never soared above the banal and the trivial. Who knows?

It was also part of a nightly drama, part of a never-ending quest to win the approval of my mother. Years later, when chemists in the country towns in which we lived displayed enemas in their shop windows, I could never walk past without a shudder. At a frivolous level my whole life since childhood has been preoccupied with how to avoid an enema. I still sometimes look deeply into a person's eyes and wonder whether they lived through the enema ordeal, just as I always look into a man's eyes to see whether he suffered as I suffered as a boarder at school. With the best intentions in the world, wanting only to do everything for my good, my mother, all unwittingly, was giving me early lessons in the kindergarten for liars. She was also planting in me the will to endure to the end, and teaching me quite unintentionally to keep out of the way of other people: they asked questions you could not answer, or, if you did, you answered in a way which left you in deeper trouble than before the question was put.

There was another puzzle. My mother never mentioned my father's family. She spoke often of her own family, of Samuel Marsden, Rowland Hassall, Thomas Hassall, Robert Hope, the Kettles in New Zealand. Nat Kettle was a mythical figure in my childhood, and Charles Kettle, the surveyor of Dunedin, one of those heroes in my mother's potted biographies of the pioneers of Christian civilisation in Australia and New Zealand. She spoke often of her brothers – of Syd, who was in a senior position in a wool firm in Sydney: of Jack (Father John), who was carrying on the family tradition as a clergyman, adding she sometimes wished he were not so 'peculiar' (he was a bachelor, and Rector of the one Anglo-Catholic church in the Sydney diocese – Christ Church, St Laurence). She spoke of her sisters – of Gladys, who was single, and played golf on ladies' day at Concord Golf Club and went to Sydney once a week to change her books at Farmer's Lending Library. Gladys loved a good book – but Gladys had never loved a man, or rather, I found out later, Gladys had loved two men, but each time her father had refused to give her permission to marry. 'Father, Mann dear, believed neither of them was good enough for your aunt Gladys.' In my mother's mind her father, like her Father in Heaven, must be obeyed. It never occurred to my mother that her father's tyranny over his daughters meant her sister Gladys began to dry up before her time, that she never knew that peace which passes all understanding – and had to make do with studying the marriages, births and deaths column in the *Sydney Morning Herald* to see what had happened to the other girls she had known at the Presbyterian Ladies' College, and to that ever-expanding cousinhood of the Marsdens, the Hassalls, the

Hopes, the Hope-Marshalls, the Waughhopes, the Macleods, the Camerons, the Maberly-Smiths, and the Oxleys – all those with a close or tenuous family connection with the 'clerical aristocracy' or the 'ancient nobility of New South Wales'. My mother told me the story of her sister Miriam, who at the age of fourteen (or was it fifteen?) had met a young Goulburn solicitor named Ernest Betts, and how he had been so badly smitten by her appearance ('Your Aunt Miriam, Mann dear, had a beautiful face when she was a girl') that every year when Aunt Miriam travelled on the express to Melbourne Ernest Betts was on the platform at Goulburn with a thermos of tea and sandwiches. When she came of age her father reluctantly consented to the marriage, though not, I gathered later, with a very good grace, because he always referred to Ernest Betts as 'that country town solicitor'.

My mother spoke of Edith who had never been married, because, 'and this is something I don't understand, Mann dear, poor Edith was born with a hare-lip.' She spoke of 'Bobbie' (Roberta), the vivacious one who had married Norman Rowe, a senior person in the Colonial Sugar Refining Company, and how 'father thinks the world of Norman'. My mother spoke of Florence; God had taken her when she was young. My mother also spoke of Marsden, her brother, who had died in Dunedin at the age of nineteen. 'I never recovered, Mann dear, from the shock of Marsden's death.' She always had a photograph of him in a silver frame in every house in which she lived. Her brothers and sisters were all very precious to her. She presented them as god-like beings, heroes and heroines who, I found later, were quite different from the way they were portrayed in my mother's potted biographies. My mother's picture gallery of the members of her family was possibly a delusion she had woven in her mind to make the world bearable for her. In my childhood I had no idea of the pain in her life which she eased and soothed with these fantasies about her own family. Nor do I know now, when it is too late to do anything about it, whether the tragedy of her life, the pains that were to come, could have been avoided if someone she respected, someone speaking with authority, someone speaking with love had stripped her of this life-lie, and asked her to face the truth about herself. She had such inner strength I believe she would have survived the shock. Who knows? Perhaps no one dared: perhaps her last fate might then have been worse than her first. Again I ask, who knows?

All I know is that she never spoke about my father's family. I was not puzzled about this at the time. My father was not in the house at Park Road at the time. I do not remember being told where he was. So I did not hear from him about his family. That came later. He always had a smile of self-satisfaction on his face when he spoke of 'my dear old mother', 'my dear old father', and 'I have three sisters, boy, Alice, Pearl and Ruby. They adore me, boy.' But in early child-hood I knew little, if anything, of my father's world. My father was not there; he had gone to the war. A veil was always drawn over those years. He did not go as a chaplain to the forces, nor as a private in the ranks; he volunteered to serve in the Ambulance Corps. Later, he never explained why. In the minute book of the Cathedral Chapter of St Andrew's in Sydney there is this abrupt entry for June 1917: 'The Archbishop reported that he had appointed temporarily the Rev. A. M. Deasey as Clerk in Holy Orders in the place of the Rev. C. H. W. Clark.' No explanation is given, no clue dropped.

The Church which claimed to represent Christ on earth was ruthless with all transgressors. They paid little heed to the divine command to forgive transgressors seventy times seven. While cats were licking the last drops of blood out of human skulls on the battlefields of France and Flanders in the European autumn of 1917, the Anglican Archbishop of Sydney was warning members of his flock of the 'dangers of over-stimulation in sexual matters', and announcing that his Church had formed a Council for 'Civic and Moral Improvement'. The Archbishop lectured his people on the evils of Popery, beseeching them not to be fooled by those who wished to restore the Cross in the services of the Church of England, because that was treachery. He denounced vulgarity in women's dress, and commercialism in sport. He wanted more British immigrants: he wanted to 'keep our people under the Flag'. He thanked Almighty God for planting 'our fathers in this land', and 'setting their feet in a large room'. He asked Almighty God to 'fashion into one godly people all those who have been brought hither from the Old Land and from other lands.'

Unlike the Galilean fisherman, Archbishop Wright did not forgive the weak, or those who could not stop. A clergyman, to whom God had given special gifts, a man full of zeal and energy, asked the Archbishop for one more chance. He was prepared to express contrition for the sin of drunkenness, but for him there was no forgiveness. A married clergyman accused 'many times of malpractices with young men' petitioned in vain for mercy and forgiveness.

So did another clergyman accused of having bought women in Africa for immoral purposes. Sydney was a diocese ferociously loyal to the letter of the law. Sydney had a morality: Sydney lacked charity.

I do not know even now whether my father resigned as a protest against the spirit of the diocese. That is unlikely, because the man I knew later was timid in the presence of authority: he hungered after a sign of recognition from people in high places, but no such sign was ever given to him. He went on courting a nod or a smile from the high and mighty until the day he died. So I find it difficult to believe he took a stand on principle against the life-deniers of Sydney. It is more likely that in a moment of rage he committed some indiscretion, some lapse from the code of conduct drafted by men with ink in their veins to trap those with hot blood. My father's heart was always hot within him: in certain moods he opted for satisfaction rather than future security.

Surviving letters are inconclusive. They tell of an estrangement between my mother and my father. Once again, as in his courtship days, my father is begging for forgiveness. Once again she is the judge, and he the accused. Once again he is making promises he may find he cannot possibly keep, and so runs the risk of hurting the person he has let down, the person who, without malice either fore or aft, has been the instrument through whom he has been made aware of his own swinishness. Once again he boasts to her how others think well of him, but begs her not to pass that on to any member of her family. My father is beginning to become bitter. My father, who professed he wanted to live in love and friendship with all men and women, who only wanted to be kind to everyone, and warm, and loving and generous, now hates 'him of the lawn sleeves' (but does not dare to say so) and members of my mother's family because they accuse him of being a hypocrite, of not practising what he preaches. In their eyes the man from St Peters has uncovered what they always knew about men from that 'element', men of the lower classes: they were unreliable – they were not 'one of them'. My father still wants Mr Hope, as he called my mother's father, to think well of him. My father wants my mother to praise him, to trust him, to believe him. But this she cannot bring herself to do, because my mother is a good woman, my mother is an honest woman, my mother can only say what she believes. So they must live together at times like a gaoler with a prisoner, a prisoner who is sometimes given an exeat to go fishing, play cricket, or watch a football game.

The crisis between my father and the Sydney hierarchy sets the pattern of their life until my mother's death. My mother cannot understand why all this has happened, cannot understand what it was in her life which brought all this to pass. She begins to look worried, to wear on her face the expression of a woman suspecting some disaster. Her eyes are never in repose. She searches for an explanation: was there something in her life which caused her suffering; was God punishing her, and, if so, for what? She must find an explanation which fits in with her own view of the world. Everything that happens is part of her Father's will. My mother will never question the goodness or the power of God. She will sing her hymn of praise to God until she walks into the night. No blows, no suffering, no pain, will ever shake her faith, or (but who can tell?) stir up one doubt in her mind. She will remain until her death living evidence of John Henry Newman's point: a thousand difficulties do not add up to one single doubt. My father is in a trap from which there is no escape. When he tries to escape, he finds to his chagrin that the jaws of the trap are biting more deeply into his flesh.

So volunteering in 1917 to go overseas as a stretcher-bearer was not a long-term way out of his afflictions. It was but a temporary relief. The life of a stretcher-bearer gave him the chance to play the role he loved most of all in life. When his ship berthed at Liverpool, my father took a bag of sugar out of the ship's stores and distributed it to the sugar-starved people near the wharf. They hugged him, and kissed him, and told him they had never met such a kind man. My father wrote all this to my mother, and added with some excitement (even now I can see his face when he was clutching at a hope that all would be well) that she must tell this to no one. I remember, too, the stories he told us of his escapades. He used to show us a photograph of himself in khaki shorts and khaki shirt holding the hand of a Ceylonese boy in Colombo. He would hold hands with anyone, except, of course, the ones who knew he was unsteady, who knew of those descents into Hell, the ones who knew he could not be trusted in anything. My father needed that hand, any human hand which might appease the insatiable hunger for recognition, the never-ending search to find someone who would understand, someone who would forgive. That was the heart of the matter. His God has told His people He is a merciful and forgiving God. He has confessed to him in secret, and asked to be forgiven. But God has not said a word. No confession to God can calm the uproar in his heart, or put an end to the self-lacerations.

There is no one to whom he can talk. His own family put him on a pedestal years ago. He has supped for years at the feast of their adoration: he cannot, he dare not, dispense with that. To rob his 'dear old mother' of her illusions about her son would be cruel – may even kill her. There is no woman in whom he can confide. Trust no man, and no woman either, was an axiom in the folk wisdom of St Peters. But he had also picked up another truism of the time, 'A man ought to be able to trust his mate in everything.' But that was the problem. All he had was men with whom he could play the goat. Slapstick humour, bizarre situations, making his life into a theatre of the absurd was his one anodyne – that and smoking Capstan cigarettes, plain (they must be plain – otherwise there was no satisfaction). He began to take comfort in making such remarks as, 'At least we can all have a good laugh' - as though to be bearable life had to be downgraded into one never-ending joke, one never-ending vaudeville turn. It was significant that one of my father's boasts about his success as a charmer was to tell us all around the dining-table, 'I managed to get them to smile.'

Years later he told me what happened when his hospital ship, *Caroola*, dropped anchor off Colombo early in 1919. 'The chap I went on shore with asked me, "How many eggs do you propose to eat?" So I told him two would be enough for me. "Two!" he said in disgust, "I'm going to start with two dozen." So I ordered a dozen. And I ate the lot. Mind you, boy, we'd had some sarsaparilla before we left the boat.' So 'sarsaparilla' became the family word for whisky, and the question, 'Did you have any sarsaparilla?', a private family joke. My mother was never comfortable when my father told stories of his adventures, stories that could not be told to the parishioners. 'I wish you wouldn't speak to the boys like that, Charlie', she would say. Sometimes her disapproval would trigger off one of my father's rages. 'God spare me days, woman, can't a man have a joke with his sons?'

There were sudden changes of atmosphere in the home all through childhood. I would giggle at my father's stories, and be 'tickled pink' when he said, as he often did, 'Manning loves my jokes', though apprehensive that he might turn from one of his stories to jokes at our expense and call me 'Pud'. When he had got what he was looking for – a wince on the face of his second son, he would rub it in with one of his favourite chorus lines, 'Manning would fall over a billiard table.' He would then turn to my brother and say, 'Russell has legs as thin as a diseased magpie.' My brother was then so thin my mother used to weep at times when she saw him in the bath, and wonder what she had done amiss, and why there was this ever-widening gap between her expectations and her experiences.

It was early in 1919, and I was four. I did not know we were all about to begin an exploration. We were soon to move to Kempsey.

Strange Goings-on in Kempsey

Early in 1919 my father came back into our lives. I have always in my mind that picture of him standing in the driveway of the garden in Park Road. I am sitting on the lawn. He smiles: he is reaching out for love and approval. He is not wearing a clerical collar, but a baggy, ill-fitting, dark-grey suit, a collar and tie, and a dark-grey hat. Years later I wondered what he did between his return in 1919 and his first appointment in the Church, which was in the Diocese of Grafton in 1920. He was no longer an assistant precentor in St Andrew's Cathedral. He was no longer a curate at St John's, Ashfield. Was he not wanted in the Diocese of Sydney? If so, why not? We children knew nothing later of our father's disappointment – or of his apparent ostracism by the life-deniers of St Andrew's. Nor do I know why he did not break with the Church, and start a new life as a teacher.

He had all the gifts – the gift of words, the gift of gesture, and that capacity to attract others to join him in his quest to find out what it was all about. He could clown his way through classes of boys and girls who took on teachers. He was a brilliant raconteur. Nature had been bounteous to him. He could hold an audience. 'Listen to me, boy,' he would say to me later, 'when I spoke to the audience last night, you could hear a pin drop.' His nostrils quivered with delight, and he drew deeply on his cigarette, and I imagined then, as I always did, that the smoke was coursing slowly down through his body until it reached his toes, and then he blew it out of his mouth in a clearly defined column. Sometimes, when he was even more pleased with himself, he would blow smoke rings. He was a magnificent showman, so magnificently alive, so much a 'heels up' man, that he never took care lest the women with the wounding tongues called him a 'cheap little show-off' or a 'music-hall comedian in clerical garb'. Then the gaiety would slip off his face, and he would sulk, and look hurt, and work out what he would say when next he met his enemy. Words were the only revenge open to him. For him, I gathered later, the world was infested with people who had despitefully used him. He would gaze in a combination of vacancy and hunger into the distance, as though someone out there would heed his petition, and satisfy his longing. I remember, too, how his voice trembled, and how sometimes he seemed to cry when he recited another passage from St Paul, 'Only Luke is with me. All the others forsook me.' I did not understand then what had planted such agony in his heart.

In 1920 he was given a chance of rescue from this conviction that he had been forsaken, that he could never enjoy the approval of the moral guardians and standards-setters in Australia. The Bishop of Grafton offered him the position of Warden of St George's Hostel for boys and girls attending the high school in Kempsey. The Diocese of Grafton decided in 1920 to establish hostels for boys and girls in Grafton, Lismore and Kempsey to counter the 'godless education' in the country districts of New South Wales, and the prevailing bankruptcy in moral and spiritual questions. The hostels were to provide a Christian alternative to the 'sweet liberty' enjoyed by country girls and boys who lived with families in country towns during school terms. The Church had to find wardens who would overcome the resistance of boys and girls to living in an institution.

My father had all the qualities required in a warden. Boys and girls liked him. He could tell stories, he could play the piano, he could sing, he could play billiards (my father could make a break of a hundred or more on one of his good nights at the table). He was not a stern disciplinarian. He had a very clear idea of the field of the possible with adolescents, and was never one to set anyone under his charge goals they could not possibly achieve. He was a man to wink the eye at anyone given to 'midnight rambles' – always provided no one else knew. He liked boys and girls: he had his own inner reasons for wanting to be liked by everyone. The salary was miserly – £6 a month for a married man, his wife and three small children, but my mother always had a maid, paid for by her father. There were fees for baptisms, marriages and funerals, because in addition to his duties in St George's Hostel my father was to be a curate at All Saints' Church. His rector was the Reverend C. E. Curtis, a Cambridge graduate, a man with a capacious heart, a man who never made the egregious error of believing that those letter-of-the-law men in the Diocese of Sydney bore any resemblance to the Galilean fisherman who had stood on that hill near Capernaum and told those stories about the Kingdom of Heaven.

St George's Hostel was in Anzac Street, Kempsey, on a hill over-looking the Macleay River. There was accommodation for fifteen to twenty boys and girls. We arrived in Kempsey in July 1920, and left in June 1921. I was then five years old. My memory of that year is very hazy. I remember talks with Buck Harris, an eccentric who lived in a hut on the river flat below the hostel. Buck Harris told me that because he lived on a diet of cabbage and cream, and washed his face in kerosene and soot, he would live forever. I remember vaguely Buck showing me a watch-chain made out of safety pins. I remember asking my mother how anyone could live forever, and her replying she wished I would not ask such questions because they only made her feel giddy, and 'Mann dear, if you ask questions like that people are going to think you are mental.' I do not remember asking my father about Buck Harris. Perhaps I already knew he did not answer questions: he put on a turn. I can imagine him now, saying, 'Buck Harris, boy, is quite a card. But at your age, boy, I was catching fish in Cook's River with a piece of string, a bent pin for a hook, and meat I cadged from my dear old mother for bait.' And away he would go with more of his stories about fishing, and I would be left wondering whether there was anyone who could tell me whether we lived forever.

I remember also a moment of terror. At the rear of the hostel there were open fields. I remember one day when we three children, my brother Russell, my sister Hope and I, all dressed to look like members of the local gentry though really belonging to the genteel poor (one of the many ways in which my mother unwittingly created a barrier between us and other children – it was as though much of the rest of the world were outside the cage in which we lived) went for a walk in the open fields, escorted by my mother's maid, Marjorie (Marge) Thompson. A white rooster flew up on to my left shoulder and pecked at my face. I screamed. The others laughed. I ran back to the hostel, ashamed of being afraid, desperate for shelter, needing to hide under someone's wing, a convert in childhood to the most insidious lie of all, namely that someone should and would rescue me from pain and humiliation. What I did not realise at the time was that a clergyman's home is a nursery school, teaching its members that others will do for you what you cannot do for yourself – that God's special servants are entitled to such services and perks. So a moment of terror might have been an instrument of illumination, but many years were to pass before I realised that the genteel poverty of a vicarage was a spur to ambition, that to rise out of it was one way of escaping all its terrors and humiliations, but that a vicarage life was also a threat to the self-reliance indispensable for such emancipation.

For my mother life in Kempsey had much to offer. She was now living not far from Port Macquarie, where her great-grandfather, the Reverend Thomas Hassall, had been the Anglican chaplain to the penal settlement. No one ever accused Thomas Hassall of improving the morals of the lower orders with the lash either of the tongue or the cat-o'-nine-tails. Thomas Hassall had also been the squire of Denbigh, a property not far from Camden. The country gentry had been the pioneers of white society on the Macleay. John Verge, architect of Camden Park, the seat of the Macarthur family, had built his manor, Austral Eden, on the river flats. Samuel Marsden had been the vicar for the Macarthurs. My mother belonged to Old Australia. Besides, down on the river not far from St George's Hostel there were families in need, families where, it was said, the man was never at home at night. My mother loved to bring what she called 'a pot of jam' to the needy. 'I think', she used to say, 'I'll take a pot of jam to poor old Mrs So and So.' The gesture could have been construed as a ransom of the gentry to the poor, an act of condescension, an act of someone who had appointed herself to membership of the superior people; it could also be taken as an act of love, an act of someone who believed in the command to give to those who were hungry, to be generous to the least of the little ones. Who knows what goes on in the heart of another person?

At least in the beginning Kempsey seemed to offer opportunities to pursue the two great passions of her life – to be a gentlewoman, and to show compassion for the hungry and needy. She could never be one of the people, but, ironically, she, who never courted their love, was adored. My father was one of the people, but, ironically, he, who hungered for their love, was sometimes eyed with suspicion, or if not with suspicion then with one of those quizzical looks women especially give men whom they do not trust.

For my father Kempsey promised much. There were stories from the past, and there were wonderful story-tellers in the district. There were all the tales from past floods. There was the story of the flood of 1864 when a pregnant woman saved herself by climbing a tree, but the flood waters rose up to her neck, and when they rescued her the waters had stripped off all her clothes, and left her naked, sitting in the fork of the tree; next day she gave birth to a child. My father loved stories in which the threat of disaster dissolved into comedy, the mixture of terror and buffoonery – life for him was a never-ending comic opera. He loved the hint of something spicy. He loved to hear an Australian from way back spinning a yarn in a deadly serious voice, but with a twinkle in the eye at the very mention of what convention and lore decreed to be unmentionable, about a naked woman in the fork of a tree.

There were great characters. One was Arthur Gill, the grandson of Silas Gill. Silas had been transported for smuggling, and had been sent as an assigned servant to the Macleay district. There he found Jesus, repented of his sins, confessed to God that he had sinned against him in thought, word and deed, that it was all his own fault, his own most grievous fault. He asked to be forgiven, and found to his joy, like Pilgrim, that his load of sin was gone. He became a 'Giant for Jesus'. Old Gill, my father used to say, must have been quite a character. What my father liked was the subsequent story of the Gill family. Silas Gill's grandson told him, 'You'd think we was horses, the way they made us work.' My father was back with his own people, the people who spoke in the only way he could understand, the people who used people's idioms – fatalists who responded to a devastating flood with the remark: 'Well, at least we can all have a good laugh' – sardonic people who often judged fools harshly,and said so, 'They say there's one born every minute.'

There was rock fishing at Crescent Head. Unlike Macbeth, my father believed the multitudinous seas could wash a man clean. There could be not much wrong with either himself or the world as long as a man could stand on the rocks on one of those days when a light nor'easter stirred the ocean into a chop which covered its surface with white water so that the 'pig' drummer could not see either the rod or the man holding it, and took the cunjevoi bait and shot out to sea as though its next stop would be Chile. There was the delight of showing the 'pig' drummer who was master, and the agony of wondering whether the line had a high enough breaking-strain to lift out a five- or a six-pounder, and the triumphant return to St George's Hostel to drop the day's catch out of a sugar bag on to the kitchen table. There was the rub. My mother did not like rock fish. She could not be enthusiastic. She thought they were 'coarse' - yes, and 'common'. Whiting were more refined; so were snapper. But my father thought then, as he thought all his life, that the rocks were for heroes, and the river or the harbour for 'old women'. There was then, I imagine, another problem. My father loved a glass of 'cold tea' (neat whisky) after a day of manly heroism and strong satisfactions. My mother could not be generous about that, she fearing it might lead to 'other things'. So my father kept his bottle in the wardrobe with his suits and his vestments.

Kempsey offered much to a man with his passions and interests. There were jokes in the local paper, the *Macleay Chronicle*. There was the joke about the clergyman who asked some young ladies to recommend a suitable hymn to be sung at a wedding; they selected 'Oft in danger, oft in woe'. My father loved telling jokes about marriage, especially jokes in which the man was the sacrificial lamb, and the woman the punisher. My mother always looked very sad when he told such stories, and sometimes sighed, saying, 'I wish you wouldn't tell jokes like that in front of the children, Charlie.' She knew she was taking a risk, as my father panicked at the slightest rebuke. She knew, to her pain, that a criticism in front of others would provoke an explosion of rage, during which her children would hear all her husband's resentments and bitterness against the snubs and slights from her family and other members of her class.

The Church of England in country areas was still the centre of a lively social life. Anglicans still observed the religious year as well as the calendar year. There was Advent, then Christmas, Lent, Easter, Sundays after Easter, Trinity Sundays and then Advent again. There was music to accompany each festival in the church year - Stainer's *Crucifixion* during Holy Week, Handel's *Messiah* at Christmas; there were hymns for every event in the Christ story. At Easter there was the promise:

> *On the Resurrection morning*
> *Soul and body meet again;*
> *No more sorrow - no more weeping,*
> *No more pain!*

My father never asked: Is it true? Or: Do I want to live like a goldfish in a bowl, with no struggle, and everything provided? During Stainer's *Crucifixion* my father always wept when the tenor sang the solo, 'Is it nothing to you, all ye that pass by?' That was the consolation prize for those who bathed their wounds with the balm of being victims, having known tribulation and sorrow in the world. For them, especially for my father, there was the claim that Christ had overcome the world: all soldiers of Christ could overcome the world.

There were the fasts. My father gave up smoking for the forty days and forty nights of Lent. That was part of his witness, evidence for all to see that he was not one of those who passed by. He believed in that day on earth when there were three crosses, and Christ told the penitent thief; 'Today thou shalt be with me in Paradise.' My father never asked himself: Did that happen? Would there be a resurrection morning? If anyone asked him he always replied, 'I'm as sure of that as I am that I'm alive.' And that was that.

He loved people who responded to his charm, those whose eyes brightened up when they saw him, when he came into a room. Kempsey offered many opportunities for eyes to meet in recognition, many opportunities for a good old laugh, many chances for the double hand-shake and the squeeze of the elbow. In September 1920 the Church of England held a village fair in the grounds of All Saints', Kempsey. There was plenty of entertainment – sideshows, raffles, a brass band, the stalls were well stocked. Admission was free. My father moved around among the customers and stall-holders, enjoying the moment when his charm, his human warmth, all the good gifts he had to offer humanity, were being used to promote a higher purpose, 'the spiritual and material welfare of Christ's Church on earth'.

There were opportunities for him as a performer. There were the services each Sunday in All Saints' Church. All those who heard him pray in the words he loved as passionately as he loved catching a huge fish, or executing a late cut in cricket, always remembered the fervour in his voice, the reverence, and the hunger – especially when he recited the words:

Ye that do truly and earnestly repent of your sins, and are in love and charity with your neighbour, and intend to lead a new life following the commandments of God . . . draw near with faith and take this holy sacrament to your comfort; and make your humble confession to Almighty God, meekly kneeling upon your knees.

Perhaps he was the only one in All Saints' Church who knew why he had to take care lest he broke down while intoning those words. For him the words were not a beautiful lie, dressing up a delusion in attractive phrases. They must be true; there must be forgiveness; there must be another chance; there must be a God who would clean a man's 'dirty slate'.

There were concerts, dances and entertainments to raise funds for the Church. My father had great gifts as an entertainer. He had the charisma, the charm, the wit and the passion to be an excellent master of ceremonies at a church concert. He threw open his arms, smiled, clasped his hands together in front of his clerical waistcoat, or, if he was wearing a cassock, swung the tassel at the end of the girdle around in a circle to rouse the audience to a fever pitch. He was always all heart, and did not bother much with things of the head. In September 1920 he recited one of his favourite poems at a church concert. It was Charles Wolfe's 'The Burial of Sir John Moore – After Corunna'. I can hear him now chanting the words; I say chanting because the poetry which moved him clamoured for music, clamoured to be lifted up into a higher medium:

> Not a drum was sounded, not a funeral note,
> As his corse to the ramparts we hurried.

For a believer in the resurrection of the dead, my father had an odd obsession with death. He was also always attracted to those passages in prose or poetry which celebrated the bond between men, the bond when there were no judges, no critics, only delight and pleasure in being together.

There was also much in Kempsey to ferment disquiet in his soul. The war had sharpened the division and antagonism between the comfortable classes and the working class in Australia. My father looked for the resurrection of the dead. My father never looked for or lived for the victory of the working classes over the comfortable classes, or the victory of the comfortable classes over the working classes. My father was a universal-embrace man; he wanted harmony; my father did not believe in class war, or class hatred, or class antagonism; he wanted them all to be nice to each other, he wanted everyone to be kind. But in 1920 the voices of the angry men, the voices of the haters, were heard in the land. The frowners denounced the 'vividness of female dress and the abandonment of modern dancing'. In Sydney 'Jock' Garden was boasting that communists would 'white-ant' the unions in preparation for a bloody revolution and the installation of the dictatorship of the proletariat in Australia. The comfortable classes were organising for the defence of White Australia against this threat. Angry words were being spoken at public meetings. At a meeting of all those loyal to King and Empire in Kempsey in July 1921 a speaker said to thunderous applause, 'If you do not like the smell of the roses, get out.' Everyone knew what he meant. There must be true loyalty in Australia.

All Saints' Church was a citadel for Old Australia, the Australia of the comfortable classes. The original foundation stone had been laid by Mrs Elizabeth Verge on 11 October 1883. She belonged by birth and conviction to the 'ancient nobility of New South Wales'. The walls of the church were decorated with testimonies of loyalty to God, King, Empire and Country. The Church advertised God's blessing on the Empire. There were no references to the compassionate Christ, the Christ who spoke tenderly of the least of the little ones. All Saints' was a temple for Jehovah, the God of power, the God of revenge, the God of domination, the God guiding and protecting the fortunes of the British Empire. My father was ill at ease when there was tension in the air. He did not believe in struggle; he believed in concord and harmony.

The irony was that there was increasing tension in his own home. After the birth of my sister my mother had prayed each night she would never bear another child. That must have imposed a strain on my father, for he was never a total abstinence man. If he had read Tolstoy's essay, 'Why Do Men Stupefy Themselves?', in which the author advocated total abstinence from tobacco, alcohol and sex, my father would have said, 'They say, boy, there's one [fool] born every minute.' Except for not smoking during the forty days and forty nights of Lent I never knew my father to abstain from anything. He was a banquet-of-life man. 'Take what's in front of you, boy', he used to advise me. He was an indulger, but never an over-indulger. The warm humid climate of Kempsey did not make it any easier for a man whose wife has put him on zero spending of one of his passions.

My mother left Kempsey early in 1921, but my father stayed on. I do not know when we children left. The diocesan report for 1921 put it abruptly, 'The Reverend Clark has left us.' They gave no reason. They did not tell their readers where he was going. I was puzzled at the time; I am still puzzled. Years later we were told that the ill-health of my mother was the reason for our sudden departure. My father was not offered a position in any diocese in New South Wales. He had to live through the warm-hearted farewells, probably not knowing what my mother proposed to do, probably not knowing what he could do. On 23 June 1921 the residents of Sherwood gave him a hearty farewell, and presented him with a cheque as a mark of their esteem. Two nights later a large crowd of Anglicans flocked into the parish hall of All Saints' Church to tender their farewell. Laymen and clergy delivered eulogistic addresses, all stressing the valuable work he had done among the sick and stricken members of the community and among the children. My father, in the words of the *Macleay Chronicle*, in an excellent address 'returned feeling thanks for the kind remarks and handsome gift; and in closing, appealed to his hearers to seek a fuller and truer sense and realisation of Jesus Christ in a greater love for each other.'

My father almost broke down. He was being praised for his spirituality, knowing his wife was back with her own family. He lived with his secret until the day he died. Years later there was a hint of what was amiss, but I never found the answer to what puzzled me about the departure from Kempsey. My father had his faith. God would confirm and strengthen in all goodness all those who turned unto Him. God would have mercy: God would pardon. But would human beings be so understanding?

I do not remember leaving Kempsey, although I was six years old. All I remember is that for half a year we three children, Russell, Hope and I, were billeted at Darriwill, near Geelong. My mother was with her own family in Burwood. I do not know where my father was, or what he was doing. In the clerical handbooks of the period his name does not appear for 1921–22. My mother's maiden cousin, Izabel Hope, the daughter of George Hope, was the châtelaine of the manor at Darriwill. The two brothers, Dr Robert and George Hope, had formed a partnership to graze sheep, grow crops and cultivate grape vines. Robert, my great-grandfather, built the bluestone manor of Lynnburn, and George the bluestone manor of Darriwill, the Aboriginal name for a place where two watercourses meet.

I remember 'Aunt' Izabel (as we called her) very well. She was ageless. By day she wore a black skirt so long that her shoes were rarely visible. The skirt was held up by a wide black belt, with a huge metal buckle. She herself was quite short – just five feet, in the memory's eye. She wore a blouse buttoned up to the neck. There was no visible bosom, but perhaps that was because the blouse fitted her body with the modesty of her class and her convictions. She was deeply religious. Every morning after breakfast all of us at the breakfast table – Aunt Izabel, her lady companion, our governess Miss Drury (I never heard her addressed in any other way, and so even now in a quite different age I do not know her first name), and we three children – went down on our knees, resting one elbow on our chairs, folding our hands reverently together in front of our faces, and recited together the Lord's Prayer. We did the same after dinner at night. Each Sunday the servants were ushered into the drawing-room after dinner (always in the middle of the day) and Aunt Izabel played the organ for the weekly hymn. I remember when it was the turn of Tom, the handyman, or Nellie, his wife, to choose; they always asked for

> Shall we gather at the river,
> Where bright angel-feet have trod.

I remember Tom taught me to catch blackfish in the Barrabool River. It was the only time I ever saw him look happy or animated. Perhaps that was why he liked the hymn about the river. Tom spoke very rarely, Nellie never, in front of 'their elders and betters'. I wonder what they said to each other when they were alone about the Hope carry-on. Our governess Miss Drury was also silent at the dining-table, not even Miss Izabel's (as they all called her) familiarities with language – such as calling potatoes 'taters' - put her at her ease; Miss Izabel and the lady companion did all the talking. Miss Izabel was a survivor from a bygone age. I remember when she spoke on the telephone to her brother, she would say at the end of the conversation 'I'll meet you in Geelong', but never name the time or the place.

Like all the members of my mother's family, she saw herself as a stewardess chosen by God and by her birth to watch over the morals and behaviour of those committed to her care. Like my mother, she was not interested in or attracted to putting on airs, or tempted to behave in a condescending way to those below her in God's great chain of being. Like my mother, she wanted everyone to be worthy of having been made in God's image. Like my mother, she was a believer and always acted as though it were God's task, not hers, to chide or frown, or even to change any part of the world. Unlike my mother, her face always expressed pleasure. Looking back now across the years I assume she believed you should enjoy the whole of God's creation, that putting on black looks, or being in a black mood, was an insult to God the Father. Like my mother she spoke of her earthly father and her heavenly Father as though they were one. I adored her. All my life I was always transported into another world in the presence of mavericks and eccentrics. Kindred spirits always recognise one another. Barriers of age, class, religion, colour or political convictions fall. Years later I was deeply moved to hear she found me very 'spirited' in 1921–22. I had always feared she might have rejected me as 'difficult', 'stormy', or even 'unreliable'.

My words have done scant justice to the mighty spirit, the lively personality encased within her tiny frame. They cannot bring to life the sparkle in the eye, the cheeks, the mouth suffused with delight as she asked old Tom each Sunday after dinner, 'What hymn will we sing today, Tom?' Off we would go, singing words which seemed to imply God's world was a better one than this world. But, if I remember rightly, all the singers, except perhaps Miss Drury (I wonder now if she ever was to know the glory), looked as though they enjoyed hugely the world in which they were living and did not want to leave it.

I remember Aunt Izabel and her companion sometimes whispered to each other the things they did not want me to hear. Some time during 1921 she told us she had some good news for us. My mother was much better, and we would all see her again very soon. I remember one scene very clearly. My brother and I were taken to Melbourne to see my mother and to visit her grandmother, Catherine Hope (née Hassall), at the home of my mother's Aunt Annie, the wife of Tom Collis, a Melbourne lawyer. They lived at Redlands in Fullarton Street, East St Kilda (not far from the St Kilda cemetery where Alfred Deakin was buried in October 1919). I mention this because all I remember of the meeting with my great-grandmother was her talk about the Reverend Samuel Marsden. Servants wheeled her into the room. She looked like a majestic waxed doll: she wore a white bonnet, the borders of which were conspicuous for their fine work with the crochet needle; her neck was kept rigid by fine whalebone supports, visible beneath the lace work covering her neck. I remember the pleats on her black bodice, and how lovingly they had been ironed. I remember the face, the face of someone who had endured with grace and dignity all she had lived through: the death of a child, who had died before being baptised; and her anxiety lest it therefore lacked the essential certificate for an entrée card to the kingdom of Heaven; and being married for over thirty years to a man with the Hope temperament – charmers who often turned nasty, self-professed servants of God who often behaved as though they were possessed by an evil spirit. Perhaps we all are.

She had seen much in her lifetime: John Macarthur raving mad in Parramatta, Samuel Marsden walking into his own 'dark night', William Charles Wentworth drunk and William Charles Wentworth sober, the Australia she loved being swept aside by the vulgarians and the new rich from the goldfields, her brother James falling a victim to the 'family complaint', and their prayers, all of no avail, to cure him of that ghastly infirmity. She had known them all. I had no idea of what she had been through at the time. All I can remember is her saying to Russell and me, 'When you grow up you'll be told that your great-great-great-grandfather Samuel Marsden was a cruel man. He was not a cruel man: he was a severe man.' I did not know at the time what she was talking about. I listened in awe, my mouth slightly open, sensing this was one of those moments which would live on, just as the memory of seeing the Keith and Ross Smith plane lived on. In childhood my mind was already overcrowded with ghosts from the past. Much of life has been a quest to learn how to live with those ghosts. I was beginning to ask questions, beginning to be puzzled, but I was still a child.

The serious person inside me ran his eyes over my great-grandmother's face, hoping, maybe, this would be one of those brief moments when everything became clear. The child wanted her to stop talking straight away so that my brother and I could resume our never-ending drama of antagonism and reconciliation. 'I do wish you boys would stop fighting', my mother used to say, sometimes adding, 'One day I will go right away.' My brother would say, 'Don't talk like that, Mummy, don't talk like that.' And I would say nothing, because fears always struck me dumb. I grieved in private, and lay awake at nights wondering what that was all about, becoming so restless, while my brother slept deeply, that my mother would come into the room to calm me down, and say, 'I don't know what's going to happen to you, Mann dear. I wonder what I have done for God to punish me like this.' She would kiss me passionately, and I knew from the moistness on her cheeks that she had been crying, and I wondered why that was so.

Often my mind was on trivial things. It would be nice to think there had been lofty thoughts in my head when we left the house in East St Kilda, possibly even thoughts about the history of Australia, or the strange history of my mother's family. But, as usual with me after an ascent into the high places, I took refuge in the banal. As we walked to the tram I was composing doggerel verses about 'Mater', the family name for Catherine Hope. The next day my mother took the three of us to Luna Park. My brother and I bullied her into giving us a ride on the ferris wheel, Russell being the most persistent. My mother had her doubts – 'Manning', she said, 'will never stand it.' That provoked me into extravagant claims that I would be all right, and many imploring, stand-over pleas: 'Please let me, please . . . please . . . please . . . please.' I remember my mother's anxious face, as she struggled with the dilemma between the desire to please and fears of disaster. She gave in. We all climbed on board; we buckled our safety belts; the wheel began to rotate. As we rose off the ground my brother was ecstatic, though in between his expressions of enthusiasm he asked, 'Are you all right, Mann?'

I was not all right. I tried during the first quarter of the cycle to hide my fear, but by the time we reached the top I screamed, and shouted, 'Stop the wheel, stop, or I'll jump off.' My mother asked the man in charge to stop the wheel. When it descended, I jumped out and buried my head in my mother's skirts and sobbed. One woman in the crowd below, some of whom had mocked and some of whom had understood my problem with heights, said to my mother, 'You were very wise to ask the man to stop the wheel. Your boy has a very special temperament.' From that time on there was always a question of what I could and what I could not abide without an emotional catastrophe. From that time on my mother was even more anxious about me, and what I could or could not endure. 'Be careful, Mann dear' became her constant refrain, her instant reaction on seeing me. My father hoped her fears were groundless. He joked. He repeated more often what he had said before, 'Manning would fall over on a billiard table.' I winced. I liked neither the smother nor the ridicule.

There was that other never-ending question: when would we all be together again? We were always on the move, always dependent on my mother's family.

In 1921 my mother told me we were all going to live together on Phillip Island. She was much better. The Archbishop of Melbourne, Harrington Lees, had offered my father the position of vicar of Cowes,

73

Phillip Island, together with the churches at Ventnor, Rhyll and Newhaven, and a chaplaincy to the Church of England boys' home at Newhaven. We were to be together again. We would see my father again. Small boys do not ask questions; they respond to the thrill of the moment. We were promised many things – a ride on a train, a ride on a boat, and a house of our own. Small boys accept; excitement stills doubt, and quietens that passion to torment oneself with the unanswerable questions.

I was not then a doubting Thomas. It was many years before I asked myself the question: why was my father not offered a parish in the Diocese of Grafton, or Sydney, or any diocese in New South Wales? By the time I put that question to myself all those who knew the answer were dead. My brother and my sister never put the question. They were lucky, they believed what they were told. But it was not long before I began to doubt everything. Perhaps life was my stern tutor, perhaps my temperament prepared me to be a doubter. Whatever the cause a passionate lover and believer became a doubter, but the doubter never lost his thirst to love or his thirst to believe. That was the cue which sent me off on a long pilgrimage.

My Swanee River

Everyone has a Swanee River – the place where their heart is 'turning ever'. Mine was, and always will be, Phillip Island, an island at the entrance to Western Port Bay, in Victoria. After the abrupt end of his ministry in Kempsey my father decided there was no future for him in the Dioceses of Sydney or Grafton. He wrote to the Anglican Archbishop of Melbourne to offer his services. On the surface His Grace and my father had little in common. His Grace was an English gentleman in gaiters, my father a boy from St Peters, who always looked as though between him and gaiters there was a great gulf set. His Grace had delicate fingers as white as the lawn sleeves of the surplice from which they emerged; my father had the fingers of a man who swung the axe, the hoe and the pick. His Grace always behaved as though God had punished him by calling on him to preach the gospel of Christ to the barbarians of the New World; my father loved Australians, my father loved his adopted country.But there was a bond between them. His Grace knew about the shadow, His Grace knew that a man often went out of his wits when possessed by a wild passion. His Grace understood. He offered my father the position of vicar of St Philip's Church, Cowes.

Phillip Island was small, both in area and in population. It had the shape of a boomerang with wavy lines. Nature had been boun-teous with its beauties, and niggardly with its wealth. The Aborigines had been birds of passage, visiting the island once a year to collect shellfish. George Bass had entered the port from the east in 1798, and Lieutenant Grant from the west in 1800. As the bay and the island were the most westerly points he had reached, Bass named the bay Western Port – a name which survived, despite it being to the east of the later principal settlement in Port Phillip Bay. He called the eastern tip of the Island Cape Woolamai, because it reminded him of the head of a fish which the natives of Sydney Harbour called the 'woolomai'. Matthew Flinders had sailed along the south coast of the Island in 1802 (what we boys called the 'back beach') and noted a 'needle-like rock', known later as Pyramid Rock. Sealers and whalers pitched camps on the few sandy beaches on the north side of the Island.

On instructions from London, Governor Darling planted a small penal settlement near Rhyll in 1826, but they soon withdrew, finding, like the Dutch in the north over two hundred years earlier, that there was 'little good to be done there'. In 1842 J. D. McHaffie settled on the Island. Later settlers named the principal landmarks after the early inhabitants – the Aborigines were forgotten except in the name of Cape Woolamai. There was McHaffie's Reef, Kitty Miller's Bay, Berry's Beach, the Nobbies, Pyramid Rock, Forrest's Caves. After the passing of the land acts in the 1860s settlers arrived to take up small blocks of land, trying to make a living on an island which had no rivers or creeks, a few springs in almost inaccessible places, low rainfall, and a prevailing dry wind. Families arrived – the McGregors of Pyramid Rock, the Cleelands, the Wests and the McLardys. The sea was bountiful; the grasses and the thistles fed the rabbits. Chicory and other crops, sheep and cattle, barely provided a living for the families of the farmers. The rabbits and the fish, the home-grown vegetables and the chooks, provided food.

The Island was a microcosm of the class system in the Australia of the 1920s. There were a few families with pretensions to belonging to the country gentry. There were the families who catered for the tourists; Phillip Island was challenging the bayside townships of Port Phillip, Point Lonsdale, Airey's Inlet, Lorne and Apollo Bay, and the Dandenongs. Just before we arrived on the Island the *Phillip Island Standard* carried this advertisement:

Come down to this Finest Pearl of the Southern Seas with its setting of crystal waters and azure skies. Leave the heat, dust and flies of summer or the cruel frosts of winter, say goodbye to the monotonous routine, or nerve-racking trouble and realise the joy of life in an island holiday where all breezes are sea breezes.

For three months every year the holiday-makers transplanted the class system of Melbourne and its suburbs to Cowes. Members of the same family belonged sometimes to different social classes. Three Spaven sisters married three proprietors of hotels or boarding houses. One married A. K. T. Sambell, the proprietor of the Isle of Wight Hotel. Sambell was a Melbourne businessman who had the ambition of turning Phillip Island into a money-spinner for the proprietors of the two hotels and the boarding houses. In 1922 his hotel catered for the noisy and flamboyant members of the Melbourne *haute-bourgeoisie*, for those with money who wanted to liberate themselves from the chains of gentility. They were the forerunners of 'flapper-dom' on the holiday beaches of Victoria.

The Phillip Island Hotel catered for types quite different from those of middle-class Melbourne. Its proprietor, Bing Edgar, was A. K. T. Sambell's brother-in-law. They were as different from each other as frost from fire. Sambell was a pillar of bourgeois respectability, an upright man, a man with one eye on the counting-house and another on his eternal salvation. Years later I saw him as a man who believed a concern for salvation was quite good for business. He did not seem to be troubled about where the profits came from, that, for example, the beer sold in his bar might lead a man on to damnation. He was not bothered when the moral improvers of the day raved on about the evils of 'flapperdom'. He was interested in 'bookings'; he was interested in all those developments which would attract the holiday-makers and weekenders to the Island. He thought big: he had ideas for a new ferry from Stony Point to Cowes, for a car punt and later a bridge from San Remo to Newhaven, and for better roads on the Island. The future of the Island, he believed, lay with the holiday-makers, the 'visitors', as the locals called them.

Bing Edgar was a very different human being. Sambell never looked at the person to whom he was speaking. As a child I remember he always looked as though he were speaking to the carpet and not to another human being. Bing Edgar only looked at the floor when he was talking to someone who did not belong to his world. His world was the world of drinkers, the fellowship of those who were dismissed in the Sambell world as not being reliable, the ones who never got things straight. Bing did not condemn or frown on liars, fornicators or drunkards; he made his living from being nice to such people, encouraging them to do what they wanted to do, convincing them there was nothing odious, deceitful, or disgraceful in being what they were. For Bing a drinker was the salt of the earth, provided he did not make a nuisance of himself, did not go too far, did not betray his fellow drinkers, and did not skite about what went on in Bing's 'night cupboard' at the Phillip Island Hotel.

I doubt whether Bing ever told anyone what went on in his heart. Years later I saw him as the eternal outsider, the man behind the bar, the man who never let anyone come near. He was always nattily dressed, his brightly coloured bow-tie always a trifle skew-whiff – like his hair, which, though immaculately brushed, always had a few hairs out of place, and often a loose fringe almost covering one of his eyes. I remember there was also something odd about his eyes. I should add that he had a superb tenor voice, and at every concert I attended as a child he made women weep when he sang 'Annie Laurie'. As a child I was puzzled why a man like Bing Edgar should be so close to tears when he sang a song about a woman. Now I know that, in my childhood, the concert was one outlet for men's confession of guilt, a way of saying 'sorry'.

Bing belonged to the man's world. Years later I remember watching him polish one of the glasses used in the 'night cupboard' of the Phillip Island Hotel. He breathed on the glass, rubbed it firmly with a tea-towel, then held it up to the light to see whether he had wiped it clean. He was as reverent and loving with a beer glass as a priest with the communion cup. The brass rail around the bar in the Phillip Island Hotel was the communion rail, not for all those who intended to lead a new life following someone else's commandments, but rather the communion rail for men. Bing, as I found later, had a bone-crushing hand-shake. With Mr Sambell my hand slipped out of his as though it had never been clasped.

Bing, I remember, played cricket for Cowes. The only dress concession he made for the game was to take off his bow-tie, and undo the top button of his shirt. Bing did not play with a straight bat. He swiped at the first ball he received, and if he fluked a hit his team-mates called out, 'Good on you, Bing.' Mr Sambell never played cricket. My mother thought Bing Edgar was 'peculiar', but I found it difficult to understand her reserve. Perhaps she was scared of the 'night cupboard'. My father, though, adored Bing Edgar. He attracted to the Phillip Island Hotel the people with whom my father knew heart's ease. The visitors who drank at his hotel were the mild non-conformists of bourgeois Melbourne, the locals were, if not the rebels against bourgeois respectability, those who found in

Bing's bar and Bing's 'night cupboard' the pleasure the frowners wanted to take away from them.

W. Dawson Davie was the proprietor of Erewhon, the boarding house for those members of the Melbourne bourgeoisie who did not want to have anything to do with bar-room culture. Erewhon had strong snob appeal. It had once been the country seat and holiday home of State Governors of Victoria, and traded on those Government House associations. W. Dawson Davie behaved like a man who had danced in the ball-room of Government House in Melbourne. He, too, married a Spaven. He and Bing Edgar and Mr Sambell were all brothers-in-law. W. Dawson Davie was a carefully groomed man: his moustache was as neat as any geometrical design, and the line along which his hair was parted was as straight as his own path through life. W. Dawson Davie was never seen in holiday dress. He wore suits which had all the *comme il faut* atmosphere and glamour of a suit illustrated in a Henry Buck's advertisement in the Melbourne *Herald* any Thursday afternoon. W. Dawson Davie was destined for municipal office: he became first a councillor of the shire of Phillip Island, and then president. His brother-in-law, Bing Edgar, never wore the robes of office.

W. Dawson Davie's wife knew what was what in the bourgeois world. She never put a foot out of place, or uttered a word which uncovered what was going on in her mind. By nature she was kindly and warm-hearted, but the lore of her tribe required that she bury all that away beneath the display garments which concealed from the eyes of the lascivious, and of at least one curious young boy, her ample bosom. I remember as a child noticing that her bosom rose and fell like the green swell on the ocean when Clarrie Williams, one of the local storekeepers, sang 'Comin' Through the Rye'. I was puzzled at the time – but not now. Mrs Dawson Davie might have had a story to tell, but the lore of her tribe required her to remain silent. She was one of the legion of conformists on the eve of the great liberation. By the time that began, she was dead. Such is life!

We arrived in Cowes early in 1922. I was seven years old. My father's mission was to minister to the locals. A clergyman kept one eye on Heaven and the other on the money in the plate each Sunday – no money in the plate, no income for the parson. The locals had little, if any, money. No man can squeeze blood out of a stone: no parson could live on the offerings of the locals of Phillip Island. My father must attract the visitors, must ingratiate himself with the world of Mr Sambell. He must render unto Caesar more than the things that were Caesar's. Once again the conditions for success as a clergyman (size of plate, size of congregation, size of audience at church concerts) conflict with the dictates of his heart. My father is again trapped. Like all animals caught in a trap he will make foolhardy attempts to break out of the trap, only to find that the teeth of the trap have bitten more deeply.

The Church had its calendar, but even that must be subordinated to the tourists' calendar. There was the season of plenty – from Christmas to Easter: there was the season of scarcity from Easter to Christmas. My father must defer to Mr Sambell, my father must cultivate Mr Sambell. My father must be careful not to give Bing Edgar the eye of understanding, because much might be construed from a glistening eye in that little world. My mother's heart was not troubled, nor was her conscience. The world of Mrs Sambell and Mrs Dawson Davie was the best the Island had to offer in the way of gentility. They were, of course, upstarts – women whose husbands had made money from trade and exploiting human weaknesses. At least she could tell them about her father's family. I am not sure they listened. My mother's world was fast becoming an anachronism in post-war Australia. That was part of her tragedy: she remained all her life a prisoner in the world of her childhood. Perhaps we all do.

For my father the Island had much to offer: once again he could perform in public; and the *Phillip Island Standard* published summaries of his sermons. At evensong on 1 January 1923 he conducted a special service to usher in the New Year; he exhorted the congregation to take resolutions for the New Year, urging them to be mindful of Christ's commandment that they should love one another. Love extended to fellow men, he added, brightened up man's short existence on this sphere. He was sure of that, indeed he was as sure of that as he was that he was alive. Loving kindness was always my father's message. I have no idea whether the message fell on stony ground. I can see now the faces of some of that tiny band of believers who gathered each Sunday in St Philip's Church. I wonder how many of them were touched by my father's message, and, if so, how long it lasted.

He played a prominent part on his first Anzac Day on the Island. After a memorial service in the Cowes Hall the people joined in a procession to the war memorial, a granite cairn erected on an enclosed triangle of lawn in front of the Isle of Wight Hotel. The Anglican and the Presbyterian church choirs sang 'Onward Christian Soldiers', 'Land of Hope and Glory', 'Stand Up, Stand Up for Jesus', and 'O God, Our Help in Ages Past'. My father, clothed in surplice and cassock and a stole bearing the emblem of the British Crown, told them that sacrifice was an inspiration to a higher and better service. All present were then asked to join in singing 'For All the Saints that from their Labours Rest'. Mr A. K. T. Sambell then offered to entertain all sailors and soldiers in the bar of the Isle of Wight Hotel.

Those were giddy days – the days of the universal embrace, the days when the clergy and politicians and publicists told the people that Great Britain was once their mother, and they were her children. But now they had grown to manhood. Great Britain granted them their freedom without exacting anything in return. The following Sunday my father dedicated two flags in St Philip's Church to the glory of God and in memory of the father of Mrs A. M. Landy and Mrs V. McHenry. The congregation sang a lusty 'God Save the King'. Why listen to 'Sinn Feiners' or 'Socialistic Bolshevists'? The Australian flag was good enough for anyone. The British flag was the only protection they had against an invader. So clergy, teachers and public men should continue to inculcate in the rising generation of Australians the need to cultivate righteousness, truth, liberty and loyalty – but beware of too much freedom, that led on to licence, and licence to decadence and Bolshevism. The boy from St Peters had become an apologist for the comfortable classes in Australia, clothing the greed of the money-changers with the mantle of divine authority.

Once again my father found himself in a situation in which reason and passion were for him 'self-division's cause'. Reason whispered in his ear: defer to the world of Mr Sambell, charm the visitors, keep away from the Bing Edgar world, and the plate shall be full, the 'Arch' will be so pleased that he will soon offer you a better parish. Reason whispered: be a servant in a cassock to the men who plan to exploit the island to gratify the post-war lust of the comfortable classes for petty pleasures. That was the great temptation. But my father could never be a servant to any man or any woman. My father knew his *Pilgrim's Progress*. He knew he was, and always would be, Mr Passion. That was why people loved him. He loved people: he loved characters – they were the breath of life for him. He belonged to the Bing Edgar world. Being obsequious to Mr Sambell, saying 'Yes, Mr Sambell', 'No, Mr Sambell', agreeing with

Mr Sambell was being a Judas to what he felt in his heart. My father came from the people, he belonged to the people. On the Island there was that same tyranny of opinion, that lore of the bourgeois tribe under which he had chafed and fretted in Sydney and Kempsey. There was also the world of the people. That was the world he loved, that was the world in which he could be himself.

Phillip Island was a people's paradise. There was the camaraderie of the cricket field. My father fancied himself as a batsman and a slips fieldsman, but to succeed on the Cowes cricket ground he needed to change his style. He was proudest of his late-cuts, his leg-glances, and his square-cuts. But on the Cowes ground long grass and rough ground meant a late-cut or a leg-glance did not travel very far. My father loved to flourish his bat after a late-cut – that was part of being stylish, being artistic, just as a violinist flourished his bow at the end of a sonata. My father loved to wear flannel trousers kept in place by a black belt, his shirt sleeves buttoned at the wrists, and a white handkerchief in one of the trouser pockets. He liked to wear a peaked cap. The locals did not wear special cricket togs: if a player wore anything on his head it was a felt hat, tilted back so as not to be smudged by perspiration on the forehead. My father batted with pads and batting gloves. So did Eric Hatfield, the Cowes school-master. But they were not locals – they belonged in a limbo halfway between the visitors and the locals. A local wore one batting pad, not two, never wore gloves, and often unstrapped that one pad and chucked it away saying, 'that bloody thing is only a fucking nuisance'.

I remember my father always looked very happy when he was showing my brother and me how to play a late-cut. 'Watch me, boy', he would say, as he held the handle of the bat loosely in his left hand and spun it a few times, and then faced up to my brother's bowling. 'Give me a short one outside the off-stump and I'll show you the late-cut.' 'No, boy, not on the middle stump, outside the off stump. Manning knows where to bowl them. Give him a turn.' I remember the cheeky way he pushed out his bum as soon as the bat touched the ball. 'You know, boy,' he would say, 'you can't play a proper late-cut on a matting-on-concrete wicket. You need a turf wicket. You should have seen the late-cuts I used to play on the Petersham oval before the war. When I played one of my late-cuts, boy, the ball went to the fence like greased lightning. They used to clap me, boy.' And he would put his arm around me and lead me towards the back door. He was a most loving man: he wanted to come near to everyone.

I remember he was not always happy with his performances with the bat for the Cowes team. They flattered him by electing him captain. The locals had a peculiar reverence for clergymen and teachers, seeming to believe they knew things the locals did not know. I remember Saturday-night tears in the vicarage when my father was in a black mood, when his comments were sardonic, and the pleasure he seemed to derive from telling about someone else's misfortunes changed his kindly face into something quite satanic. Years later when I read the *Phillip Island Standard* I found the reason. In the first games of the cricket season in which he played he was dismissed for a duck. But by January 1923 the same paper was reporting the Cowes players were 'glad to see their captain, C. Clark, show a little of his practice form'. The previous Saturday he had made 28 not out; the following Saturday he and E. Hatfield made a 'quiet start' in the Cowes innings.

By then Mr Hatfield ('Hattie') had become a great favourite with the boys and girls in the Cowes school. I remember Hattie very well: I remember the alpaca coat he wore in all seasons of the year, the stiff white butterfly collar, the dark tie. I remember the tension when he took us for mental arithmetic, how he started with very simple sums, and coaxed us into believing we could give the answers to more difficult sums. I remember thinking at times that what Mr Hatfield meant by the word 'mental' was not what my mother meant when she said to me, 'I wish you wouldn't say such strange things, Mann dear. People will think you're mental.' I enjoyed the days when I was good at Mr Hatfield's 'mental'; I also secretly enjoyed it when my mother warned me I might one day be considered 'mental' by 'people'. It seemed to me then that some people liked it when I was being 'mental'.

I remember my father enjoyed the attentions of the boys and girls in the school. In March 1923 he was elected to the school committee. Once a week he came to the school to give religious instruction. He loved an audience. He was superb at holding boys and girls spellbound with his series of stories from the Bible: 'All eyes on me,' he would begin, 'I want you all to keep looking at me.' He would survey them all with his eyes, giving the recalcitrant ones his famous 'quelling look'. ('Boy,' he would often say, 'as soon as I start to speak you can hear a pin dropping.') 'What's your first duty on Sundays?'

The boys and girls knew the answer my father wanted. 'Go to church', they chorused. My father moved so swiftly from one side of the room to the other he seemed to be dancing. He always wore a smile on his face, except once I remember when one of the older boys asked him how did he know Christ rose from the dead. My father stood stock still, the smile was replaced by a frown, much puckering of the eyebrows, a quick quiver of the nostrils, as he said: 'Look, Frank' (it was Frank Towns, if I remember rightly, the son of a council road-worker, and cornet player in the Salvation Army band. It was one of the many contradictions in my father's character and behaviour that although he was a people's man, he was incensed if any child or adult from the people challenged his arguments. 'A man, boy,' he used to say, 'should not be treated as though he were a butcher's assistant'), 'I am as sure of that as I am of anything living.'

Frank's position in society may have been 'lowly', as they would say in those days, but he was no fool. 'Mr Clark,' he said, 'you haven't answered my question.' I remember my own alarm on seeing the sudden change in my father's face, all those hints of an explosion, the tension before the storm. But in public he generally managed to control himself. We heard about it later. So did my poor mother: 'God spare me days, woman,' I heard him raging, 'why should I be laughed at by a young guttersnipe?' He went on to make her responsible for all he had to endure, shouting that her family had poisoned people's minds against him. I did not know then what he was talking about. I do not know how all that fret and fever in which they lived could ever be avoided – or whether they knew what it was doing to one of their children.

My father could not abide contradiction. He wanted everyone to agree with him. He went to pieces – dignity, the desire for approval, the hope of being highly esteemed by the men in power, the value he placed on self-respect – nothing could restrain him. He was Mr Passion: he wanted everything now. He never could and never would stop. That was part of the cross he had to carry through life. That was what made it certain that what he wanted most in life would never be. The angry man inside him always cheated him of the prizes he coveted.

I was aware at the time that there was something terribly amiss. I was puzzled. Every Sunday morning I heard my father tell the congregation in St Philip's Church a story from either the Old or the New Testament. He was a superb story-teller. I listened entranced as he told the story of Balaam and his ass, or Joseph and his brothers, or Noah and his Ark, or the Prodigal Son, or the Good Samaritan. He stood in the pulpit in his robe of white linen, his black cassock, his stole, every hair of his head in place, his face a picture of the sun of love in his heart, his eyes glistening, sometimes moistening, with tears of ecstasy.

From those sermons I wrote in my mind my first history of the world. It went something like this. In the beginning God made the earth, the sky, the sea, and all that lived on the earth, and in the sea, including human beings. God made everything for human beings. But something went wrong – though what that was I did not understand at the time, nor do I understand now. God, my father told us, loved the world. To put things right he sent his only Son into the world to fix up the world. (Later I found out the meaning of the phrase – 'to redeem the world'.) This Son, Jesus Christ, taught us what God was like: he was loving, and forgiving. But men and women did not like their Saviour. They arrested him, charged him with being a 'blasphemer' (I did not know what that meant at the time), and sentenced him to be crucified. Men and women killed God's only Son. But God was not defeated. Three days after his Son was taken down from the Cross he rose from the dead, and ascended into Heaven. My father never told us where that was, though as a child I had a picture of Heaven in the sky – that is, just above as far as I could see on one of those days when there were no clouds in the sky. My father never told me what people did in Heaven, nor did he say whether there were bodies or spirits there. He only told us that all those who obeyed the will of God would meet again in Heaven, but then lapsed into a prose poem about the life in Heaven: God would wipe away all tears from our eyes, and there would be no more weeping, and father, sister, child, brother and mother, would meet once again.

This seemed an attractive idea at the time. I was not bothered about the ones who did not get to Heaven – I do not remember my father ever referring to Hell, or to the punishments God would inflict on those who did not obey His laws. That was not in my father's account of God's plan for all of us. God would forgive everyone, God would understand. So I did not have to decide whether I liked a God who sentenced a large part of His creation to eternal torments in Hell. I liked the idea of this place in the sky where we all met again. Well, not quite. Rather, I made my own Heaven, a place where I could meet again the people I liked. My Heaven did not include the whole of humanity. I thought of Heaven then as a place of refuge, a place where I would at last be safe from the people who hurt me in this world. Heaven was my funk-hole. Years later I read that for sailors Heaven was a place where there was no more sea. I knew what they meant. For me as a child Heaven was a place where I would not hear my father's rages, or ever again hear my mother say, 'There are things in my life, Mann dear, I hope you will never hear about.'

I needed an escape. The world was a painful place, the world was unbearable. I could fantasise, and I did fantasise about a world quite different from the world I knew. In my childhood I became a Heaven-on-earth man, a person who needed to believe there would one day be a different world from the world I knew – either here and now, or in some future time and place. Childhood fashioned me into the person who was to spend his life thirsting to believe there could be a Heaven on earth, or a Heaven in the life of the world to come. But that thirst was never slaked: that thirst clamoured for satisfaction all my life. That was one of many satisfactions which eluded me. For me, there was never to be a drink at either of those waters.

The world was a strange place: the world was a painful place. Just at the moment when everything seemed clear, when the mood of the moment gave me confidence that everything would be all right, the wounding words were often said. I remember one morning in the church at Cowes. My father had preached the words of hope, telling us of Christ's promises that we would all meet again beyond the grave. (Years later, when I searched feverishly through the Gospels to see what Christ said, I found to my dismay that he made no such promise.) We had all sung the confidence-building words 'With the Cross of Jesus/Going on before', and my father had pronounced the benediction 'The peace of God which passeth all understanding', and my father walked reverently towards the vestry. I felt so sure of everything that when Louie Burke told me her mother would not be calling for her for half an hour after the service I took an enormous risk. I said, 'That's good, you'll be able to play with me.' I can still see the sneer on her face. She looked at me with loathing and contempt, and hissed through her teeth (I remember her lips were rolled back so that I could see the bands on her teeth), 'Who'd want to play with you?'

I did not know what to say then, nor do I know now. I never forgot. Her words and her face lived on. It was one of many remarks which

My mother before she met my father

My father: 'that ye have life, and have it more abundantly'

My father on his ordination day

My father's world

My father as a stretcher-bearer

My father and a Ceylonese boy at Colombo, 1917

My mother

'Pud', 1916(?)

Mother, Russell, Hope and self, 1919(?):
'there are as many kinds of love as there are hearts' – L. Tolstoi

might have taught me to keep out of the way of women's character sketches, but I learned such wisdom late in life. It was years before I learned to wear a mask, years before I learned to keep out of the way of the women driven to punish the vulnerable – the women for whom I provided the sport they loved. I found later some women had an unerring eye for the sore spot in a man, an unerring eye for weakness, and an innate knowledge of the most painful whip.

My father liked me to go with him when he was visiting the sick. We travelled in a jinker, a single-seater carriage drawn by a horse. 'Boy,' my father used to say, 'help me to back Ginger between the shafts.' That was not easy, as Ginger was not all that keen on the role of pack-horse for a country clergyman. He used to express displeasure by showing the whites of the eyes, by digging his hind legs into the soil, and by snorting with rage at the indignities my father and I were inflicting on him. My mother came out to the stable too. I heard her whispering to my father not to let Manning see or hear anything nasty, because he was too sensitive for that sort of thing. My father replied, 'Manning will be all right. He's a thoughtful customer.' And he would say, 'Jump up, boy', and as I sat down next to him he would say, 'Don't forget, boy, you're here because you're the thoughtful customer. You understand.'

Yet when I spoke to him on the way back, on a moonlight night when the moon seemed to be travelling the same pace as we were, and my father was enjoying the moments when Ginger raised his tail gracefully and farted with every step in the stately trot he turned on when the world was shrouded in the beauty of the night, he shied away from my question. I was frightened. I wanted the moon to stop moving, but it wouldn't. So I asked him, 'Dad, who created God?' My father was startled. He took a quick look at me, then drew the whip out of the whip-stand, rose slightly out of his seat, whacked Ginger quite hard on the backside, fell back into his seat from the jolt of Ginger's sudden spurt, turned to me and said, 'Boy, that's my great subject. You wait till you're a bit older, and we'll have a long talk about it.' But he never did. I was still waiting for him to tell me when he died in 1951. He was still calling me a 'thoughtful customer'.

I remember another time at Cowes when my father drove me in the jinker to the local cemetery for the burial of a local, who had been crushed to death by the wheels of his dray on his drunken way back to his house after a long session at Bing Edgar's 'night cupboard'. Once again my father and mother whispered to each other before we set out, my mother imploring my father not to tell me much about this man, and my father giving the non-committal 'Leave it to me' type of answer. The man was probably ugly in childhood, and years of heavy drinking twisted his face into a caricature of the ugly and the grotesque. He was a slobberer, slovenly in dress, the stomach so swollen that the bottom half reached almost to the knees. On the way back, as we were driving through the swamp on the old Rhyll road, with the tea-tree the appropriate setting for such a sombre occasion, I asked my father one of my questions. 'Dad,' I said, 'will he be the same on the Resurrection morning?' My father, if I remember correctly, tightened his grip on the reins, and flicked Ginger on the rump. 'What are you getting at, boy?' he asked. I said that I wondered whether God would want to change him, because no one liked looking at him when he was alive. My father said, 'Boy, when you grow up you'll read a lot about St Paul. He said we were all going to be changed. In a moment, boy, in the twinkling of an eye. The trumpet shall sound, and we shall be changed. Listen to this, boy.' And my father began to sing the aria from the *Messiah*, 'Behold, I tell you a mystery . . .', to which, but perhaps I am embroidering the story, old Ginger farted in time. Resurrection was my father's great hope – though I did not understand at the time why his voice hardened when he mentioned the name of St Paul. I do now. 'You mark my words, boy, on the Resurrection morning body and soul meet once more.' But by then we were out of the tea-tree swamp, and onto the metal road leading into Cowes. In the presence of that vast sky, and the emptiness, the air of mystery and wonder had vanished. We had left behind the world of make-believe.

My father was not generous about the ministers of the other denominations. He was a superb mocker of any rival. The rivalry was about the number in the congregation, that being the source of the 'plate', which in turn was the only measure ever mentioned for the success or failure of his work. The Presbyterians were the only other congregation on the Island. The Catholic church, the Star of the Sea, was at San Remo on the mainland. I only heard of one Catholic on the Island, Ethel Saw. My father told me she had a house full of cats. He thought that dealt with her. My mother told me Ethel Saw was 'mental'. I did not know whether my mother meant Catholics were 'peculiar' (in my mother's meaning of the word) – they had cats, and were dirty and slovenly. My father had a sympathetic eye for

Catholics and eccentrics, but was careful not to let anyone know what he was thinking.

On the subject of the Reverend Mr Dann, the Presbyterian minister, my father was unmerciful. 'Boy,' he would say to me, 'you ought to take a geek at the Preso reading from the Bible to the men repairing the piles of the Cowes pier.' ('I wish you wouldn't use low and common words when you're speaking to the boy', my mother would say.) My father would wink at me once he was sure my mother could not see, and continue the story with a surge of gusto. 'Old Dann wears a clerical black boater on his nut, a black coat, buttoned up to his neck and reaching down to his knees, yes, and black gaiters, boy, as though the lower half of him was an archbishop, and the top half a puritan relic from the past. And he stands there and reads verses about how God will punish sinners. You should hear the language, boy, of the men shifting the piles.' It did not occur to me then to wonder why my father mocked so many people. It did not occur to me then that there was anything odd about a man professing Christ-like love for all human beings deriving such pleasure from ridiculing the behaviour of so many of God's children. Perhaps that was why he was always sarcastic about my brother's skinny legs, and my dreaming. I doubt if it ever occurred to him that we might be hurt. His hunger for such satisfaction was so voracious, clamouring as it did for immediate relief, that he seemed never to discipline his appetite. Nor was he ever contrite – though I imagine now that he was contrite about other things, but only because the pain they brought him was more than he could bear.

At the time I adored my father – he was the magician, the one who worked great marvels. It was nesting time for the birds, and a magpie in the pine tree was terrorising my brother and me. My father took his rifle, a twenty-two single shooter, put a bullet in the breech, took aim, fired, and our tormenter fell dead out of the tree.

My father was our saviour. He told stories about his parish work in which he found much to amuse him while preparing the souls of the locals for their eternal salvation. 'I always put the rifle on the floor of the jinker, when I'm out on my rounds. Your mother likes a fricassee of rabbit. A wonderful woman, your mother, boy. I hope you'll learn to love her as much as I do. One of the Jenner boys was sitting next to me. He's a good chap, but he stutters, he doesn't stammer, he stutters . . . Do you know the difference? A stutterer, boy, can't start to speak. All the Jenners have eyes like a hawk; most of the locals do. Nature has sharpened their eyes, even if it hasn't sharpened their wits. But the age of miracles isn't past. Where was I? Oh yes, as old Ginger was farting his way up the hill after the Ventnor turn-off, the Jenner boy grabbed my arm, and pointed at a rabbit asleep in a lair about five yards from the left wheel of the jinker. I stopped Ginger, picked up the rifle, took careful aim – I always aim at the eye, boy, because that does not damage the part of the flesh we eat. Your mother's fussy about that sort of thing, boy. Well, just as I squeezed the trigger – never jerk a trigger, boy – Ginger breathed, the barrel of the rifle went up, and a rabbit one hundred yards away leapt into the air and fell down dead. The Jenner boy was after it liked greased lightning. When he came back he was so astonished he said, "Geez Mr Clark, I thought you were aiming at the one close to the jinker." Well, boy, I didn't let on – and, boy, I didn't stop again, though my companion kept tugging my arm and trying to say "L-l-l-look, Mr Clark, at th-th-that beauty." But I said I thought we ought to keep moving as the wife might be getting anxious.'

There were more stories about the Jenner boys and the rifle. 'Did I ever tell you, boy, about the other time I was driving along the Ventnor road with another Jenner boy? He pointed to a rabbit asleep in a lair. I was so anxious to fire before Ginger breathed that I missed. Believe it or not, the rabbit cheekily rubbed its nose with one of its paws before it scooted off. Alan asked me what happened. I didn't like to tell him Ginger breathed, if you see what I mean, because that might have destroyed my reputation with him. So I told him I aimed at the eye and he said, "Geez, Mr Clark, w-w-why didn't you sh-sh-sh-shoot him in the g-g-g-guts?"'

Looking back now the mystery is why he, a clergyman, never referred to God – he never discussed whether God would be pleased with Alan Jenner. Alan Jenner respected my father; that was, I suspect, his great attraction.

My father did everything with such grace. I remember how he twitched his nostrils after inhaling smoke from a cigarette. It was like the last two bars in a piano sonata, classical in form, but romantic in its inner meaning. On the rocks at the back beach he moved with the grace and agility of a rock wallaby. The movement of his body when casting his line into the ocean had the same grace, there being always an air of distinction emanating from everything he did. He never got his line caught in the kelp; he had a contempt for anyone whose hook or sinker was held fast. In the pulpit and the classroom he was like Toscanini conducting an orchestra – it all led up to some emotional extravaganza: 'The only difference between me and the man I have been talking about is that that man was the Son of God. I'm as sure of that as I am of anything living. That's why I'm standing here before you today as a witness to that truth.' My father was always putting himself up for judgement, as though he were not confident of the result. Perhaps that was why he was a seventy-times-seven man – a man who needed a forgiver who was as extravagant and as generous in his pardons as my father was extravagant during his passage across the stormy seas of life.

My father was my first enthusiasm. There were to be many more. I could not live without an enthusiasm, painful though it has always been to discover the reality behind the myth my brain conceived to feed the hungers of my heart. There had to be an idol. There had to be the love which transcended all offences, the love which nourished terrible delusions. I was to find myself many times in life defending the indefensible, the heart is a lonely hunter. That began on Phillip Island.

I remember one painful, though illuminating, experience. I was one of a group of boys out bird-nesting. Part of the trouble was that I was never able to become one of 'them'. My mother insisted that I should always wear a tie, and put on boots and socks. 'I don't want you, Mann dear, to be low and common.' That created a barrier. But perhaps it was deeper than class pretensions, or a clash of lore, my mother's lore of the gentry and the locals' lore – that lore for breaches of which transgressors were savagely punished. I knew nothing of that at the time. All I knew was this yearning to belong, to be accepted, and this fear that I was the outsider. Perhaps I should add that there was one other fact which singled me out from the others. On bird-nesting excursions I could only be the observer. I knew already that heights were not for me: I became dizzy, I became quite odd, a figure of fun, a boy to be despised, or to be pitied. 'Mannin', as the locals called me, 'is a bit odd.'

So there we were – Frank Towns, Colin Twyrold, Frank Walker and some others – looking for nests in trees or hollows in the trunks of dead trees where parrots might have nested, or for skylarks' nests among the tussocks, or goldfinch nests in the clumps of sword grass. We started an argument about whose father was the best. They, I believed, must choose my father. He was in touch with God, he had been chosen by God, and he was so graceful when he played a late-cut at cricket, and told such wonderful stories, and, anyhow, everyone loved my father. Besides, there was not much they could say about their fathers. One was the local night-soil man. How could this son possibly claim his father was superior to my father who told those wonderful stories about the Kingdom of Heaven, and about the man who fell among the thieves during his journey from Jerusalem to Jericho? So when the argument started with 'My Dad's better than yours', and the reply 'No he isn't, my Dad's better than yours', I found to my surprise that neither reason nor passion swayed my companions. I took it for granted that anyone who conducted a religious service in a robe of white linen was superior to a cornet player in the Salvos' band. But my opponents did not agree.

It took me many years before I shed my mother's mythology about human society. I was a people's boy wearing the clothes and presenting the arguments of the 'ancient nobility of New South Wales'. I was for the people, even if they were not for me, or eyed me with suspicion or mistrust. I was never at home in my mother's world – even though it was a great temptation, the temptation to believe one was something special, one of the elect for whom Christ had promised the days would be shortened. I had no idea what that meant at the time – nor do I know now. All I knew then was that my mother often stood between me and my discovery of the world.

That was a misfortune for both of us. The past manacled her mind. There were bizarre events – part-comical, part-tragical. She was always asking me to promise her faithfully I would not do the things her code taught her I should not be doing. 'Mann dear,' she said to me, 'I want you to promise me faithfully you will never speak to Mr —.' I asked her why. She replied, 'Mann dear, Mr — and a lady' (in my mother's code you never mentioned the lady's name) 'go into the tea-tree and take their clothes off.' I made it my business to see him as soon as possible. He owned a shop in the main street of Cowes. Nothing would stop me having a look at the Don Giovanni of the Phillip Island tea-tree scrub. I persuaded my father to give me a penny to buy something from the penny tray – I loved the four liquorice blocks you could buy for a penny, or the two liquorice straps, and was planning to ask if I could have one liquorice strap and two liquorice blocks for my penny. That would prolong the time in the shop.

Well, it was quite a let-down for a romantic boy. Don Giovanni wore carpet slippers, and looked as though he had not shaved for two or three days. I left the shop with my penny's worth, but not even that heady taste in the mouth, the sliding of the tongue around the block which had always before given me such pleasure, could rid my mind of the fear of discovery. I had again let my mother down: I was not worthy. Once again I wanted to be forgiven, but I could not even tell her what I had done – not out of fear of punishment, but rather, well, we never really spoke to each other – or perhaps I was afraid of losing her love, that the betrayer would be neither understood nor forgiven. Who can tell? I sat through the evening meal in silence, fearful of discovery, fearful that I would be accused of many other deeds of shame, and going silent, as I was to do all through life, when my father or anyone else used me as their whipping boy.

My mother responded to all my flights of fancy, not with minatory words or the words of condemnation, but rather with the words of alarm. 'I wish you would not talk like that, Mann dear', she used to say when I tossed up one of my fantasies, 'People will think you're mental.' Another time she would reply, 'Don't go on like that, Mann dear, you're making me feel giddy.' She was not easy to please, it was not easy to win approving words from my mother. My father was always enthusiastic and generous, except when in one of his rages. My mother had her own ways of warning me that the world may judge me harshly. 'Mann dear,' she would say when I came up with one of my plans, 'I think you should ask the others and see what they think.' I realised later that was her gentle way of teaching me that what was going on in my mind would make some people very angry. I did not know then who these 'others' were who drew up the laws, who were the law-makers, prosecutors and judges in our society, or what they did to those who either could not or would not obey their laws. I hear still my mother's voice at Cowes, 'You'll make yourself very unhappy one day, Mann dear.' I see her sad face – but she was never able to tell me why this would be so.

Perhaps she knew it was of no use to talk to me. Women generally do. Perhaps that was why she often looked so sad, and uttered the despairing words, 'I worry, Mann dear, what we are going to do about you. I worry about what's going to happen to you.' But I was young, only a child, no use to talk to me. I wonder now what would have happened if I had said, 'Please don't talk like that, Mum, please.' Perhaps she never knew her words would haunt me always – like ghosts from the past, ghosts from which I could never rid my mind.

I remember also a game of doctors and nurses in the tea-tree in the vicarage grounds, not far from the stable in which Ginger was munching his hay. My partners were my sister Hope, Esme Grubb and Charlie Walker. Charlie stuttered. Charlie, who was at least a year older than I, had already begun to instruct me on the facts of life, but his stutter meant it was taking him a long time to come to the point. The very delicacy of the subject, the air of mystery in which it had been shrouded by the mores of the times, also prolonged the prelude to the revelation. Well, on this day in the tea-tree I suggested we would all learn a lot more about the body if we took off all our clothes. We were beginning to do that when the call came to go inside at once. My mother looked troubled. 'What on earth have you children been up to all this time?' We dared not divulge anything except a guilty 'Playing hide and seek in the tea-tree.' I may say that life was to be unkind in many ways to all four of us – all four who were impatient for a moment to leave behind the innocence of childhood.

Not long after the tea-tree encounter Charlie recommenced his lectures to me on the procreation of the species. I have already mentioned Charlie's stutter. The shame of what he was to say to me aggravated both the stutter, and the blush which suffused his whole face when he was talking of forbidden subjects. I don't remember the details of his lecture. I do remember noticing darkness was beginning to descend, and Charlie had still not told me what was what. I was anxious because I knew the back door would soon open, and my mother would utter the words of her well-known call, 'Are you there, Mann dear?' Well, if I remember correctly, I had just asked Charlie the key question, 'Where did you say he puts it?' Charlie was struggling hard to get out the words, 'He p-p-p-puts it her c-c-c-', but the call came before Charlie got out the words. When my father was saying grace that night before we began our tea, and we three children were standing reverently behind our chairs, with our eyes closed, I cheated yet again. I stole a look at Mum and Dad. I could not believe they did that sort of thing – perhaps my father wanted to, but my mother must surely think that sort of thing was 'low and common'.

There was no one with whom I could share my thoughts. A boy always spoke to a boy, never to a girl. My brother always said before saying his prayers, 'I'm looking forward to having a long talk with you, Mann.' But he never did. He was always asleep before I finished my first question to him. So I lay there in the dark while the wind blowing down Bass Strait sighed in the pine tree just outside our bedroom window. My mother opened the door, and stood there with her hand shielding the candle against any draught from the wind buffeting the house, her hair down, and brushed back so that I could see the shapely brow, her left hand oscillating between the duty of being a candle shield and a support for her chin, as she said again what she always said on such occasions, 'I don't know what we're going to do about you, Mann dear.' Not even in the dark could I tell her what was troubling me.

There was no one to whom I could talk. My brother lived in another world, not interested in the questions in my head clamouring for an answer. My sister's world was not mine. My mother did not or could not speak about such things. 'I wish you wouldn't bother me with such questions, Mann dear, you're making me feel giddy', or at other times she would say, 'I wish you wouldn't talk like that, Mann dear. People will think you're peculiar.' My father held out the promise that he knew the answers. 'That's my favourite subject, boy', he would say when I asked him during those trips in the jinker when night was falling over the island, and there was an absence of uproar either from man or from nature – a setting for a revelation. But the spell was soon broken. When my father did not know the answer he always lapsed into clowning. Ginger would help him by lifting his tail high and starting to fart. 'Listen to that, boy,' my father would say, 'it's perfect three/four time. Hear it, boy? One, two, three – one, two, three.' And when Ginger lowered his tail my father would rise a little in his seat, pick the whip out of its stand, flick Ginger gently on the rump, and smile at me and say, 'He likes a bit of a tickle after he's got rid of all that wind.' I got the message that my father did not want to peer into the darkness.

I was puzzled by a young man named Rex Boughton. I had first seen him sitting on the deck of the S.S. *Genista*, the steam ferry which ran between Stony Point and Cowes, Rhyll, Newhaven and San Remo each day except Sunday. There was something odd about Rex. He slobbered; he spoke no intelligible words; he grunted like an animal; his eyes roamed about as though there were no brain controlling them. I was puzzled. I was also fascinated, not able to take my eyes off him, though I knew from my mother that it was rude to stare at people. I remember being quite mesmerised by the sight of this strange human being. I was only a boy of seven. The moment did not last for long. There was so much to do on a boat, especially in the days when the green swell from Bass Strait rolled deep into Western Port Bay in search of some sport with the *Genista*, while my brother and I ran around the decks looking for passengers who were turning green.

Rex's face was to become part of the picture show my brain turned on when I was brooding over the questions no one wanted to answer. This time I asked my father why God had made a person like Rex Boughton, or rather blurted it out, fumbled for the words, not knowing then what was bothering me. Perhaps I was close to asking, 'If God is so good, if God loves us, why did He make Rex Boughton?' I asked my mother, too, but again she silenced me with one of those 'I wish you wouldn't ask me such questions, Mann dear. People will think you're mental' or 'Don't talk like that, Mann dear. It only makes me giddy.' That silenced me, but did not satisfy me. My father was his usual theatrical self. 'Boy,' he said, 'that's the question of questions. I've told everyone Manning's the thoughtful customer in the family.' My father always played a lively overture, but, alas, the curtain never went up on his opera – or if it did it was always *opéra bouffe*: clowning, jokes, laughter, they were his tricks for avoiding a look into the darkness. I can still hear him saying, 'At least we can all have a good laugh.'

There was a sequel to the Rex Boughton episode. Not long after I had seen him on the deck of the *Genista* I went for a walk down Lovers' Walk (not as a participant or even an aspirant) during which I passed the house in which Rex and his family spent the summer vacation. Rex's brother Guy (or is memory again playing tricks?) was a boarder at Geelong Grammar School. I saw three or four young men dressed in Geelong Grammar School light-blue blazers, with gold braid trimmings, and a huge monogram on the breast pocket, beside or under which were letters I did not then understand, such as XI, XVIII, A (surrounded by a laurel wreath) or a pair of crossed oars. I gaped in awe and wonder at these godlings. I did not think of it then as a temptation. It just seemed that it would be wonderful to be as graceful, as elegant and beautiful as Guy Boughton. I did not realise then that in my garden of Eden, my childhood paradise, it was not a woman who tempted me, no serpent urged me to take the forbidden fruit.

Something inside me was tempted by that sight down Lovers'

Walk. Such scenes planted in me the idea that to be like Guy Boughton and his friends would be a happy issue out of all my afflictions. It took me years to convince myself that such a move was not open to me: it took me almost as long to persuade myself that such an ambition was evil. Maybe my mother's family was living on in her prodigal son, but if so their values were always in collision with the values of St Peters – although as a child I had no idea what my father had lost by his futile doomed quest to win the approval of the respectability-mongers of Sydney. I did not understand at the time that he was never able to tear that hope out of his heart. It may be he knew what was driving him to his own destruction, his own pain and loss, but was not able to do anything about it. Perhaps for his generation there was no alternative to this pursuit of the approval of the self-appointed directors of the standards laboratory. My father never could win their approval. Yet he wasted his substance professing his desire to observe the commandments of bourgeois Australia. There is madness in our hearts while we live.

Phillip Island was my nursery school in madness and folly. Later there were to be many finishing schools in the same subjects – alas, often the top of the curriculum list in my heart. There were lessons in the trivia of that subject. My father had a passion for rock fishing. He was always fantasising about hooking and landing a five- or six-pound bluenose (a member of the *Wrasse* or parrot fish family which abound off the south and east coasts of Australia). He dreamed of deep-sea leather-johnnies, the ones with the light purple skin, delicate yellow fins and tail, and of sweep which, 'boy, are as greedy for sand worms as you are for liquorice blocks. I know you, boy.' But generally he had to be content with a few green and black parrot fish, and an occasional one-pound leather-jacket, lacking grandeur both in size and colour. My mother did not like rock fish; She loved whiting, she loved snapper, she loved flathead. That meant going fishing with Arny Brown in a boat, but my father was not keen on that. He had been out once with Arny Brown, but at the end of the day, when he was about to jump from the rowing boat on to the lower platform of the Cowes Pier, Arny Brown said to my father, 'Put all your fish in my basket, Mr Clark.'

My father never fished again in the bay – and my mother never ceased yearning for a whiting or a snapper. My father made no move to gratify her longing. My mother went on telling us how she would love to collect shells again at Shelly Beach (not far from the Nobbies). My father never accommodated her. He had his mad dream: one day there would be a north wind, the tide would start to move in about two hours before dusk, and the bluenose, and the sweep, and the deep-sea leather-johnnies would be ravenous. But, though perhaps I exaggerate, the north wind always seemed to blow on a Sunday. By Monday, my father's day off, a southerly gale would be blowing, and he would say he knew a place on the west side of the Pyramid where you could always get your line in, even if elsewhere the seas were mountainous. If it was not school time, he would ask me if I was game to come with him.

My own relations with the other boys were rather like attempts to find a good spot for the cat's whisker in the days of the crystal wireless set. Most of the time there was static, rumbling, but no communication. At other times there was a promise, an awareness of the harmony, the serenity I had heard of in church, that peace which passed all understanding. Noel Cleeland invited me to his farm to go hunting on Saturday afternoons. His two older brothers were already heroes for the young boys on the island. Clyde was a horse-breaker; he could keep his seat even when his stallion reared up on his hind legs and pawed the air with his front feet. Clyde could sit it out, Clyde was the lord of the beasts. I never saw him perform this feat; I never knew anyone who had seen it. But we all believed it. Jack Cleeland was so huge he had no neck, no visible wrists, and no visible knees. He could press down the spring of a rabbit trap with his little finger. Jack was special. Rumour had it that he could not fit into any of the seats provided in the Cowes Hall. Clyde, I remember, was thin and never smiled; Jack was fat and always chuckled at everything people said. Their younger brother Noel was my friend. The Cleelands had a farm not far from the turn-off to Newhaven on the road from Cowes to the back beach. I had no idea at the time why they were more comfortable than other chicory farmers on the island. Their house was larger, their front garden was larger, their stables, cow-yard, wood-heap and back fence had an air of elegance. No fowls ever pooped in the Cleeland's back room.

The Cleelands had a pack of dogs for rabbiting – two greyhounds, which slobbered, and held their heads down, some whippets, and a fox terrier. Noel and I did not talk very much during the hunt. I wanted to talk his language. I wanted to say 'Skitch him, skitch him!' and 'Tear his guts out, Tiny!', but could not bring myself to do it. I noticed during the chase that the greyhounds were the swiftest dogs, but they rarely got a rabbit between their teeth. The 'foxy', the slowest dog in the pack, was often the killer. Years afterwards the words in Ecclesiastes would have leapt up in my mind, 'The race is not to the swift'. But just then that part of me which always stood apart from everything in which I was engaged was not distressed by the squeal of the rabbit just before the teeth pierced its sides, or engaging in any inner soliloquy on what brutes we all were. I was wildly excited by it.

After the hunt there was always cake and a glass of milk back at the farm. Then Noel and I jumped on one of his ponies and set off for the vicarage at Cowes. Noel and I never really spoke to each other, it was a bond without words. It was the first of the friendships that mattered. From that time there always had to be someone to whom I felt I could speak, someone who understood even though I already knew it was never wise to let the other person know how much the awareness meant to me. I was a lover who never made declarations, a lover who had to believe the other one understood, and did not dare to bear witness to my love, because that might mean I would have to suffer the worst wound of all – the wound of rejection, the equivalent of Louie Burke's 'Who'd want to play with you?' Perhaps even then I was frightened that there never could or would be another.

This secret stormy emotional life, and an impulsive temperament, led me sometimes into quite painful experiences. My mother gave me a football for my eighth birthday, on 3 March 1923. She told me not to play with it when the grass was wet and water was lying around. But nothing could ever stop me. I played. The football was soaked. My mother said it would dry outside. I wanted it to be dry straight away – Mr Passion, I found later, always wanted everything now. So did I. I put the football in the oven. My mother warned me what might happen. No use to talk to me – I wanted the ball dry straight away. I opened the oven door. There was no longer a football, but a lump of ridges, the leather so stiff it would not budge no matter how violent my blows. I wanted the football. But that could never be.

That night there was a school concert in the Cowes Hall at which I was to recite a poem. ('My second son has a phenomenal memory for things he likes. Show him a piece of poetry and within an hour he will recite the whole blessed lot to you. But show him something that does not touch him and he won't learn a line.') At tea-time my mother asked, 'Are you sure you'll be all right, Mann dear. Are you sure you're not still too upset about the football? Do you think you should go, Mann dear?' But I would have none of that. Of course I would be all right. I have forgotten the words of the poem now, though vaguely I remember it was about a country I had never seen. As I began to recite, the picture of the football in the oven floated before my eyes, like some evil act haunting and tormenting a man, never letting his soul be quiet. I began to shake. Soon I was blubbering. My mother signalled to me to stop, but that expression of alarm on her face, that look of terror, only angered me. I went on to the end; as a man I came to believe in enduring to the very end. Some sniggered, some looked sad. When I rejoined my mother she put her arm around me, and cradled me as though I were still a little child. There are many people inside one human being: there are many voices. One side of me in childhood was prey to the winds of passion, to all the pains of surrendering to a passionate heart. It took years to hide that from the straiteners and the life-deniers.

There was another person inside me – the one who knew what was happening, the observer, the serene one, who, so far, seemed powerless to rein in, to put the brakes on Mr Passion. Some only saw the stormy, moody scowler, and warned him of what would happen if he did not mend his ways. When I took no notice, never expressed contrition, never asked to be forgiven, their prophecies became more threatening, a 'You'll be sorry' with many extras. I still took no notice. There was, I believed, this other person who was watching, listening and storing up. I had faith in him. That was my faith, my impenetrable fortress, which gave me the strength to go on. I did not pin my hopes on my father's judgement of me as a 'thoughtful customer'. That did not interest me. I pinned my hopes in my mother's words, 'Manning understands a lot, but he doesn't say very much.' Perhaps the torments of childhood fed this understanding. Who can tell?

There was always so much to observe. The Island was a stage, and its inhabitants all players in a never-ending tragedy, relieved at times by brief intervals of comic opera.

Clarrie Williams and his father owned one of the two general stores in the main street of Cowes. You could buy almost anything there – groceries, shoes, boots, hurricane lamps, fruit, vegetables, clothing – everything except meat and fish. You bought meat in Jack Bell's butcher's shop, next to the vicarage – Jack Bell, with his butcher's apron, offering nourishment for the body, and my father, next door, offering nourishment for the soul. Clarrie Williams already fascinated me. On Anzac Day each year (we were on the Island for two Anzac Days) he wore the uniform of a captain of the Light Horse. I liked the feathers on the side of his Digger hat, the highly polished Sam Browne belt, the well-Brassoed buttons on his tunic, the leggings, and the boots. He had the air of a proud man – and yet he never smiled. I do not remember him ever looking happy. He used to sing in my father's choir, his face just as morose in God's house as behind the counter in his store. There was a reason for this. His wife was dying – or so I gathered from remarks by my mother. Death was one of the great unmentionables. My mother's words always required a translator: 'Poor Mrs Williams' meant death was not far away.

I was puzzled, at the time, why believers in the life of the world to come should speak of death as loss. My mother was not a 'oncer': she believed we would all see each other again. By chance I had seen the young Mrs Williams in her bed. I had knocked on the side door of their store, and heard her feeble 'Come in'. There she was in her bed, her body (what I could see of it) almost a skeleton, her face a mirror of that pain from which at that time there was no relief, and a smell of decaying flesh in the room. She was warm to me: she knew there was a bond between me and her son Harry. No words were spoken. It was one of those moments when words were inadequate. She was dying: there was nothing that could be said. But the scene in that room became part of my 'picture show', one of those pictures which came again into focus as the story of my association with the Williams family unfolded.

I remember one evening after the young Mrs Williams had died seeing Clarrie Williams, one of the two general store owners, standing with one foot on the front door-step of Linda Burke's drapery shop. I had never seen her face so animated before. In my childhood world she belonged to the army of women who frowned whenever I came near. I had never seen her smile before. The two were so engrossed with each other they did not notice a small boy watching them. She was a war widow with two daughters, Louie, who had inherited her mother's sharp tongue, and Queenie, who had a generous, loving heart. But nature had fallen a-doting with Queenie. She wanted to give, but the only gift she had was her body – a gift that would bring her much pain years later. But not then. As a child she loved to lie on the beach in the sun; the earth was the first of her lovers.

Clarrie Williams married Linda Burke – but from that moment things went wrong for all of them. Not long after we left the Island the store was burnt down. Clarrie Williams borrowed money to put up a new store worthy of his new bride. But the depression cut his income. There was not room for two general stores on the Island, and Robb's store won the competition for the local market. Clarrie Williams sold up and decided to try his luck on the mainland. My father, generous as ever to those in need, asked Mr Lee Neale, the general manager of the Myer Emporium, if he would give Clarrie Williams a trial run behind one of their many counters. The message came back that he was 'too slow on the uptake' to work in a big emporium. The last time I saw Clarrie Williams was in Swanston Street, Melbourne, in 1936 or 1937. It was winter-time. His overcoat was shabby, the lapels raised to protect his face against a chilly wind, his eyes quite dead, looking straight ahead into an empty distance. The man who used to sing 'Mother Machree' with such tender passion, such an appealing longing for something he seemed to sense he would never know, was a wanderer in the streets of Melbourne. He did not see me.

I was glad he did not see me because I too was nursing a pain which I was to find would never go away, just as he was living with the worm of failure – the knowledge that it had all gone wrong. I do not suspect Clarrie Williams ever speculated about primal fault in the universe or some mole in his own being which had inflicted such a terrible punishment on him for being an overreacher both in love and in business. I had my own private hell in the heart about Clarrie Williams and his family. In the year after the death of Clarrie Williams's first wife my friendship with Harry Williams flowered. We were more than friends, we were mates before my family left the Island – and became even closer during our annual holiday there each year. He had a quite absurd idea of my gifts – just as my mother inflated a minor talent into a promise of, no, a certainty, of a man who would be remembered for years to come. Harry had absolute trust, absolute faith. There could not be a Judas: lovers were never betrayers or betrayed.

He called me Charlie. He thought I knew everything – even what happened to us when we died, so great was his faith, so mad and foolish his adoration. I did nothing to rid his mind of his delusion, if only because that would have been very cruel, possibly even more frightful for him than discovering the truth one day. If we fished off the rocks he assumed I would catch a big fish; if we were shooting rabbits he could not believe I would ever miss, and, when I did, as happened from time to time, he would say to me with a fervour it is painful even now to recall, 'Geez, Charl, there must be something wrong with the gun.' Such was his faith. He asked me questions such as: Who made the world? Do we live again in another world when we die? How are babies born? Where do they come from? It was as though I were an all-knowing god, and he an adoring disciple.

Melbourne Grammar was to cast a shadow over this poem of friendship on Phillip Island. Harry was frightened. 'You won't want to speak to me anymore', he said at the end of my first year there. I told him not to be so 'fucking well mad'. Of course, I'd always want to speak to him. Not long after his father moved his family to Melbourne during the Great Depression Harry went out of my life. But not entirely. In the early summer of 1934, when I was playing cricket for the Melbourne University team, a shabbily dressed, pale-faced boy rushed up to me as our team was walking towards the dressing room, grabbed my hand, and looked at me with the same faith, and said, 'Charl, don't you remember me?' Of course I remembered. I remember everything that touches me deeply; it lives with me all the time. But life had done something to me. I wanted the respect and admiration of those who were not in Harry's world. I pulled my hand away and said I would see him after we were changed. I did not see him, for Harry had fled. Mockery and beer soon blotted out guilt. The heart had become so corrupted that I was not aware of the enormity of the offence.

Harry would not go away. In 1942 or 1943 someone asked me whether I knew Harry Williams had been killed in Malaya, and added, 'I thought you would be upset.' Well, I was not ready then to let anyone know my grief, my loss. By then I knew damnation was loss, I was beginning to see through all the delusions I had put between myself and the truth about life, to recognise all the drugs I had indulged in so ferociously to soothe my pains, and had already confessed to myself the evil I had committed against Harry.

But I was not going to let anyone know about my suffering. I told my questioner I did not know Harry very well really – which was another denial, another betrayal. By then I had another hunger, a hunger for someone, somewhere, either on earth or in Heaven who would understand, someone who would forgive. I was aware of an ever-widening gap between my 'simple self that was' and the man of the world; I was beginning to wonder what 'crass cause' had merged the Swanee River boy into the one who searched frantically for someone who could teach him how to regain the 'simple self that was', where and how to find grace. The Harry Williams experience taught me again we were all both betrayers and betrayed. I later met Judas on every committee, Judas was everywhere. My sympathy with Jimmy Scullin in the sixth volume of *A History of Australia*, my never being able to read one paragraph about Jimmy Scullin in that volume without tears threatening to run down my cheeks, came from those events in life which taught me about treachery – taught me that no waters would ever wash away that guilt.

Another experience on Phillip Island probably shaped my later view of human behaviour. My father liked the company of a woman when he went rock fishing. There always had to be someone who was prepared to listen: women were good listeners, and good servers. They did those things which my father ought to have done, but rarely did. They collected bait by prising limpets and 'cochineal' shells off the rocks. My father knew how to coax women to do the menial tasks. 'Are you game?' he would ask them when they sat down beside him in the jinker. They loved that. Then, as Ginger grunted his way along the dusty road to the Pyramid Rock, my father would ask them if they had sharp eyes. He had a most persuasive smile. By the time the three of us were on the rocks the woman was so much under his spell that she would ask my father to show her where he kept the knife. Later he would charm her into gutting and scaling the fish.

May Sambell was different. She was not a server. She was one of the daughters of A. K. T. Sambell, the businessman who wanted to convert Phillip Island from a place for chicory farmers into a tourist resort. She fished, and when she was not fishing she sat apart. She was the only member of the Sambell family with whom I ever felt at ease. Her face was a map which I was never able to read. She sat or stood on the rocks at the edge of the ocean, wearing a soft hat with such a wide brim that, like the sea, it had crests and troughs. My mother used to say to me, Don't stare, Mann dear. People don't like it when you keep looking at them.' But I could not keep my eyes off May Sambell, aloof and apart though she always was. There was an air of mystery about her: it was as though she knew things of which other people were unaware. She always looked so sad. I do not remember ever seeing her smile, except when my father paid her one of those compliments which always delighted his rock companions. 'It's always a pleasure to be on the rocks with you, Miss Sambell', he would say, and she would smile, but not for long. The mask of melancholy would soon return, and she would gaze again at the sea.

My mother hinted all was not well with May Sambell. 'Poor little thing,' she would say, 'the doctors don't expect her to live for long.' I could not understand why God would want to take away from us a woman of such beauty, why God would consume her beauty away, like a moth fretting a garment. I had heard my father read the words about the life of man being as grass, which grows up, and is cut down, and then is seen no more. I had heard my father say, 'You'll learn about things when you grow up, boy.' But that did not satisfy me. I wanted people like May Sambell to stay alive: I needed her, with the promise in her eyes that she had seen into the heart of the mystery which was to puzzle me all my life, that she knew something which I wanted to know, that, maybe, one day she would tell me.

I did learn something from her, but not from what she said to me, because we never spoke about the things I wanted to talk about. (I was beginning to wonder whether anyone would ever speak to me about the things I wanted to know.) I learned a lesson about life from what happened to her. She was engaged to be married to James Waterman, known to his friends as Jimmy. Everyone said, 'You must meet Jimmy Waterman. He's so amusing, he's such wonderful company.' But when I met him I was at a loss to understand why people were drawn to him. Jimmy Waterman was a theological student at Queen's College, at the University of Melbourne, a candidate for holy orders in the Methodist Church. The people he was courting were all Anglicans, all members of Yarraside in Melbourne, who had holiday homes down Lovers' Walk, or on the coast between Ventnor and the Nobbies. Jimmy Waterman announced he had decided to seek ordination in the Church of

England, and the Archbishop of Melbourne had accepted him. My father was delighted. In his eyes all those who were not either Roman Catholics or Anglicans were 'Prots' – targets for his ridicule. He was not interested in membership of the Church of England as a prerequisite for all those who hungered for admission to the drawing rooms of Yarraside. My mother believed that the Church of England was a mansion with many rooms, the best rooms being occupied by all the upright and God-fearing people. 'Mr Waterman, Mann dear,' she said, 'is peculiar.' And that was that.

May Sambell's health declined. Doctors in Collins Street were consulted, but they could do nothing for her. Jimmy Waterman broke off the engagement. May Sambell died. Jimmy Waterman married another woman, and I heard of him no more. The face of May Sambell lived on in my mind. Years later I thought of her when I read the first verse of Thomas Hardy's poem 'The Riddle':

> *Stretching eyes west*
> *Over the sea,*
> *Wind foul or fair,*
> *Always stood she*
> *Prospect impressed;*
> *Solely out there*
> *Did her gaze rest,*
> *Never elsewhere*
> *Seemed charmed to be.*

May Sambell was always a riddle to me.

Jimmy Waterman was to come back into my life. During the war I gave a talk in Geelong, in which I took as my theme W. H. Auden's point that at the end of a 'low dishonest decade' the British and the French found themselves defending the bad against the worse. As soon as I sat down the Reverend James Waterman, the loyal servant of Yarraside, rose to his feet and told the audience he wondered whether it was his duty to report what had been said to the people responsible for security in Australia. I wondered how many of those people in the room would ponder over why the Church of England, Christ's representative on earth, should attract into its ministry men who seemed to enjoy frightening the vulnerable.

There was always the sea: the mighty monster or the redeemer. I used to wonder what May Sambell thought as she stood or sat on the rocks, 'Stretching eyes west/Over the sea'. I wanted to know what went on in the heart of another human being. I know that for my father the sea rarely behaved as he wanted it to behave. For him there were so often those deep pools in the ocean just around the corner, where the bluenose, the deep-sea leather-johnnies and the giant sweep fed, but, as he so often had to say, 'You can't get there today, boy. The sea's up', and he would then stretch his eyes to the south, the direction from which the mountainous seas rolled in from Bass Strait. He had to be content with a position out of the swing of that vast sea, and hope that the black and green parrot fish would start biting before the tide rose so high that we had either to get off straight away or be stranded until the tide dropped again. About midday he would throw out hints it would be a good idea if his companion and I collected driftwood for the fire on which to boil the billy. 'Make sure, boy, the billy does not spill, because that's all we've got.' Over lunch he would tell his stories – about how old Charlie McGregor was standing on the rocks opposite the Pyramid when a freak wave came up out of the ocean, and Charlie dived in to escape certain death, and swam 200 yards around to the shore. There were stories of how Charlie and Gordon West picked crayfish off the shelf under the rock, 'the part, boy, which the sea has eaten away'. I would ask how long that would take, and my father would say billions of years – but I knew by then not to ask if there were human beings on the earth then, because that thump of the ocean on the rocks, that rattle of the rocks as the wave receded, had already intimated to me that it was all much more complicated than those stories I had heard in my father's church. I shuddered. I still do.

The ocean was a greedy monster. The sea was as treacherous as human beings. There were currents in those innocent-looking waters off the front beach, near the Cowes jetty, and near the old baths. I remember the commotion when news was passed around that a man had been drowned. My mother asked me to promise faithfully I would not look at the body of the man. 'You'll never stand it, Mann dear.' But at that time, maybe always, there was no use telling me what to do. I did see the man as they carried him up from the beach. My mother was right. I was never able to look at a dead body again until my mother died, and that was the experience which altered all, the experience which persuaded me of the shallowness of the secular humanists on death, just as my experiences in life convinced me of their shallowness on evil.

There were so many characters on the Island. It was possibly the best theatre show I ever attended. I loved both the setting and the people. 'Old' Matthews, as we called him, one of the church-wardens, was the one I remember most because when he took up the plate at morning prayer or evensong, he always seemed to be looking at the floor when a worshipper put his contribution in the plate, but at the critical moment his eyes flew towards the fingers of the giver, and then back to the floor, as quick as you could say Jack Robinson and possibly even quicker. Old Matthews (I'm not sure to this day what his first name was) always had a hang-dog look in his eyes, and bowed shoulders as though he were carrying some intolerable and unjust burden. He sighed a lot. He was a man of few words. Whenever he was told some story about the goings-on of his fellow islanders his whole body would heave, and he would say, eyes firmly on the ground, 'What more could you expect?', or sometimes he would be wordless, and content himself with an expressive, long-drawn-out sigh. Old Matthews did not need words to speak to other people.

After evensong each Sunday he had supper with my father. On Monday morning, my father's day off, my father would say with a twinkle in his eye that Old Matthews had his 'sitting britches' on again last night, and my mother would say she found them both asleep in front of the fire, and how it was well after midnight. My father would wink at my brother and me, making sure my mother did not see him, and say Old Matthews was really a 'decent chap', and that there was a lot of good in all people, while my mother fussed over whether we three would eat enough porridge. Porridge was good for character building; her father ate a bowl of porridge for breakfast every day of his life, and that had made a man of him. One Monday morning my father told me over breakfast that Old Matthews had told him he had had enough abuse from his wife ('I wish you wouldn't talk to the boys, Charlie, about that sort of thing') and he was going to tell her the next day he had had enough, and he was going to leave. I don't know whether he ever managed to say it. But I do know that every January when we went back to the Island for the holidays Old Matthews was still to be seen, eyes down, head lowered, fossicking around in his backyard. So perhaps he never succeeded, or if he started to say it perhaps she silenced him. I can't tell. I never saw Mrs Matthews, the one Old Matthews was going to have it out with. I began to wonder whether, no matter who his companion was, he would always have the down-cast eyes, always look as though he were the victim of some terrible injustice, whether perhaps he could not live without a grievance against other human beings, and why a man who had heard the 'glad tidings' of Christ to all who truly turned to Him should always look so desperately unhappy.

There were others, like Mr and Mrs Charlie Pryor. On fine days Charlie Pryor sat on a seat just off the main street yarning with the other retired men. Water poured out of his eyes. I remember he was always mopping it up with his handkerchief. He always looked as though he were about to speak, but then the water flowed again, and Charlie would miss his turn because he had to dry his cheeks. He never looked like a man who would fight for his place in a conversation. His wife was also a woman of few words. I never heard anyone use her first name, though I assume Charlie must have known it. My mother called her 'little Mrs Pryor', and that was puzzling because, thin though she was, indeed so thin she always looked as though the wind would blow her away, she was very tall. She was an agreer. She said a wheezy 'Yes' to every remark, and then moistened her lips with her tongue. My impression then, even at the age of seven, was that the waters of life had stopped flowing years ago in Mrs Pryor's body.

There was Mrs Archie Finlay, a mountain of flesh, always dressed in a black cotton smock, which was never gathered a-midriff by any girdle or belt. She had such an ample spread that her girth had its maximum reading just at that spot where the 'fashion plate Fannies', as my father called them, hoped for a minimum reading. Mrs Archie Finlay had an ample form, but that part of it visible to the eye had lost the whiteness of maiden flesh, and taken on the appearance of a plucked fowl. Her voice was like the screech of a cockatoo. But Mrs Archie Finlay had a heart of gold, her eyes belying coarseness of body and voice. Her eyes were always magnificently alive, always full of light. By then I had heard with some astonishment how the righteous found accommodation in Abraham's bosom, and wondered how he could find room for all of them. I thought maybe there was a similar space and a similar welcome on Mrs Archie Finlay's bosom. My mother told me I was not to think of such things, because people would think I was peculiar. She never seemed to realise how keen my search was for a haven.

Old George Wylie, the painter, lived on a house-boat. My father ridiculed him as a crack-pot: 'They say, boy, there's one born every minute.' Old Wylie hoped one day that the sea in Bass Strait would be so quiet that he could anchor his boat between the Pyramid and the Island, and paint the rock. But the sea was no more generous to Old Wylie than it was to my father with his dream of dropping his line into that deep pool right opposite the Pyramid. There were so many people on the Island dreaming of things that could never be. I heard chicory farmers say with a sad voice they hoped the wife would speak to them again properly just as she used to speak when they were first married. I heard a woman say if the wind continued to blow she would kill herself. But before I could sort out those remarks I would be called to a bird-nesting party, or to help set the rabbit traps. Life always rudely irrupted at the moments of revelation. They had to be stored away in the memory, part of a store from which one day I would sort out what was what – to be used as ammunition on the days when I was angry, and then used again when life had taught me to look on all with the eye of pity.

There were the visitors. I remember the Wilson family. They put on an entertainment each year in the vicarage grounds to raise money for the church. My father was at ease with all the Wilsons. Like him they were all actors, but not rivals or competitors, because their show was in the open air and my father's show was in the church. I remember Mr Wilson waxed his moustache and his hair, both of which were tinged with a becoming whiteness. He and his sons put on a mock operation in which the surgeon, played by Mr Wilson, dressed in long white coat and white skull cap, extracted yard after yard of sausages from the patient anaesthetised on the table, to much clowning by Mr Wilson and his assistants. It was as funny as a Charlie Chaplin film.

My father then told the people they were in for a real treat. 'Dame Nellie Tree Chaplin' (Mrs Wilson's professional name) had agreed to sing to them. Dame Nellie was past it. Her appearance was as extravagant as her gestures, the crown of her hat was decorated with sundry fruits and flowers, and her plunging neckline, rescued as it was from gross indecency by a many-jewelled clasp, was somewhat daring for those times. Dame Nellie went through all the motions of a woman possessed by some wild passion. Her bosom shook, her hands were as lively as the hands of a performer in a deaf-and-dumb show, her eyes were the medium through which she let the world know that she was the victim of a sorrow to which neither words nor music could give expression. Dame Nellie was an over-treater: not even the most brilliant posturing could hide what the passage of time had done to her voice; an octave leap was beyond her – she had to settle for a sixth or even a fifth. The visitors clapped politely. From what I can remember now, the locals looked as though they knew they ought to enjoy her singing, because their vicar said *he* did, and all the respectable people, all the la-di-da people praised Dame Nellie, but she did not touch them at all. They liked Mr Wilson the clown, the toff who put beeswax on his hair, although he did not belong to their world. They liked to hear Bing Edgar sing 'Mother Machree' or Clarrie Williams sing 'Annie Laurie'. They had no songs of their own, no ballads, no doggerel verse expressing their feelings about life. They were borrowers of voices from overseas. They could speak to each other, and they understood each other. They had a lore for their own tribe. They knew Dame Nellie was singing because they could hear her voice, but it meant nothing to them – or so I came to think later on.

Their way of life was doomed. The motor-car, the aeroplane, and the wireless were about to change their world. In 1922, the year of our arrival, visitors drove cars, locals travelled on horseback, in a jinker, a buggy or a dray. Picnic parties travelled to the Nobbies, Pyramid Rock, Berry's Beach, Forrest's Caves or Cape Woolamai in a drag – a six-wheeled wooden carriage drawn by four or six horses. There was always much doubt among the passengers in a drag whether the horses would be strong enough to pull the vehicle to the top of the long pinch after taking the turn-off to Ventnor. Parties travelling to Rhyll were always glad when their vehicle did not get bogged in the Rhyll swamp. There was always uproar and commotion during a trip in a drag. Snakes, the oldies said, could wind themselves around a wheel of the carriage and slither into the passenger area. Those stories were told to frighten us. Droves of rabbits crossed the road in front of the drag. The wind from the south-west never ceased to blow, and left me with the impression that it was never going to stop, that it would blow until the end of the world, that to hope for something different was like my father hoping a day would come when he could drop his line in the deep hole right opposite the Pyramid.

111

The locals were pitifully equipped to meet the challenge of the wind, the dryness, the absence of fresh water, the poor soil and the developers from the mainland. Changes in transport and communications were giving outsiders the equipment the locals lacked. In the main street of Cowes in the holiday season between Christmas and Easter cars were now seen. The locals gawked at them, seeing them like invaders from outer space. But their way of life was doomed. Old Charlie West told my father a horse would go into places where you could never take a car; 'Give me a horse any day', he said. I did not know then what they were talking about, though I had a vague intimation about victims of changes. In the church my father often read with a voice of unwonted sadness, 'All the rivers run into the sea, and yet the sea is not full. From the place whence the rivers come thither they return again.' I already in part believed that some things would never change.

I was puzzled by many things in the world around me. There always had to be someone I could admire, someone about whom I could be enthusiastic, someone whose feats were so extraordinary that in my eyes he was god-like. But I was always let down; there was always the moment when my eyes were opened. Bern Denham was my hero in the Cowes football team. On the Cowes football field he defied the laws of gravity – in my eyes he leapt so high to mark the ball that I wondered whether he would return safely to earth. A League club in Melbourne invited him to train with them, but Bern Denham soon returned to the Island. He was not good enough – my idol was too slow! Exit Bern Denham.

I was puzzled by the behaviour of the locals during the Anzac Day ceremony on 25 April each year. Men in uniform, many with gold and silver medals dangling from ribbons on their breasts, spoke of loyalty to King and Empire, of courage and sacrifice, but their words did not seem to touch the locals at all. After the ceremony I saw men embracing each other, and weeping, some saying 'I should have gone myself', and some just managing to say 'I know, I know' – but what it was they knew I had not the slightest idea at that time. Their world was the world of Phillip Island. They had their own lore, and they expected all the members of their tribe to conform – to toe the line, or get a belting.

The world outside the Island was in convulsion. Communists were predicting the imminent collapse of capitalist society; conservatives were predicting the victory of the communists, unless men were prepared to take special measures to defeat these destroyers of the three pillars of civilisation – private ownership of property, the family and religion. Anarchy and destruction reigned for two nights in Melbourne during the police strike in November 1923. Senior army officers from the war were recruiting ex-diggers into a White Guard, or an Old Guard, to protect bourgeois society in Australia from the Bolsheviks, the Sinn Feiners, the 'Wobblies' (Industrial Workers of the World) and other revolutionary movements. Ortega y Gasset had prophesied a revolt of the masses. T. S. Eliot has likened the post-war world to a 'waste land'. The flappers and drunken diggers were corrupting the morals of the young in the cities. Billy Hughes, the 'little digger', had outlived his usefulness to the comfortable classes of Yarraside and Potts Point, and Stanley Melbourne Bruce had become Prime Minister. Lenin died in Moscow; Mussolini marched on Rome; the Turks confronted the Allies at Chanak. Of all these events I never heard a word on the Island, only those snatches of conversations about the motor-car, and the truculent confidence of the locals that they would overcome that challenge, as they had met every change since their families began to settle on the Island after the passing of the Selection Acts.

I was as divided then about the changes as I would be all my life. I had a bond with the Island in its pre-industrial, pre-commercial innocence – a rustic paradise where men, women and children lived out their days of innocence. But I already knew they were not like children in a Garden of Eden. I remember one night after the football a small crowd gathered near the Cowes dressing-room to watch two players 'have it out'. There was a thud. One of the fighters collapsed to the ground, with blood pouring out of his nose and his mouth, and the victor standing over him, saying, 'That'll teach the bastard a lesson.' They were an-eye-for-an-eye people. The law punished those who broke the laws. They had their own lore: they punished transgressors almost as savagely as the criminal law in England at the end of the eighteenth century. Fathers thrashed their sons. There was a story of one father tying his son to the trunk of a tree with a rope and horse-whipping him for some offence.

I wanted change, but I also wanted my Swanee River to continue just as I knew it – to hear old Dann reading from the Old Testament to the labourers on the jetty, to see Charlie Pryor trying in vain to mop up the moisture flowing from his eyes, to hear the voice of Mrs Archie Finlay, and to listen to one of my father's stories about his days as a gaol chaplain in Sydney. ('Did I ever tell you, boy, about Geordie Richards? You would have been interested in Geordie, boy. He was quite a character.') But I already knew that our days there were numbered. My father and my mother were already whispering to each other about a letter from the Archbishop; my father had been summoned to Melbourne to have a talk with the 'Arch'. My mother became agitated; her chin was to be seen cupped in her left hand, her eyes motionless, then darting swiftly from one side to the other, like frightened small fish in a rock pool.

Soon we were told the reason. We were to leave Phillip Island and go to Belgrave, a country town twenty-six miles east of Melbourne. We were going from the sea to the mountains. I had a sense of foreboding, fearing things would never be the same again. There was a special reason for my anxiety. By then I had a new hero, a new lover: my dog Jumbo, the only lover who never answered back, the one who was always pleased to see me. My mother has told me Jumbo must be left behind. I implore her please, please, to say yes. I cry. I storm. But my mother does not bend to my will. No one can ever persuade her not to do what she believes is right. She can't be flattered, bribed, cajoled, threatened, bullied. Her decision on a moral question does not vary with the mood of the moment. She says, 'Mann dear, you can't take Jumbo to Belgrave.' And that is that.

My mother, Russell and Hope set off first. My father and I stay on with Mrs Archie Finlay. No one can console me in my grief. Jumbo must be abandoned. Jumbo must be betrayed. I cry too much. My father gives me lollies, and tells me I will get over it. 'You'll forget the dog, boy, in a week or two.' But I never forget. I can't decide why I am so sad – whether it is leaving Jumbo or leaving my Swanee River – I do not know then, I cannot know then, that from that day that's where my heart is 'turning ever'. I remember now leaning on the rails of the S.S. *Genista* and watching the coastline of the Island disappear over the horizon. Even now, sixty-four years after that day with the load of lead in the heart, I want to sing to myself the first verse of Bach's 'Magnificat' as I cross the bridge from San Remo to Newhaven, and I drive straight to Pyramid Rock. At such moments the joy is so intense that I believe maybe there is a kingdom of God, and maybe we shall all meet again – that is, those who can talk to each other. It may be it is because the survivors from my years in the Island are always so pleased to see me that I have this moment of grace, this epiphany. Who can tell? Not even the sight of the fibrolite holiday homes at Forrest's Caves and later at the Nobbies can spoil the moment. I am remembering my happy land, the land in my crude verse:

There is a happy land
Far, far away
Where Arny Brown and son
Catch fish all day.

My Swanee River has been commercialised: the developers and the money-changers have had their victory. Now surfies turn their 'trannies' on full-blast at Pyramid Rock, and skin-divers spear those huge fish my father dreamed would one day take his bait. But nothing can tear my Swanee River out of my heart.

Belgrave

Not long after we arrived in Belgrave in 1924 my mother told us one morning at breakfast that as we three children no longer believed in Father Christmas there would be no Christmas presents for us on 25 December. We were not generous in our response. We protested that of course we believed in Father Christmas, everyone did. What we were really upset about was not the loss, but rather how could we answer the question of other children: What did you get? My mother believed we should be strong, not sensitive to what others thought. That puzzled me because she was always advising me, 'Ask the others, Mann dear, and see what they think.' My father was the servant of the others, the important people in the parish. I was beginning to smoulder within when that argument was used. I could not see then what was special about them. I did not like them, standing as they often did between me and everything I wanted to do. They had no warmth. They were not embracers and touchers. So I was angry with my father and mother, and used my imagination to prove they were wrong, shouting at them in a childish tantrum, that even if I did not believe in Father Christmas, I did believe in Christmas as a time of giving. My father said, 'That's rich, boy.' That only incited me further to the wild threat that I would tell the parishioners my parents did not believe it when they professed in public that it was more blessed to give than to receive.

Once again my passions have caused me to be unfair to my father and my mother. I did not know then what I was doing. I was in a fog, thrashing around in search of the light, in search of the way out, hurting others, hurting myself. My father and mother were short of money. My mother was not greedy, or avaricious. My mother's mind was manacled to her past as a member of the patrician class of New South Wales. We must be genteel, even though we are poor. So we must live the life of the genteel poor. My father no longer had a horse or a jinker to carry him to the outlying churches in his parish. My father could not afford a motor-car. So each Sunday afternoon he must walk either to South Belgrave (Lockwood) or Ferny Creek for an afternoon service, and then walk back to Belgrave in time for Sunday tea and evensong in Belgrave.

Marge Thompson, the maid at Kempsey, came back into our lives. My mother must have a maid. I did not know until many years later that my father and mother had generously offered to pay for Marge, her father and mother to move from Kempsey to Moray Street, South Melbourne. I remember Marge went to Melbourne once a month, and we were told she was visiting her parents. My mother and my father were very generous to her. Of this I knew nothing at the time, and it was many years before I knew why my parents could not afford Christmas presents in 1924. All I knew was that there was something I must not know. I was puzzled. I wonder if it would have been better if I had been told. But then what could they possibly say?

One of the great pleasures of my life was getting to know Marge. The new house and Marge brought a spaciousness into our lives. My sister had a room of her own. My brother and I shared a room next to our parents' room. There was a bathroom with a chip-heater. There was a dining- and sitting-room large enough to accommodate my father's three-quarter-size billiard table. Gentlemen and 'probationer gentlemen' always played billiards at home. There was also a set of ivory billiard balls, which my father used to juggle in the air; and my mother would cry, 'Careful, Charlie, you might drop one.' My father would say 'I never drop a billiard ball', and Marge, having made sure my father could not see what she was doing, would give me a wink.

There was a study for my father, large enough to house his roll-top desk (another wedding present), the glass-fronted bookcase in which he lovingly kept his copies of the novels of Walter Scott, the Chapman and Hall edition of the novels and stories and the American notes of Charles Dickens, the works of Harrison Ainsworth, the poetry of Byron, Tennyson, Longfellow, Cowper, Wordsworth, the essays of Charles Morley, *The Scarlet Letter* by Nathaniel Hawthorne, Aylmer Maude's two-volume life of Tolstoy, the works of Shakespeare, the works of Bishop Gore, a Cruden's Concordance, and Watch Ditchfield's *Who Moved the Stone?* ('That's my pet subject, boy. You wait till you're older and you'll know what I mean.' I am still waiting.) There were no books on the history of Australia; no novels, short stories, plays or poems by Australian writers. My father was a spiritual exile, a searcher who never looked for answers in the works of Australians.

There was a kitchen, and next to the kitchen a bedroom for Marge. I never entered her room. The kitchen quickly became Marge's kingdom, the place where she held court. She did all those things which my mother was not accustomed to doing: she washed, she ironed, she chopped the kindling for the kitchen stove, the sitting-room fire and the chip heater. My father chopped wood for the kitchen stove and the log fire. I loved watching Marge work in the kitchen. Her two strong points as a cook were making a batch of scones, and pastry for a meat pie, a jam tart, or an apple pie. Marge was an artist with the rolling pin and the knife used to cut the dough into the required shape; my mother was an artist at jam-making. Marge was also an artist in the preparation of the small squares of bread for the 8 a.m. Communion service each Sunday morning. She rolled the bread flat with a reverence, a loving care appropriate to a substance which within a few hours would be referred to by the vicar as 'the body of Christ'. Marge, I remember, observed a silence as she rolled the pin over and over the bread until the surface was as flat as polished marble, and the bread could be sliced with a sharp knife without any fear of crumbling. Her squares of bread were so beautiful I had no difficulty in believing as a child that they might perform the marvel my father claimed for them, that they would 'preserve thy body and thy soul unto everlasting life'. But perhaps life had already so manured the soil of my heart that I longed for just such a miracle. Even as a child I yearned for what could never be. I will go on hoping all my life it was not true that what mattered most could never be.

Marge's kitchen was my land of make-believe, when she was in a good mood. No one had told me about women and the menstrual cycle – I knew that some days my mother was warm and loving, and other days remote and likely at any moment to utter one of those cries of desperation in the words which I could never tear out of my heart. Marge was the same. On her good days she would tell me of her dreams. She would sing in her unreliable soprano voice:

> *I'd like to sing in opera,*
> *I've got that kind of voice.*
> *I'd like to sing in opera,*
> *If I could have my choice.*

That was never likely to happen!

At night, after an early tea, and after the washing up had been finished, Marge sometimes had visitors. There was Bella Green. The unkind in Belgrave laughed at her because, as they put it, Bella had 'at least one screw loose'. My father befriended her. My mother did not need to be reminded of Christ's counsel to his followers to show compassion to 'the least of the little ones'; she liked to comfort and relieve all those 'who were in any way afflicted or distressed in mind, body or estate'; she did not need to be told. My father liked the display side of being nice to those on whom God had set a mark, but he had no theology on the question. He giggled and winked at any pretty woman in the room if an agnostic or one of those silly Melbourne rationalists asked why a loving, caring God could create a Bella Green. My father was a skilful subject-switcher. 'Have you met old Green, Bella's father?' he would ask. 'He runs a boarding house for holiday-makers and week-enders. The old codger wears a turban on his nut, with a tassel dangling down the side. He plays cards with his guests. Whenever he is served a bad hand he bangs the cards on the table and says out loud "Good Lord God Jesus Christ All bloody Mighty". He's quite a card. I've told him he might get more guests if he didn't use such fruity language.' I gathered my father knew old Green would never stop, indeed, secretly hoped he would never stop. My father would laugh, and hope, presumably, that no one would raise awkward questions.

I liked Bella. She giggled a lot: she laughed so much I thought one day she would have a fit, or one of those giddy turns to which my mother was always darkly referring. Bella sang in the choir, and so did Marge – both in the back row. I never heard Bella's voice, but judging from the black looks she received from the ladies in the front row – the ladies who thought they could sing and also fancied themselves for other reasons, chiefly the social standing of their husbands – Bella was well off the note printed on the stave. What I did notice was Bella's face, the wild ecstasy, the desperate longing in her eyes as she sang the words:

Jesu, Lover of my soul,
Let me to Thy bosom fly,

Poor Bella believed that after the storm of life, after this world in which so few seemed to want her, there would be another world. Bella had to believe.

There was also Lottie Hale, the housemaid to a well-known Collins Street specialist, Dr Strong. My mother hinted Dr Strong knew things other people did not know. Dr Strong was a healer; Dr Strong understood. Lottie spoke very little. I gathered she adored Marge – but how much she knew of Marge's earlier life I was never told. Lottie was a server, an agreer. She knew only one master. Not even my father's charm, not even my father's get-you-in question to prospective suppliers of the needs of a fisherman, his 'Are you game?' would ever persuade Lottie to join the family during their annual January holiday on Phillip Island. Lottie served Dr Strong and that was that.

For me there were magical moments in the kitchen with Marge, Bella and Lottie. Marge was a queen of her own tiny kingdom. I can hear now the hiss and the thud as she brought the iron down hard on the sheet she was ironing. I can see her testing the temperature of the iron by placing it so close to her right cheek that she looked as though she were blushing. I can see her delicate movements with the rolling pin. Marge was a superb mimic. She loved to imitate anyone who put on airs, the pretentious, the hypocrites, all those who lacked the virtues they professed to practise. Marge never made fun of either my father or my mother. Nor was she ever obsequious to them. She looked them in the eye. She would do anything for them. I did not realise at the time why she had such a bond with them, why there was a hint of love and devotion as she called my mother 'Mrs Clark', or why there was an almost a lyrical note in her voice when she asked my father whether he would like a glass of 'cold tea' before the evening meal.

Lottie Hale wore the traditional maid's uniform when working in Dr Strong's house, but Marge never wore any such uniform. She sat at table with us except when there were visitors. I had no idea what she believed. Her face in church never betrayed any of the enthusiasm which lit up the whole of Bella. I suspect now that as a country girl she was suspicious of any promise that life would ever be any different. Marge came to life when she sang about how she wanted to sing in opera, she having that kind of voice, or when she twiddled the rolling pin before moulding the dough into shape. Marge was magnificently alive – she also looked happy when waltzing with one of the more daring young men in the Belgrave Memorial Hall. I remember my mother always seemed anxious when the blood rushed to Marge's cheeks, and her eyes sparkled, and she drew closer to her partner. Sometimes my mother signalled something to my father, but I could not understand then why she should want to do that. Marge's face was radiant as she made a entire twirl and curtsied to her partner after the music stopped. But that, if I remember correctly, only rang the alarm bell in my mother's mind. By then I was only too familiar with her alarm signal: she cupped her chin in her left hand, the furrows in her brow above her nose deepened, and her eyes darted swiftly from side to side as though searching for a reassuring sign.

My mother feared most of all that she or a member of her family might be exposed to some public shame. One of the themes in her litany of life was expressed in the words, 'It's a right down cruel shame!' She was not afraid of annihilation; in her faith there was no such thing. She believed in the life of the world to come, that we would all see each other again, though she never made it clear whether we would be spirits, or whether she believed in the resurrection of the body. She never spoke of Hell, never threatened any of us with Hell if we did not mend our ways. She was never a threatener, never a one to warn us that Hell was the final resting place for liars. She dropped mysterious remarks, such as, 'I do not know what is going to happen to you, Mann dear, if you do not change.' She meant that I might expose them all to shame, to disgrace, to losing the approval of the important parishioners.

My father gave us much advice on how to play a straight bat ('There are only two strokes to learn in cricket, boy: how to play forward, and how to play back'), on how to make a late-cut or a leg-glance, how to tie a fish-hook, how to split wood ('Aim for the grain, boy, and then it's as easy as cutting butter with a knife'). He never told me how to behave. Perhaps life had so filled him with doubt, that he no longer believed he had any lessons to impart on how to live. Not so my mother: 'There are two things to remember, Mann dear. Never look inside a lady's handbag, and never climb a staircase beneath a lady.' At the time I wondered why. She made strange requests. 'Mann dear,' she said one day to me in the vicarage in Belgrave, 'I want you to promise me faithfully you won't speak to Mr — ' (mentioning a man she knew I was infatuated with because he moved so gracefully on the cricket field) 'and his lady friend.' My mother would never mention a lady's name if she was about to condemn her behaviour. I asked her, 'Oh, why not?', in an aggrieved tone of voice. 'Well, Mann dear, you will be sorry to hear they play with each other's private parts.' Well, I was not at all sorry. (Years later the man, by then a mature-age student at the University of Melbourne, came into my room at the university for an oral examination. I was so nervous I had to ask my fellow-examiners to put the first question to the 'player' of the mountain districts who now seemed to have his mind on 'other things'.) I found my mother's request irritating for another reason. The woman I believed she had in mind – I was already beginning to notice such things – worked in a shop next to the tobacconist and hair-dresser's which my mother had already put out of bounds for her son.

The tobacconist and hairdresser was Lal Philips. My mother recommended us to have our hair cut by Mr Johnson, one of the churchwardens, a man who could wield the hair clippers, snip with the scissors or take round the plate in church without betraying the slightest emotion. To speak he opened his lips the very minimum to permit sounds to come out of his mouth. I also did not like him because he always commented adversely on my behaviour in church while running the clippers over the back of my neck. To emphasise his condemnation he tore a hair or two just as he hissed the word 'disgusting' or 'Your father ought to give you a good hiding. That would keep you quiet.' I was never one to enjoy a character sketch by one of the straiteners.

Mr Johnson was so neat, so tidy, so clean. His barber's coat was as snow-white as my father's surplice after a Marge Thompson scrub, rinse, and ironing. Mr Johnson never smoked while performing his duties; Lal Philips always had a cigarette dangling out of the left side of his mouth, and when he talked he balanced it on his lower lip. Lal Philips's barber's coat was grubby, and the floor of his saloon often covered with hair he had not swept up; Mr Johnson used the broom after every customer. There was always a car parked outside Lal Philips's shop every Saturday morning. At its back there was a blackboard with these words chalked on it:

Self, in photograph of junior grades, Cowes School, 1923(?):
'There's where my heart is turning ever' – Stephen Foster

Hope, self and Russell, Phillip Island, 1923(?):
'In my end is my beginning' – T. S. Eliot

Russell (*left*), self (*2nd from right*) and three others, Phillip Island, 1923(?)

The Scholarship Boy, 1927:
'It will make a man of you, Mann dear' (self and Lindsay Wilson)

The Cricketer – or Grammar leaves its mark, 1928
(self and H. M. Ross)

Russell, Hope and self, Belgrave, 1933

'Listen to me, boy'

'There are things in my life, Mann dear . . .'

Get you drunk for a bob.
To the Gully and back for only a shilling.
Driver guarantees to remain sober.

My mother would never tell me what that meant. My father replied with his usual laugh and the enigmatic words, 'That's rich, boy.'

When my father asked me to buy him a box of matches, I would always run so that I could do my business with Lal Philips, and return home so quickly that it would sound plausible when I told my mother I had just bought my father a box of matches at Johnson's, hoping she would not check up on me. Happily for me nothing could shake her belief that members of her family (the *Hope* family) never fibbed. In Lal Philips's shop I could hear the click of the billiard balls from the snooker and billiard saloon behind the counter. I could hear glasses clinking, liquids being poured, and tantalising snatches of conversation such as, 'Did I ever tell you the limerick about the girl from Wyanna/Who played on a moll-house pianna?' And Lal shouting back over his shoulder, 'For Christ's sake, break it down. The parson's kid is in the shop.' That was greeted with guffaws, and a blurry voice saying with an emphasis the sober rarely used, 'You've got to learn some time.' When Lal was embarrassed he used to move his lower teeth up and down with his tongue.

Unlike his sisters Lal never entered my father's church. That alone damned him, proved he was 'peculiar'. Besides, he had committed the unpardonable offence – he was friendly with Harry Luscombe, the Catholic soda-fountain, sweet-shop and newsagency proprietor who did business (if I remember correctly) across the street from where the car for the drunks was parked each Saturday morning. I adored Harry Luscombe. He had a generous mop of white hair which grew luxuriantly above his prominent forehead. He had a brush-back, a hair style no gentleman ever affected, just as no true man ever parted his hair in the centre. In the winter Harry Luscombe wore a grey coat, which he never managed to button up correctly. He also left his hands in his coat pockets when he was speaking to a lady, and this, too, no gentleman would ever do, no matter how cold the weather, or how great his need.

Harry Luscombe had something which the vestrymen and the other leading parishioners in my father's church lacked: he had a generosity of heart; he looked pleased when I did things which were, in their turn, pleasing to him. With much misgiving, much hesitation, my mother finally allowed me to sell the *Herald* and the *Sporting Globe* on Saturday afternoons, and the *Herald* on weekdays during school vacations. My mother urged me to be on my guard with a Catholic. She used the vocabulary and the rhythms of the Litany in the Book of Common Prayer. I gathered I was to be sober (at the age of ten or eleven that was not difficult) and to be vigilant because my adversary, the Devil (the Catholic Harry Luscombe with his endearing smile, and the tender look in his eyes when he sang, 'God bless you and keep you, Mother Machree') was roaming about 'seeking whom he may devour. Whom resist steadfast in the faith!' Well, I was a traitor to my mother. I loved Harry Luscombe. He used to give me a bag of lollies if I sold more than five dozen papers. The payment was threepence a dozen, plus tips.

My mother told me I was not to accept a tip from any drunken man, but give it back. I quickly became a casuist about who was and who was not drunk. My father had more than a sneaking regard for Harry Luscombe. To the dismay of my mother my father always put on an ingratiating smile for local Catholics. He also had his own patter for them: 'We all worship the same God', he would say, and was sometimes quite hurt when a Catholic replied politely 'Not quite'. He was puzzled why, no matter what the weather (the skies in Belgrave specialised in a soaking rain – indeed so much so that I remember once in a daydream thinking Heaven would be a place where there was no more rain), Harry Luscombe, Oz and Garnet Fanning and others could be seen every Sunday morning just before eight o'clock walking briskly towards the Austral Hall where Mass was celebrated. Fifteen or twenty minutes later I noticed the fervour in the sounds coming out of that hall. At breakfast my father would say wistfully, 'I wonder what gets them in?' He was still puzzled. My mother would then make the conversation-stopping remark, 'I wish you wouldn't speak like that, Charlie, in front of the children.' Marge would look nervous, and remain so until grace was said and we began to eat our porridge. My father was generally in a good mood at breakfast on a Sunday morning, as indeed are most human beings after a few ports on an empty stomach. That wisdom came later.

Belgrave had so much to offer. Each year there was a concert for the blind in the Austral Hall. The performers, all blind, were led on to the stage by the master of ceremonies for the evening. That prepared us all for the emotional bath which was to follow.

There was laughter, there were tears. A tenor sang the words:

> *Maxwelton braes are bonny,*
> *Where early fa's the dew,*
> *And 'tis there that Annie Laurie*
> *Gied me her promise true.*

That was the heart-softener. My mother became very tender to me.
I noticed she was crying, but not in her sad way, as she did when
the memory of what she had lived through became too much for
her, when she feared the ghosts from the past would never go away.
She squeezed my hand when the blind tenor sang the passionate
words:

> *And for bonnie Annie Laurie,*
> *I'd lay me doon and dee.*

There was more to come:

> *Her brow is like the snaw-drift,*
> *Her neck is like the swan,*
> *Her face it is the fairest*
> *That e'er the sun shone on.*

My mother was strangely moved. At the time I did not know why.

She was also amused by the two comedians who swapped jokes
with each other. There was one I still remember because it was the
only time I ever knew my mother to laugh at a risqué story. A man
came home early from the office, tip-toed into the kitchen, put his
hands over his wife's eyes, and kissed her passionately. The wife
said, 'Two of brown and one of white today, please, baker.' My mother
did not laugh. She first said, 'Oh, oh, oh . . . goodness', and blushed
and turned to me, and began to laugh as she put an arm around
me. That was also the only time I ever knew her to be amused by
a joke which had a faint connection with treachery. For her, treachery
and betrayal were the sins against the Holy Ghost.

Nor did she ever see anything funny in jokes about drunks. Not
long after we arrived in Belgrave I remember her making another
of her requests to me, another appeal to me to be faithful, 'Mann
dear,' she said, 'I want you to promise me faithfully you won't speak

to Mr Dennis when he's "peculiar".' I had no idea at the time that she was referring to the author of *The Sentimental Bloke*, who was struggling to observe the command to be 'sober', but from time to time cutting bizarre capers, to the great amusement of the gossips of the mountain district. I made it my immediate business to see Mr Dennis on one of those days when he was 'peculiar', and so had my first lesson in the meaning of the word 'peculiar'. It was rarely possible for a boy to be faithful to his mother's requests.

There was a never-ending clash of wills, she striving to confine me within the walls of her world, and I catching glimpses of another exciting world. But my mother was not one of those vulgar 'King and Empire' people who were beating their drums even in that lovely mountain district. Jack Mahony, the local real estate agent, urged the locals to get rid of the Bolsheviks, Sinn Feiners, Wobblies and socialists. That was not my mother's kingdom: her kingdom was not of this world. God's only Son had made that clear. My mother believed simply that in the world a man would always know 'tribulation and sorrow'. She had a narrow view of how to behave if you wanted to enter the 'narrow gate'. Her eye was single. She knew. So when I started on my journey of discovery she was worried. 'Be careful, Mann dear', she said.

Other voices were calling to me. Across the road from the vicarage, builders erected a two-storey stone house for the new doctor, Olaf Jorgensen. The doctor for the vicar and his family was Dr Shirley Francis, the son of a retired chemist who had put on the cloak of gentility after a successful business career. The doctor's wife, Constance, a tall and slender woman, always wore an expression of ineffable sadness on her face, as though for her too there were things in her life about which she either could not or would not speak to anyone. My mother was strongly drawn to her; 'I think I'll take little Mrs Shirley Francis a pot of my jam', she would say. My mother had an unerring eye for those who understood.

Perhaps that was why she was never at ease with Olaf Jorgensen. He was a Catholic, or said to be. He was a Bohemian, that is, one of those post-war young men who snapped their fingers at the laws of God and the lore of his tribe. Olaf Jorgensen was the brother of the artist Justus Jorgensen. Rumour had it in Belgrave that Olaf Jorgensen wanted human beings to liberate themselves from all restraints on their behaviour. Rumour had it that behind the high hedge in front of the new Jorgensen mansion men and women lay on the grass naked. Doubtless there were other rumours at the time, but they would have been about behaviour so hideous, so disgraceful, that it must not be mentioned in front of a boy – goodness me no, what is the world coming to?

So once again my mother presented her request. 'Mann dear,' she said, 'I hope you won't talk too much to Dr Jorgensen.' This time she gave no reason. What to do? I was already a secret admirer of Olaf Jorgensen. Like Harry Luscombe he had a mane of white hair. He wore a suit, he wore a stiff white collar, and a bow tie – but the latter was never tied quite right. He put his arm around me, and drew me to him, and began to unfold to me a world quite different from the world of 'When I survey the wondrous Cross/On which the Prince of glory died', or 'Foul I to the fountain fly/Wash me, Saviour, or I die', different from all those hopes and dreams of which my mother sang with such fervour in church each Sunday. Olaf Jorgensen showed me the light, showed me a world where we were not all 'miserable sinners', or grovellers before the throne of grace. I remember he told me that when I grew up I would want to read the books of a man called Freud. But I remember most of all that he introduced me to the world of painting and secular music.

In our house the paintings and the drawings were few. There were no religious paintings. We did not eat our daily bread with a sorrowful or saccharine Christ pleading with us, or asking us, 'Is it nothing to you, all ye that pass by?' There was no painting or drawing of the Mother of God. My mother never referred to Mary, she believing all worship of the Virgin Mother to be idolatrous. She needed no intercessors: she was a straight-through person, straight through to the one on top. My father also was silent about Mary. Maybe it would have been a comfort to him to know the Russian legend that Mary had once visited Hell and had been so shocked that she interceded with God the Father to forgive those sinners; and God had relented, and they had been saved. My father needed something less bleak than the religion of the *quod erat demonstrandum* men: my father needed to be shown that two and two did not always make four.

In his study my father had a drawing of Napoleon on board H.M.S. *Bellerophon* which touched my father deeply – for the proud and the stiff-necked would one day be humbled. There was a drawing of a man dressed in the clothes of some ancient civilisation biting the finger of a woman. What puzzled me as a child was that the woman seemed to enjoy the lover's bite. No one ever told me why. Also in my father's study there were photographs of Dr Yarnold, the vicar of the church where he had first met my mother, and of the Reverend Manning, my father's fellow chaplain at Darlinghurst and Long Bay Penitentiaries. In the sitting-room there were photographs of a sketch of Eliza Marsden, the Reverend Samuel Marsden's wife; of Marsden, my mother's deceased brother; of Florence, her deceased sister; of Charles and Mary Hope, her father and mother; of my father and mother on their wedding day – she with a face of astonishing beauty, the face life was to ravage so mercilessly, and he enjoying the moment of having arrived, with the face of a man who wants all of us to be nice to each other because he goes to pieces if anyone is not nice to him.

So Olaf Jorgensen was tilling virgin soil when he introduced me to the world of art. I do not remember much of his early instruction. I was only eleven when he started to talk to me. There were many unpronounceable names, names there was no point in pretending to have heard before. I was interested in faces. I was interested in stories. I was interested in the reproductions Olaf Jorgensen showed me of paintings based on stories from the Old and New Testaments, but that presented a difficulty for both of us. He wanted me to be revolted by Christian art – the sorrowful Christs, the bleeding hearts – he wanted me to acknowledge that most religious art was propaganda for the life-deniers. He wanted me to notice how the principal characters in all those dramas lived in great darkness. He wanted me to see that the characters in Greek and Roman mythology lived in the bright light of the sun, that they knew a gaiety, a joy to which the Christian miserables were total strangers.

I was tremendously excited by what he showed me. There was a special reason for this. Olaf Jorgensen was one of my heroes. Olaf Jorgensen moved on the cricket field with the grace and beauty of one of those Greek athletes he had drawn my attention to. He was like one of the gods he told me had once walked the earth, and worked their great marvels, and performed their god-like deeds. Olaf was a slow left-arm spin bowler. He had played cricket for the University of Melbourne. He could spin the ball sharply from leg to off when bowling to a right-hander. My father loved fielding in the slips when Olaf was bowling. 'In the slips, boy,' he would tell me, 'never keep your eye off the ball from the moment it leaves the bowler's hand. Don't worry about the bat. Just keep your eye on the ball.'

128

Somewhat to the chagrin of Olaf Jorgensen, I was not an enthusiast for that time when the gods lived on the earth. That was make-believe. That was a fantasy. That had nothing to do with the world I knew. I was not bothered by his hints that maybe God did not exist. That was no loss to me, because the God I heard about in the church, the Sunday School, school, and sometimes, but only rarely, at home had seldom been part of my world. What I could not do without were the remarks Christ had made. Even at ten, and certainly at eleven, I believed in Christ. I was a 'lilies of the field' boy. I was 'a man went down from Jerusalem to Jericho' boy. I was a 'neither do I condemn thee' boy, though I did not know what Christ was not condemning. I was an 'anti-money-changers' boy. I already had an idea that the Pharisees Christ condemned were people like Mr Sambell and Mr Johnson, frowners, life-deniers, straiteners (a word I was not familar with at the time). Christ loved the people I loved – people like Bing Edgar, Marge Thompson and Bella Green. I could not do without that Christ: to deny him, to betray him, to disown him, would be a loss I could not endure. I was never willing to abandon Christ. I hoped one day to believe in God. What mattered to me was that there had been such a person as Christ. In later years this passion, this adoration, this love, was to cause me many problems. I was growing up at a time when God took a high place on humanity's list of missing persons. The secular humanists had no time for Christ. I mixed with them, seemed to be one of them, but was really like a foreigner in their country. I had the first intimation of a coming alienation from the modern man and the modern woman when Olaf Jorgensen talked to me about painting.

Olaf Jorgensen also spoke to me about music. So far, apart from English, Irish and Scottish ballads, I knew only religious music. *Hymns Ancient and Modern* were a gloomy, dark view of the world, or sometimes unintentionally funny. Consider the words, 'There is a book, who runs may read.' Now I heard a song I have never forgotten:

> *Gin a body meet a body,*
> *Comin' thro the rye.*
> *Gin a body kiss a body*
> *Need a body cry?*

I also heard a man sing on the gramophone, 'Oh Shenandoah, I long to see you'. They were very different from the Psalms, Morning

Prayer, Evening Prayer, a sung communion service and Stainer's *Crucifixion*. I once heard an Anglophile tell my father the *English Hymnal* was superior to *Hymns Ancient and Modern* in both music and poetry. My father winced, and winked at me. *Hymns Ancient and Modern* were to live with us forever, the words and the music never going away. Anyone who had heard the choir and the congregation at Belgrave sing 'Nearer my God to Thee, nearer to Thee' must have realised these people feared their God to be a long way away, and that he ought to be nearer, much nearer, but, alas, he almost certainly never would be any nearer. Singing hymns was an outlet for their emotions, their hopes, their longings for all those things which could never be. There was the question, 'Will he say me nay?' There was the confident, reassuring answer, 'Not till earth, and not till Heaven pass away.' I was worried by the answer. I thought Christ's kingdom would not come until the end of the world. My father silenced my doubts with one of his smiles, and his 'I'll explain all that to you, boy, when you get older.' But he never did.

The hymns reflected what that little world believed you ought to talk about, and on what you should be silent or refer to only in whispers so that children would not hear. A change from an *mf* to a *pp* or a *dim.* told all:

(mf) Angels, martyrs, prophets, (dim.) virgins,
(ff) Answer 'yes'.

The hymns gave choir and congregation a chance to testify to their depravity, not in any hole-and-corner way, but openly, as though they were making a confession about themselves:

I am not worthy, Holy Lord,
That Thou shouldst come to me.

There were the hymns where choir and congregation professed to believe the impossible was possible:

JESU, gentlest Saviour
Thou art in us now,
Fill us with Thy goodness,
Till our hearts o'erflow.

There were the hymns of resignation and acceptance, the hymns which kindled what I learned later was identified as the 'oceanic feeling'. There were moments in the church in Belgrave when I sensed we were all being translated from the world we knew into quite another world. 'Abide with Me' took us all on a journey out of this world. My mother's face was transfigured as organ, voices, faces worked the great marvel:

> Abide with me; fast falls the eventide;
> The darkness deepens; Lord, with me abide

We were away. My father's face was beatific. Marge looked very happy, and Bella Green was so happy it seemed to me as a boy that she might cry, or shout for joy, or embrace everyone.

Yet, outside the church, these men and women who had just experienced this spiritual ecstasy, these men and women whose voices had given expression to some higher harmony, some yearning for a universal embrace, quickly lapsed back into the world of gossip and back-bite. I remember one episode which puzzled me at the time. Mrs — had a most beautiful soprano voice; she sang like an angel. But Mrs — was said to be the local Mary Magdalene. I remember one morning after church hearing one woman say to another through pursed lips, 'Did you notice her dress when she came into the church? No one will convince me that she came straight from her home to the church.' And the reply, 'Yes, and did you notice how flushed her cheeks were?' 'Yes, I certainly did, and we all know what flushes cheeks, don't we?' I was puzzled. I noticed also that no matter how exalted we all seemed to be during the singing of the hymn the expression on the face of Mr Johnson the barber never changed. He still frowned. He still had only a wintry smile for me after the service.

While singing a hymn, members of the choir and the congregation revealed how they felt towards each other. As we all joined in singing the words:

> Sun of my soul, Thou Saviour dear,
> It is not night if Thou be near

those who were fond of each other exchanged a loving smile. I noticed young Mr Critchley, who was said to be very much in love with a young woman but could not afford to marry her because times were hard, looked at her with eyes of longing. When I was seated near him I thought I heard a sigh, even a groan, escape from him at such a moment. My mother, rising to the mood of the music, sometimes put an arm around me, and pressed my arm as she sang with fervour of the hope that someone would be near. I did not know then how great was her need: I do now. I remember, too, the look of hope in the eyes of Marge, Bella and Lottie as they sang the words, 'Hath He arms to lead me to Him?' The hymns were a consolation prize for all those who were never to know the prizes they coveted. They provided the opportunity for the deprived to sing of their hopes and their longings. They believed

> There is a happy land,
> Far, far away.

In the beginning at Belgrave I kneeled, sat and stood as I listened in wonder to all these hopes, all these confessions of unworthiness, all these acknowledgements of powerlessness to change their own world. Within a few years I began, inwardly, to be angry with all of them for entertaining all those delusions. Now, looking back, I see them all with the eye of pity and the eye of love. Perhaps they knew that such things could never be, that there was no one to whom those that travailed and were heavy-laden could go and be refreshed, but that did not stop them hoping that it might be true. Perhaps they knew there was no 'help of the helpless', but thought there ought to be, there must be, or life would have no meaning, and all their suffering be in vain. So why be angry with them, why view with contempt people who promised each Sunday to sacrifice to their God 'all the vain things' that charmed them most? Why mock and sneer at people who besought a God who was probably not even there, or if He was, adopted an air of indifference to the millions of petitions sent up to Him each day and night? They sang of how they saw with a lively interest 'the sights that dazzle' and heard with some promise of future delights 'the tempting sounds'. They knew, they said, that if only He remained their Master and friend all would be well.

For a while I believed we should all face the truth about ourselves, should all rid our minds of such delusions. But now I wonder whether for the great mass of humanity that is bearable – I wonder whether, if they did not have a 'carer' in the sky, whether they might not abase themselves before some monster on earth, and commit terrible crimes against other people to prove their devotion to their monster. To change the image, hymns were a crutch, just as the words in the Prayer Book, 'Hear what comfortable words our Saviour saith to all those who truly turn to Him', were a crutch. The question is: Can human beings dispense with a crutch?

Belgrave was probably the flowering time in the life of my father. His ministry began with one of his usual brushes with the gentry. There were two sisters – I think their surname was Elliot, one was Hettie, but, alas, I have forgotten the name of the other. Paint and powder imprinted on their faces the pomp and splendour to which they believed their birth entitled them. They both wore fox furs around their necks, and Hettie always stroked the nose of the fox affectionately with her left hand as she spoke to other people. They both believed the 'elect' to whom Christ referred were those born as the self-appointed members of the local gentry. Hettie always moved the little finger of her right hand – provided it was glove-less – across her well-lipsticked lower lip just before making some withering remark to someone she judged to be her social inferior. My father could never abide women who put on airs, women who behaved as though being socially important meant more to them than love, or even affection. Hettie Elliot's upper clothing, I remember, seemed designed to attract the attention of the men of the parish to her prominent partition. I knew nothing about that sort of thing at the time. But now, looking back, I wonder why Hettie preferred social power to love, why the furs and the jewels, and not the partition, were the ruling passions of her life. I wonder now whether that was why her eyes were always cast downwards, as though she were looking down on everyone with disdain and contempt.

My father went to pieces when a woman treated him as an inferior, as someone ineluctably, irreversibly tainted or flawed. He and Hettie clashed over music. Hettie, who was not lacking in the arts of the masterful, assumed that as organist she had the right to decide which musical version of 'Abide with Me' would be sung. My father must always be in charge, would never share power. When Hettie said the wounding words, accusing my father of being a sentimentalist and not a musician, that ignited my father's powder keg. Angry words were exchanged. Hettie Elliot resigned as organist, and joined the neighbouring parish of Kallista, where the Church of England vicar was a more obliging servant of the local gentry. My father never forgave Hettie Elliot. She joined the ever-increasing number of those who had done him great evil, those whom the Lord would reward according to their desserts. My father would never speak again to anyone who had hurt him; the very sight of any of his wounders was enough to stir the madness in his blood.

When my mother spoke to Hettie Elliot – my mother finding it easy to be in love and charity with everyone, and not easy to understand the unforgiving – my father shouted at her, 'Spare me days, woman, do you know what that woman Elliot is saying about me all around Belgrave – and yet, you, my wife, fawn on her.' My mother was puzzled why a man who loved much should also be such a hater, why nothing she could do, nothing anyone could do, healed the wound in my father's heart. He had to live all his life with many such private hells in his heart; no one could rescue him from himself. He had to go on asking his God to 'cleanse our hearts and minds' each day, knowing no one would ever work that great marvel for him.

In boyhood I was puzzled when these gusts of malevolence swept over my father's face. I remember the puzzles, I remember the doubts. I remember the doubts being swept away, as organ, voices and faces held out that promise of 'other things':

> Lord, in this Thy mercy's day,
> Ere it pass for aye away.

The calm never lasted for long. That last sentence in the hymn triggered off another anxiety. Was it all to end in nothingness? The words always sent a chill of fear through me. That fear did not last, for there was the petition:

> Grant us 'neath Thy wings a place,
> Lest we lose this day of grace
> Ere we shall behold Thy face.

Then I wondered about the size of the wings, I wondered if we could all find a place. I wondered also whether that meant that Mr Johnson, the respectable barber, would have a place under the wings, and that Lal Philips, the naughty barber, might also be there. I clung to the hope, a hope which was never to leave me, even though it was to drop to a very, very shy hope in later years, that I would meet again those I had loved. So, when we sang the 'Amen' after declaring the desire to see Christ's face, those who had a bond with each other exchanged smiles, as though they were saying I want above all to be under those wings with you.

Yet as soon as we moved out of the church into the bright light of day, the never-ending war of humanity broke out again. Children tormented each other, children competed with each other: 'Touched you last.' 'No, you didn't, I touched you last.' 'You're a big fibber. Everyone knows what you are.' Embarrassed parents told their children to control themselves, women apologised to other women about the dresses their daughters were wearing: 'You'd never think that only yesterday I'd washed and ironed the dress she's wearing.' Those who were of 'riper years', as the Prayer Book puts it in one of its many glosses on what we do not like to see, as it were, face to face, were displaying their talent for insinuation. 'I'm surprised that – feels qualified to take Communion. Mind you, I'm sure everything's all right, and I don't wish to imply anything about her. But it does make you wonder, doesn't it? I mean, I wonder where she got to after the dance in the Memorial Hall?'

I used to move around from group to group, standing always a pace or two apart, listening to what they had to say, and puzzled why, after they had destroyed someone's character and reputation, they would then shake hands so warmly, and look at each other with such eyes of trust and love, having just made it clear, or so it seemed to me, that they trusted nobody. And when I risked asking my father about it he would say, '– is really a very decent fellow.' Then my father would move the blade of the carving knife deftly over the steel, and prepare to carve the Sunday roast. The puzzles of boyhood would be swallowed up in satisfying at least one of the hungers of the body. At such moments, when my father looked so very happy, no one would ever believe that he had dark moments chewing over schemes of vengeance. Later in life I was told that on their death-bed the vengeful are often reconciled with those who have hurt them, because they know there can be no other wounds. But I believe a shadow would have crossed over my father's face if, say, Hettie Elliot had appeared at his bedside. That was one of the questions to which I never found the answer.

But that was in the future – when there would be retribution for all of us. No one would have foreseen what was to happen. During the early Belgrave years my father played cricket with the Belgrave team in the summer, and there was no longer any need to seek sympathy from the afternoon-tea ladies. On the cricket fields in the mountain district the grass was short enough for one of his late-cuts or his leg-glances to race to the boundary. There were men he could speak to in his team – men like Olaf Jorgensen, a Catholic renegade with a secret hope that maybe what the Jesuits had taught him at Xavier College was all true; Alf and Sutton Leonard, Melbourne businessmen, who wore proper cricket dress; the 'old codger'; Bert Deasey, the wicket-keeper who had the good sense to acknowledge that my father held spectacular catches in the slips; and Vance Palmer, the writer, who played cricket for Emerald.

Cricket, in my father's mind, was a game for poets, for those who moved with the grace and poise of ballet dancers. There was 'Bunny' Gramlick, another man with a touch of the poet and melancholy eyes which suggested the sadness my father always found becoming in any man who had dared to launch out into the deep. There was a pavilion, ostensibly a changing room, the walls of which provided ample cover for men who preferred something stronger than the brew prepared by the tea ladies. I remember still the twinkle in Marge's eye when she asked my father on his return home from a cricket game, 'Cold tea for you, Vicar?' You have to learn to translate early in life; at the time I was a literal translator, but life later taught me how to translate the metaphors of those who were close to me.

Belgrave gave my father the opportunity to display his skill as a choir-master. He was lucky in his choice of an organist to replace Hettie Elliot. Mrs Bleakley, the wife of the school master at Belgrave School, had the qualities Hettie Elliott lacked, or disdained. She was a server: she had the gift to perceive what the Vicar wanted, and was not irritated by her subordinate role. She had warmth. I always felt you could tell Mrs Bleakley anything, and she would try to understand, even though it might be difficult for her to condone what was being said. She was a Belgrave paragon of St Paul's precepts for stewards – that they be found faithful. I remember the right eye of Mrs Bleakley watching for the signal from my father to play the introduction to a hymn. I remember, too, the vigour with which she pressed the keys and the pedals of the organ when my father, with a flick of the hand, called for more volume. I remember Mrs Bleakley and my mother shared a love for the hymn 'When I survey the wondrous cross,/On which the Prince of glory died.' I did not understand at the time why that was so, but I do now. They were both carrying a cross. I remember my mother often spoke of taking 'another pot of jam' to 'little Mrs Bleakley'. That puzzled me, because Mrs Bleakley was quite large – rather like her heart, capacious and full of comforting words and gestures for those wounded by the world.

My father loved the work with the choir. Every February he began to train them for the singing of Stainer's *Crucifixion* during Holy Week. Generous parishioners helped to buy the copies of the music. 'The great work about betrayal, boy, is Bach's *St Matthew's Passion*' my father used to say to me, 'but, boy, they are not up to that yet. But you just wait.' My father was fortunate to have two visitors from Melbourne each year as soloists – a tenor, Mr Searle, as the Evangelist, and a bass, Mr Robertson, as Christ. He was also lucky to have Mrs Smith, wife of the schoolteacher at Kallista, as his principal soprano. The performance each year was quite an occasion. My father, as the conductor of the choir and the accompanying organ (Mrs Bleakley's eye fastened on my father's baton), wore a becoming clerical black suit, a black silk stock and a white clerical collar. He never liked anyone to call it a dog collar ('A man is not a dog, boy'). The male soloists wore black dinner-jackets, white shirts and butterfly collars and black bow-ties. The women soloists wore long white dresses buttoned up to the neck, symbolical, I learned when I reached riper years, of the mystical purity between Christ and his Church. The men in the choir wore dark suits, and the ladies white dresses, cut with such ample cloth that one was not aware of the curves behind the white linen. The unreliable singers were in the very back row – Marge, Bella and Lottie could scarcely be seen from where we sat in the front row. My father commanded them to sing pianissimo even in the loudest of the many choruses, and his will must be obeyed.

Years later the musicians I knew looked down their noses or curled their lips into an expression of contempt if I risked asking them what they thought of Stainer's *Crucifixion*. They were just as high and mighty in their comments on *Hymns Ancient and Modern*. Bad music and bad verse. *Exeunt* Stainer's *Crucifixion* and *Hymns Ancient and Modern*. I said not a word. Stainer's *Crucifixion* was my first discovery of a work of art. Maybe it was middle-brow, maybe it was dripping with sickly sentiment, maybe it was an emotional bath for the mediocre. For me it was my baptism, my initiation into a story of betrayal. It was more than that. I was attracted to Christ as a person, and not interested in the claims of the Church that Christ was the Son of God. I was already feeling ill at ease with those who claimed to be Christ's followers and interpreters. Later it meant much to me when I read the description of priests, parsons, ministers, prominent laymen and laywomen as those 'who had corrected Christ's work'. Already as a boy I had formed in my mind a picture of a good human being, of an innocent human being – that is, someone who never harmed or did injury to anyone else, someone who understood everything, and forgave everyone. Years later I wept when I first read Grushenka's remark in *The Brothers Karamazov*: 'If I were God I would forgive everyone.' As a boy I already knew for certain that if Christ were to come back on earth and pass through Belgrave he would have spent his time with Lal Philips, Harry Luscombe and 'Bluey' Carter, and the woman with the lovely voice, whose clothing, according to the women in the ladies' guild, told a tale of having 'loved much'. I saw Christ outside Mr Johnson's barber's shop, using the words of condemnation: 'Woe unto you . . . who build monuments to the ones your ancestors killed.'

For me as a boy Stainer's *Crucifixion* was a story in music, an opera, except that the singers did not wear costumes, or employ gestures. In it we were introduced to an innocent man who was crucified by the men in charge of the world – the ones with whom I would always feel so ill at ease, the ones whose morals I never could observe, and never wanted to observe. As Henry Lawson would have said, 'That's the whole bloody trouble.' Those people ruled the world – be it Belgrave, Melbourne Grammar School, the University of Melbourne, Oxford, Bonn, Canberra. Wherever I worked and lived THEY, the men and women dressed in black, who put on black looks if ever I risked coming near, were everywhere. I was to consume far too much time and energy denouncing them in extravagant language, ridiculing, mocking the bourgeoisie of the Melbourne suburbs, calling Sydney University the 'last citadel for the defence of British philistinism in Australia', and so on. That provided immediate satisfaction at the price of long-term fear and remorse. The laughter of the listeners was the only satisfaction. I was never to find an answer to the problem, except to keep out of their way. Despite all the anguish and torment, that solution, and silence in their presence, were to be my only shields against their attacks.

Even now, at the age of seventy-three, I find that some of my terror dreams are about THEM. Recently I dreamed THEY arrested me and charged me with inciting the young to sedition and depravity. The judge sentenced me to twenty strokes on the back with a cane. The next scene in the dream was the flogging. Terrified, I looked up at my flagellator. It was a man in whom I had placed an absolute trust. I asked him how many strokes I would receive. He said, 'Twenty'. On waking I could not understand why the judge and executioner should be a friend, a gentle spirit. In the next scene (dreams change the scene as swiftly as a fast-moving film) I was in a car driving to the university. A professor from the Australian National University, well known for his humane views, a liberal in politics and a libertarian in morality, asked me why I looked so pale. I told him what was troubling me, and begged him to help me against my tormentors. He said that at any other time he would love to help me, as, like many others in Canberra, he owed so much to me, but this was the wrong moment to ask the men in power to take any action which would offend a large number of voters. Once again, in a dream as in life, I faced the terrifying fact that possibly no one would ever help. We were all strangers to each other.

As a boy it meant much to me when the choir sang, 'Is it nothing to you, all ye that pass by?' I already felt a bond with those who cried out in anguish, 'O perishing souls, it's to you I cry.' At that time I believed there must be someone who would understand, someone who would forgive. I believed my father felt the same way, but some ghosts in his past of which I was then ignorant checked him. Now I understand why my father trusted no man, and certainly no woman; why he had many acquaintances, he being one of Australia's great charmers, but no close friends; why, to give a trivial example which may tell much about him, he would never allow anyone to see the contents of his wallet. The charm was the mask.

Now, when it is too late, I begin to understand why Stainer's *Crucifixion* touched him so deeply. There was that menace in the music he knew so well in his own life, that menace of the men in black that they would be satisfied with nothing less than death. There was the response of the well-orchestrated mob when they had their chance to recognise the sort of person who was on trial before Caiaphas and Pontius Pilate. They shouted in anger, 'Crucify Him, crucify Him, crucify.' There were those enigmatic words from the Cross, 'Jesus cried with a loud voice, saying "My God, my God, why hast Thou forsaken me?"' What did that mean? Why did my father always bow his head while the bass sang those words? Why did his nostrils quiver? What was it all about? My father seemed to long for the reassuring last words from the Cross, 'Father, into Thy hands I commend my spirit.' My father seemed reassured when the tenor sang unaccompanied, 'And he bowed his head and gave up the ghost.' Those last words were a trouble to me all my life. What did they mean? I wondered later why not even Christ, the innocent one, could overcome death?

My mother needed no such comforter. She trusted Christ's promise to the repentant thief, 'Today thou shalt be with me in Paradise.' My mother also had her own reasons for believing one of Christ's other promises about the Kingdom of Heaven, 'In my Father's house there are many mansions.' In between I hoped singers and organists would get it over quickly so that my brother and I could hop into the meat and mustard sandwiches, the cream puffs, the sponge cakes and the chocolate éclairs cooked or prepared by the members of the ladies' guild. That was one voice inside me, the voice which knew quite early, though the words came later, that there is no sin, there is no crime, there is only hunger. There was by then another voice, another part of me which wanted to be there when 'everyone suddenly understands what it has all been for'. I was grateful to Stainer because he provided some food to appease briefly that great hunger in my life. Later I would never be able to hear 'Abide with Me' without tears streaming down my face. It persuaded me that no matter how much the 'darkness' of human behaviour 'deepens' there may be those 'certain certainties'. There may be another kingdom than the kingdoms of this world – but that hope never lasts for long.

There was another discovery during the years at Belgrave. One winter my father presented a series of sermons on great books; I do not remember now the order in which he presented them. I remember there was one on *A Christmas Carol* by Charles Dickens. Happily for me my father was not a literary critic, not given to close examinations of either the words or the ideas. Contradictions never bothered my father. 'Let me tell you, boy, dry souls gloat over contradictions.' My father was an appreciator, an enthusiast. His story excited me. He quoted with gusto the Dickens description of a dinner. My father wanted everyone to be jolly when they sat down at the banquet of life. He spoke with approval of how the eyes of Bob Cratchit glistened when he saw and smelt the amply-filled bowl of punch, and the steam rising from it. My father spoke of Tiny Tim. He quoted Bob Cratchit's description of Tiny Tim in the church:

Somehow he gets thoughtful, sitting by himself so much, and thinks the strangest things you ever heard. He told me, coming home, that he hoped the people saw him in the church, because he was a cripple, and it might be pleasant to them to remember upon Christmas Day, who made lame beggars walk, and blind to see . . .

and said Bob's voice was tremulous when he told his family this. So was my father's. I thought he was going to cry.

I remember the tremble in his voice recurring as he quoted Dickens on the human situation: we are all 'fellow passengers to the grave'. The dead should make us more tender to each other. He quoted the hope of the man who had erred and strayed, as the Prayer Book put it, and was seeking desperately for some water which would 'sponge away the writing on the stone'. I did not understand at the time why these words moved him so deeply. All I knew at the time was that this was a voice, the Dickens voice, I had wanted to hear for a long time. Here was someone talking about things which interested me. Perhaps books would give me the answers my father, my mother and my teachers either could not provide or withheld because of my tender years and my growing awareness that 'sorrow, wrong and trouble is the lot of all mankind'.

I was too young then to notice the difference between the optimism in the New Testament, and the pessimism in the Old Testament; too young to heed the comments in the Psalms, the Book of Job and Ecclesiastes about the life of a human being. I had heard, but had not felt, the words. They were not as yet part of what Henry James called 'the quantity of felt life'. I had heard my father read with a becoming melancholy the words, 'My heart was hot within me, and while I was thus musing the fire kindled . . . Thou makest his beauty to consume away like as it were a moth fretting a garment . . . Every man therefore is but vanity.' I had heard him read the verse in Ecclesiastes, 'There is one alone, and there is not a second', and did not even wonder why that touched him so deeply. That came later. Life was preparing me to be tempted to believe that message. My father's sermons held out the promise that the answers for which I hungered might be found in books. There was that ever-recurring piece of advice: 'Get wisdom'. But how? And where? And what was this wisdom? I remember my father loved Ecclesiastes: 'That's great stuff, boy.' My mother said she did not care for it. She told me such verses as

For that which befalleth the sons of men befalleth beasts; even one thing befalleth them: as the one dieth, so dieth the other; yea, they have all one breath; so that a man hath no pre-eminence above a beast: for all is vanity

were 'peculiar'. I can hear her troubled voice saying to my father, 'I wish you wouldn't talk about such things in front of Manning, Charlie. He's a worrier.' I can hear, too, my father's angry reply, 'God spare my days, woman, what do you expect me to do?'

My mother was pained by my father's sermon on *The Scarlet Letter* by Nathaniel Hawthorne. I do not remember now very much of what he said that evening in the pulpit at Belgrave. I had no idea then that everything a man writes or says is a fragment in a gigantic confession about his own life. I remember the picture my father portrayed of Hester Prynne, and how she was condemned to wear the letter 'A' on her breast because she had committed adultery. She had broken the seventh commandment: 'Thou shalt not commit adultery.' She had transgressed against the letter of the law; she must be punished. My father often quoted Christ's words; 'The letter killeth.' I remember, too, my father's description of the scene where the Reverend Mr Dimmesdale met Hester Prynne and their daughter Pearl in the forest on the bank of a river. I remember how my father faltered when recounting the magical moment when Hester Prynne and the Reverend Dimmesdale had their chance to go off into the forest, and start a new life free from the load of sin, and how Dimmesdale declined because he believed his guilty stains could be washed away only by a public confession of his sin, and a humble petition to God and his congregation to forgive him his 'trespasses'. I remember, too, my father's interest in Roger Chillingworth. I did not know at the time, but I am sure my father had known ever since his confrontation with the letter-of-the-law men in the Diocese of Sydney, that the Chillingworths are everywhere, that they are an ever-present reminder of exposure, of public humiliation and shame – they are the ones who drive lovers out of their Garden of Eden, out of their Paradise.

I remember the scene in the vicarage after evensong that Sunday. My father still hungered and thirsted after praise and approval. He mopped up the flattery outside the church. Women parishioners shook him by the hand, and whispered in his ear, 'I can't tell you how much your words meant to me.' Bella Green laughed her semi-hysterical laugh, and said, 'Thanks, Vicar.' Marge looked strangely sad and thoughtful. She always looked as though she understood everything, though I doubt whether she ever read a book in her life – she *knew* the book of life.

My father was no fool. What he coveted was the praise of the discerning, the recognition of those who had weighed him in the balance and found him wanting. He hungered for words of praise from my mother. My mother said not a word. Perhaps that was why in later life one line in Thomas Hardy's poem 'The Going' made me quiver when I first read it – and lived with me always: 'Why, then, latterly, did we not speak . . . ?' I wonder now whether she was always silent when reminded of what she called 'those things in my life, Mann dear, which I hope you'll never know anything about'. That night my father was preaching to her, hoping for forgiveness. But she, a most loving and forgiving woman, could not respond. So in a moment of public triumph, in the full after-glow a performer knows after one of his creations has succeeded with his public, my father discovered again that what he wanted most in life could never be. He had to make do with his adorers, and his flatterers, hoping God would give him the strength to endure the pain which never went away. Besides, there was always the hope that a huge bluenose would swallow the bait the next time he dropped a line at Pyramid Rock – that would be one source of satisfaction.

One Sunday evening that winter he preached on Victor Hugo's novel, *Les Misérables*. My father knew some Latin and Greek, but no modern European language except Australian English. Again I do not remember much of what he said. I have a picture in my mind of a man wearing the white surplice, the symbol of the mystical purity between Christ and His Church, the black stole, the hood of a diplomate in theology, and the face of a hunter, of a man who was pleading for someone to tell him where it had all gone wrong, and that, late though it was, there was still time for that amendment of life to which the Prayer Book referred, he having despaired by then of ever being forgiven or forgiving himself. Perhaps I have read too much into his face – memory's picture often tells more about the observer than the observed.

I do remember that my father presented *Les Misérables* as a story about forgiveness. He was selective; he had to be with such a long-winded work. My father was a magnificent story-teller, and he held us all spellbound as he told the story of the bishop and the candlesticks. 'Boy,' he would often say to me 'when I'm in good form in the pulpit you can hear a pin dropping.' That was one of those occasions. The convict, Jean Valjean, steals the bishop's candlesticks. The French provincial police arrest Jean Valjean and bring him back to the bishop's house for him and the candlesticks to be identified by the bishop, but the bishop, mindful of Christ's words, 'neither do I condemn thee. Go and sin no more', tells the police he gave the candlesticks to Jean Valjean. Forgiveness is not barren: Jean Valjean prospers. Forgiveness pays, with a glow in the heart of the forgiver, and money in the pocket of the forgiven. But that was not my father's only interest in the story. As in *The Scarlet Letter* there was the one who knew about the past transgressions of Jean Valjean, the man bent on exposure, the punisher, one of God's destroying angels – those who would never let the Arthur Dimmesdales and the Jean Valjeans of this world know a moment of peace, a moment of heart's ease. Dimmesdale collapsed and died under the strain of those all-seeing eyes; Jean Valjean had to endure the years of servitude. I listened in awe and wonder. I did not understand at the time; I do now. My father was initiating me into the world as he had experienced it. There would always be the eyes of the ones who knew about the past: they would never go away.

There was also a sermon on *Vanity Fair* by William Makepeace Thackeray. I remember now two scenes from that sermon. My father told us a good writer tells the reader about life by painting scenes. My father read with great passion Thackeray's paragraph on the battle of Waterloo. Here it is in part:

All our friends took their share and fought like men in the great field. All day long while the men were praying ten miles away, the lines of the dauntless English infantry were receiving and repelling the furious charges of the French horsemen. Guns which were heard at Brussels were ploughing up their ranks, and comrades falling, and the resolute survivors closing in . . .

No more firing was heard at Brussels – the pursuit rolled miles away. Darkness came down on the field and city: and Amelia was praying for George, who was lying on his face, dead, with a bullet through his heart.

'You mark my words, boy', my father would say later. 'It's what happens to the individual which is the stuff of history.' Perhaps that was why he also dwelt in his sermon that night in Belgrave on the odd throws of chance. Jos Sedley might have proposed to Becky Sharp if he had not got drunk at Vauxhall Gardens. 'Don't forget, boy', he would often say to me later, 'Jos Sedley got drunk at Vauxhall Gardens.' The words, the image, became part of my store of knowledge of the human scene – of what painful and terrible events often follow one act of folly, one act of madness. I was not surprised to hear that even in the last years of his life, when much had slipped away from him, the light came into my father's eye when he urged young men to read the story of Jos Sedley, Becky Sharp, George Osborne and his wife Amelia.

My father was my first teacher about life. In these sermons he turned my mind towards the things that were to matter to me in life. Great actor that he was, an *artiste manqué* dressed in clerical garb, he coaxed me into reading books, holding out the hope that there I might find comfort, there I might find answers to some of the puzzles of childhood. Books, like life, were schools for those seeking wisdom and understanding. From that time on I was to devour every book which touched on my subject. Novels, short stories, poems, plays, moving pictures, newspapers, words of songs – I found food everywhere. I was then and was to remain all my life a contents man – the beauty, the poetry, the music, always being secondary to the idea. From that time on, and possibly earlier, I had a secret life of my own, a quest for I knew not what. Years later I stumbled on the words which made me say to myself, 'Yes, that has always been my secret life.' They were the words of Ivan Karamazov in Dostoevsky's *The Brothers Karamazov*, 'I want to be there when everyone suddenly understands what it has all been for.' I never risked letting anyone know what was going on in my mind. My father threw out his hint he knew something was brewing inside me. 'Manning', he used to tell people, 'is the thoughtful customer.' But we never really spoke to each other. My mother was troubled by my long silences; 'I worry, Mann dear,' she used to say, 'about what's going to happen to you.'

It was a good time and place to begin such a journey. The schoolmaster at Belgrave State School, Mr Bleakley, was the husband of the organist. He believed in education as a means of getting on in the world. The boy or girl who got sums right, mastered the rudiments of spelling, punctuation and grammar, had a secure footing on the bottom rung of the ladder of worldly success. Mr Bleakley knew his place in the world. Neither he nor we must expect to climb to the top, but knowing how to multiply, how to add up, subtract and divide, knowing *ei* comes after *c* but *ie* is better after any other letter, being quick at mental arithmetic, and knowing how to spell 'their' and 'there' might later mean the difference between being able and not being able to earn your daily bread. Education meant virtue and respectability, the one sure way to avoid a life of drudgery. In the school room at Belgrave I carpeted many floors, wallpapered many walls, calculated the interest on huge sums of money – all part of my training for 'getting on'. But I added not one jot or tittle to my inner life. That all happened outside the classroom.

I remember some of the boys with great affection. There was Cecil Carrington, whom Mr Bleakley insisted on calling 'Ceecil' to our amusement and his discomfiture. On Saturday I used to see Cecil dressed in a butcher's apron serving in his father's shop. I wonder whether knowing *ei* always came after *c* helped him in later life. There was Kevin Hernan, the son of a local sweet-shop proprietor. We had a strange bond, he being tongue-tied on all the things that mattered to me. He must have remembered something, because many years later when the self-appointed defenders of bourgeois society in Australia were accusing me publicly of giving lectures which were 'soggy with socialist sentiment', Kevin, by then a warder in Pentridge Gaol, sent me a message that he had a comfortable cell for me in Pentridge if I got into serious trouble! Once there were loyalties which transcended differences in ideology, class or interest! There was Bill Hayes, a big, burly boy, with sad eyes. Later he played football for Richmond, and later still he had a stroke. There were others. They all meant much more to me than I seemed to mean to them. That strengthened the lesson first learned at Cowes: do not risk showing your heart to anyone.

One episode in the playground at the Belgrave school (located in Tecoma) lives with me forever. A returned soldier named Weaver climbed through the fence at the far end of the yard and walked towards us. I say walked; really he hobbled, as he was permanently lame. I could not take my eyes off him. He limped towards me, bent me over, and kneed me hard in the bum. It was not the kick which hurt; it was his words. He hissed at me, 'That will teach you not to stare at a lame joker.' He was carrying a horse-whip in his left hand. I remember the moment of terror, of fear, that if I angered him again he might horse-whip me. I remember also no one sympathised with me: there was no one with whom I could share what had happened inside me when Mr Weaver's eyes took control, first of my eyes and then of my whole body. A time would come when fear, anxiety or uncertainty would rob my mind of the power to control my body. But no one foresaw that on the day Mr Weaver kicked me in the arse, and my classmates laughed, as we all do when we discover this time we are not the victim but the observer of cruelty. My father never wanted to hear about such things. His attitude to any illness either of the mind or the body was, 'Rub it off, boy, with a rough towel.' He was not callous or cruel, he just did not want to be bothered. From that time my mother sensed there was something amiss. Once again she said, 'I don't know what we're going to do with you, Mann dear.'

On the Eve

It was not all darkness. There were many discoveries, many experiences which persuaded me later this was a flowering time in my life. On my way back from Lal Philips's barber's shop and billiard saloon I sometimes stopped to talk to Bluey Carter. He used to sit on a stool outside the garage and service station he shared with Dick Geyl. They also ran the United Services service car which carried passengers, mail and parcels between Fern Tree Gully and Upwey, Tecoma, Belgrave, Sassafras and Ferny Creek. Beside Bluey Carter there was always an open kerosene tin full almost to the brim with sump oil. Bluey, as his name suggests, had red hair, his being wiry and unruly. He had heavily lined cheeks, dark lustreless eyes, and never smiled. He wore greasy oil-stained overalls, though he never seemed to do any work in the garage except to pump petrol into the bowser. I liked watching the froth; I was always attracted to anything frothy.

One day Bluey Carter asked me whether I had ever heard of the Russian revolution. I had to say no, I hadn't heard of that. He told me during many talks of how the communist revolution in Russia would spread all over the world, ending the division of the world into the rich and the poor, the oppressors and the oppressed. Then there would be no more revolutions, no more wars, no more people living in poverty. The churches would become museums in which people could see and laugh at the ignorance and superstition of their ancestors. I wanted to ask him whether there would be no more people like Mr Weaver, but that seemed silly and unworthy in the presence of the grandeur and harmony Bluey was foretelling. I wanted to believe it. So far the only hope of which I had heard was that what was painful to me would cease in the life of the world to come – there and then God would wipe away all tears, men and

148

women and children would neither hurt nor destroy. Here was Bluey Carter telling me a day would come in Australia, and indeed on the whole earth, when human beings would no longer hurt or destroy each other. I wanted to believe him: I needed to believe him.

I also wanted to believe what I heard in church: that we would all see each other again, that Christ had overcome 'the sharpness of death' and 'opened the Kingdom of Heaven to all believers' – that Christ would come again to judge both the living and the dead. I spent much of my life wanting to believe in a Heaven on earth and a Heaven in the life of the world to come. I wanted the lot. Maybe I was greedy; maybe I was hungry for life. Who can tell? I could not have the lot. Life in God's world meant my mind was to be stony ground for the seed of the Enlightenment.

In Belgrave in those years there was so much to discover, so much to explore. Once a year, David Unaipon, the Aboriginal preacher, visited us. I do not remember a word of what he said in the pulpit. I remember the talks with him after the bounteous meal Marge cooked for us each Sunday. We stood together near the trees beside the vegetable garden where my father was then preparing to start a new life as a grower of potatoes. In Belgrave there was never much light. There were the open patches in the forest, into which the light streamed, surrounded by the darkness under the trees. I thought of it later as a place where there was very little light for a man to stand up in, a place of drip and gloom. Perhaps that was yet another reason why the hymn 'Abide with Me' meant so much. In Belgrave we were sometimes like pagans singing to the sun: 'Shine through the gloom . . .' So there the two of us, David Unaipon and I, stood in the light. We talked to each other as fellow hunters – I was by then a trapper of rabbits to make pocket money from the sale of the carcass and the skin, and he had been a food gatherer in the years before he became a missionary for Christ to his own people. He told me how the Aborigines robbed eggs from a duck's nest, how they swam underwater until they reached the clump of reeds in which the eggs had been laid. He told me how underwater swimmers grabbed the legs of a duck, wrung its neck, and then brought it on shore to be thrown into the coals for the evening meal. He told me how they stalked the kangaroo.

His eyes glistened as he spoke, and his whole body came alive; he was a different man from the man who before lunch seemed embarrassed and ill at ease when he told the Belgrave congregation what Jesus meant to him. He mesmerised me. While he was enchanting me I became aware of another world different from the world I knew, a world of many wonders, many delights, a world of magic. It was as though the trees were persons, the birds, the possums, the earth and the sky – everything – were all one. I became aware also of what I learned later to call 'otherness'. I had never felt 'otherness' in a church: I had known many other moods: awe, and the canker of doubt, the first intimations of what was to trouble me all my life (Can this be true?). But here, on the edge of the gloomy, ever-dripping gum trees I was carried away into I knew not what. His eyes, and the soft, gentle voice, live with me always. So perhaps it was not surprising that my first published work – in the *Melburnian* at Melbourne Grammar School – was to be about the Aborigines.

I did not risk uncovering in that article what had happened beside the gum trees at Belgrave. By then I had learned it was sometimes wise to hold my tongue in the presence of the philistines of Australia. I can only hope that he was with me when I wrote about the Aborigines and the white man in *A History of Australia*. In volume 6 of that work I made David Unaipon a forerunner of a great awakening in Australia, and included a photograph of him, knowing that could never do justice to the eyes and the body so brim-full of life.

One of my greatest delights was the discovery of the wireless. With luck, or rather with good weather, you could hear the Melbourne radio stations on a crystal set. Bern Brent, the local chemist, taught me how to build a crystal set. That was all I or my parents could afford, money always being much shorter than goodwill in a vicar's house. Bern Brent always had a cigarette hanging down from the corner of his mouth. While talking to me he would pause and roll the cigarette along his lips from one corner of his mouth to the other, but before I could get a word in he would start talking again, as the 'joeys' whistled in his loudspeaker. My mother liked Mrs Brent, because she attended the Ladies' Guild; 'A dear little thing', my mother called her. My mother was not so keen on Bern Brent. He never went to church, but spent his Sundays fiddling with wireless equipment. My mother was not even sure it was wise for men or women or children to listen to the wireless. She always seemed to fear clever people were the enemies of God's world.

With money earned from selling newspapers and lollies at the Saturday night picture show in the Memorial Hall, I bought headphones, the cylinder on which to wind the aerial wire, the insulators, the crystal and the cat's whisker. Bern Brent taught me how to wind the wire on the cardboard cylinder (bakelite being outside my range), how many turns to make to ensure the set would receive the stations both at the bottom and at the top of the dial. I do not remember now the elation on first hearing a human voice or music in the headphones, but I remember my brother's mixture of doubt and fear about his younger brother's powers: 'Manning's sure to make a mess of it – my little nipper [as he sometimes called me when he wanted to remind me of my rung on the family ladder] could never make a wireless.' Yet he was always keen on having a role in every family achievement. 'Good on you, Mann,' he said, 'I always knew you would do it' – and this immediately after expressions of scepticism and lack of faith. I had to get used to living with that, with his strange blend of pessimism and optimism, his never-ending fear about his own ability, and his generosity to all those with gifts different from his own.

There were strange scenes in the bedroom in which the crystal set was kept, the room I shared with my brother. There was a table in between our two beds, and that was the place for the crystal set. There were arguments about the aerial wire. Was it possible to bore a hole for the aerial wire in the sash of the window without breaking the glass? I said it was. My mother said, 'Be careful, Mann dear.' My brother made the menacing remark, 'What do you think you're doing with your mother's good glass?' My father was worried about what the vestry would think if the window were damaged. The hole was bored, and that crisis ended with the usual encomiums from my brother ('Good on you, Mann, I always knew you could do it') and my father ('I always say Manning's the thoughtful customer'). Then there was the nightly crisis of finding the right spot on the crystal set for the cat's whisker. Once a spot was found, and a signal received, there were further questions: Was this the best spot? Might there be a better spot? That always led to a flurry of opinions and fears: 'How do you know you can find the spot again?' 'I tell you it's not as good as last night.' 'I tell you it is.'

There was another problem. Any movement in the room might dislodge the cat's whisker from the long-sought-for spot. Hence the cardinal law of the bedroom was 'Don't move'. But if you did not move you could not find a better spot. What to do? We never found an answer. Listening to a crystal set introduced a new list of sins, and at least one addition to the prohibitions in the Ten Commandments: 'Thou shalt not move'. I remember too that my mother and sister were not allowed in the room during that sacred hour when an announcer was reading the results of the football, or the scores in the cricket. 'God spare my days, woman . . .' my father would say to my mother if she dared to interrupt our male communion. We three males assumed my sister had no rights or interest in the 'man's world'.

For me the wireless had other pleasures. There was the music – especially what was later called 'pop' music. I remember one night in 1926 or 1927 (it being easier to remember the night than the year) when I heard a man sing, 'If you were the only girl in the world and I were the only boy'. I remember thinking then that maybe if that were to happen, then maybe I might be successful. I remember also the chilly moment when the thought crossed my mind that maybe even then the girl would not be impressed. I do not know now what made me take such a black view so early in life about the chances of one human being taking pleasure in the company of another. Looking back now I know the awareness, the attraction, meant much to me. What I feared was that others did not share my hunger. I remember also hearing a tenor sing a song from *The Student Prince*:

> *Overhead the moon is beaming,*
> *White as blossoms on the bough.*
> *Nothing is heard but the song of a bird*
> *Filling all the air with dreaming*

and then he went on to declare his great passion:

> *From your window send me greeting,*
> *Hear my everlasting vow.*

I dreamed of one day making such a vow, of making the confession of a passionate heart. At that time I wanted to make it to my mother. But she always seemed to be far away. About that time she dropped another one of her enigmatic remarks, so terrifying to a boy for whom the world he knew was always threatening to descend from the lofty heights of 'love divine, all loves excelling' to a 'vaudeville of devils'. 'One day,' she said, and she would go on saying it until she 'walked into the night' in 1941, two years before she died, 'one day I'm going to go right away.' My father looked frightened, my brother, who could not face the bleak world, and clung desperately to anything which pasted over the cracks revealing the darkness underneath, said 'Don't talk like that, Mum, don't talk like that.' And I stood there, puzzled, frightened, and stripped, robbed of what I wanted most. How could I ever speak to her about what was going on in my mind? How could I answer her remark, 'I don't know what's going to happen to you, Mann dear'? I didn't know either!

So there we were, so close, needing each other, both having a capacity to understand each other, but not able to speak about what mattered most to both of us. At that time I did not even chew over or brood over why we did not speak about such things, or about what kept us apart, or why we could not comfort each other. I knew she cared. What bothered me then, and overwhelms me now with regret, is that I do not know whether she even guessed at the depth of my grief. Now I have to feed on the hope she knew there was someone who understood, someone who never forgot. It was possibly my first lesson in my own inadequacy, perhaps also my first lesson in how pitifully equipped we all are to respond to the needs of another person. A hand reaches out – we either cannot or dare not grasp it. The laws of God, the laws of men, the lore and conventions of our own tribe, the ghosts from the past check us whenever anyone comes near. Life is a pilgrimage to find how a man or a woman can know both liberty and grace. The 'whole bloody trouble', as Henry Lawson once put it, is that we find out too late: we find out when our own powers to do anything about it are waning fast.

My mind then was not always searching frantically for answers to the unanswerable questions, nor was I always scanning anxiously the faces of other people for signs that maybe they knew them. I still believed there were answers. I certainly told myself there must be answers – chaos and meaninglessness were not for me – without answers it would be too unfair, quite unbearable.

There was always so much going on. Bern Brent told me the wireless reception was more reliable with a valve and battery set than with a crystal set, and now I had to learn how to construct such a set. Money had to be found for A and B batteries, a valve, a condenser, a bakelite cylinder for the aerial coil. I needed a soldering iron, solder, a copper pipe and copper wire to fasten to the earth pipe, and the materials with which to build a loudspeaker. First I built a one-valve set, then, reaching as ever beyond the capacity of my pocket, I built a two-valve set. That required another piece of equipment, namely a condenser. I added to my very limited wireless vocabulary when I learned there was a detector valve and an amplifying valve. I also learned to work with aluminium – to cut a neat rectangle, to trace the holes for the valve sockets, and then to fit them precisely. Once again I needed money. Once again, I behaved shamefully when my father pleaded poverty, calling him 'Tightness', and hoping fondly that my character sketch would not trigger off a rage.

I saw myself then as a labourer worthy of his hire, or a grant – a worthy experimenter – not knowing how limited was my father's wealth. One of the many troubles with genteel poverty is that it creates in the eyes of dependants a delusion there must be wealth somewhere. I believed then it was in that wallet of my father's which he was cunning enough never to let us have a peep into. At the time I harboured a grudge – one valve only cost the same as five packets of cigarettes. It all seemed unfair then. The judgements of young boys on their fathers are not only impulsive, they are harsh. They live on in my mind as part of the huge burden of remorse which torments me now that it is not possible even to say sorry, let alone to be forgiven. The only remedy for the guilt about the past is to cry out when alone, but that is only a temporary relief. It is like alcohol: it is a temporary pain-deadener, which, after the satisfaction evaporates, is followed by the old pain, plus a new pain, the knowledge, nay the certainty, that there is no escape, that no matter how fast I run guilt will always keep up with me.

In boyhood there are other anodynes – or so I found. There was the weekly reading of the *Triumph* and the *Champion* – both arriving from England once a week on the mail boat, and finding their way to Harry Luscombe's newsagency where I bought them for threepence each. I had to sell a dozen copies of the *Herald* or the *Sporting Globe* to earn the money for the *Triumph*, and another dozen for the *Champion*. My drug at the time was the stories about soccer. I remember even now the agonies I endured puzzling over the solution to the problem of how the hero, the champion goal-kicker, could possibly get to the ground in time for the kick-off for the final match of the season, he having been bound, gagged and knocked unconscious by the 'baddies' in the preceding week's instalment. That was the end of my addiction, for the next week's number began: 'When [my hero] arrived at the ground his team was already on the soccer pitch.' That cured me. Would that all my addictions had been so easy to cure!

There were also the sporting pages in the newspapers – read free of charge by courtesy of Harry Luscombe. In their very simplicity the words had overtones of tragedy and disaster. They were my substitute theatre. I remember the headlines in one Saturday edition of the *Sporting Globe* or the *Herald*: 'South [i.e. South Melbourne] by good kicking defeated the Dons [Essendon]'. In Melbourne morality pervaded even the popular literature on sport. Doing the right thing, having the right thoughts, won approval. I remember those who did the wrong thing on the sporting field were dismissed as 'animals': 'He's a real animal.' The articles in the sporting pages of the *Argus*, the *Herald* and the *Sporting Globe* discussed the fitness of a player. There were two questions: Was he physically fit? Was he morally fit? Did he have 'guts', pluck, courage, or would he 'crack' under strain? They were my kindergarten in writings about character and behaviour. They were my first experience of an ever-recurring theme in my life. My enthusiasms were always for the players with great gifts and great weaknesses.

My first enthusiasm was for 'Cargie' Greeves, the winner of the first Brownlow Medal, the Geelong centreman, a player who moved on the field with grace, beauty and, so it seemed to me, an inner confidence and serenity. He also had the cheekiness of the talented footballer. He was not a taunter, a jeerer, or a sneerer. He rested the ball in the palm of his right hand, held it out to an opponent, as though he were inviting him to grab it if he could, and then, when the opponent made his dive, he withdrew hand and ball, and rushed past his opponent as the latter stumbled towards the ground. Cargie Greeves was a magician, Cargie ministered to my secret delights. But Cargie had a weakness: his knee had been twisted in one of those turns he so loved to make to evade an opponent. The *Argus*, the *Herald* and the *Sporting Globe* wrote my first serial: the story of Cargie and his knee. Can Cargie, the wizard of the football field, overcome nature? I believed he could – heroes can overcome anything – just as Christ overcame death. But not my Cargie. One winter's day at Corio Bay Oval in 1926 or 1927 (I forget which) Cargie Greeves fell. No trainer, no doctor, no masseur, could ever put Cargie's knee together again.

In time I would put away these childish things, and graduate from footballers to the great tragic characters of literature and of our time.

I would see Bob Menzies fall; I would weep over Henchard in Thomas Hardy's *The Mayor of Casterbridge*, and mourn with Hester Prynne. But footballers as tragic heroes will never leave me – nor will I ever shed the fate of conceiving a wild enthusiasm for the player, the politician, the writer, or the man or woman doomed to have a great fall.

My other source of inspiration in boyhood was the motion picture, and advertisements in the *Herald* about silent films. It was the great era of the silent film. I remember my mother took us to see *The Ten Commandments* at the Capitol Theatre in Melbourne. I do not remember how we got there, but I remember the many splendours inside the theatre, the ever-changing lights in the ceiling, the performance on the Wurlitzer organ, the orchestra, conducted (if I remember correctly) by Tarczinski, who interested me because of the extravagant gestures with his baton (I always loved over-treatment, provided it did not go too far) and the expression of wild ecstasy on his face during the coda of the piece they played. Like all performers he played in part for the applause: he got his claps that matinée. The film did not touch me at all. I could not understand why there should be such a fuss when a man with an off-putting face, no lover he, read out ten things we were all to do or not to do. That told me nothing about life – Jehovah never 'turned me on' (to use the popular language of today).

It was different with the advertisements for films. The Friday-night *Herald* was my land of dreams and enchantment. I remember once reading a snatch of dialogue from a film then showing in Melbourne – a film I would never see because the theatre was too far away, and 'Mann dear,' as my mother said, 'it's not really suitable for young boys.' 'Morally,' my mother was to say often to me later, 'we are all hoping everything is all right, Mann dear.' This was to come when my morals were by no criterion 'all right'. My mother always knew. Perhaps she even knew why her second son pored over the advertisements for the pictures in the *Herald*. Who can tell? I remember even now that advertisement, quoting a remark by a man to a woman: 'It's Fanny Braund. It's five years since you broke your appointment with me in Eden Park. And ever since then . . .' Well, maybe we have premonitions even in boyhood of what is to come later in life, for those words lingered on. Years later, when I too knew that most painful of all wounds, the wound of a broken appointment, the wound of rejection, of showing what was going on in my heart to other people and their not responding to what mattered so much to me, I discovered Thomas Hardy's poem, 'A Broken Appointment'. Historians are parasites: they feed on the words of the creative. When I first read the Hardy poem I knew he knew the pain; I could only say to myself, '. . . and that's true too':

> You did not come,
> And marching Time drew on, and wore me numb –
> Yet less for loss of your dear presence there
> Than that I thus found lacking in your make
> That high compassion which can overbear
> Reluctance for pure loving kindness' sake.
> Grieved I, when, as the hope-hour stroked its sum,
> You did not come.

In my life many a 'hope-hour stroked its sum'. For me the words 'You did not come' conjured up those ghosts from the past, that terror in childhood of 'doom' – or what I later labelled damnation, or loss.

There was other food for my heart to feed on. My father had been a gaol chaplain at Long Bay and Darlinghurst, and he often spoke of the mind of hardened criminals. He was fascinated by what fascinated me later, that a man or a woman guilty of the most abominable crimes, of, say, murder with mutilation, or deliberately impregnating a woman and then tormenting her about her future ostracism from the society of the cosy and the respectable, can also be loving and tender, can have lofty and noble thoughts about life. A man or a woman can weep when they hear a song or a poem about the day when all men will be brothers, and then rush out and commit some horrible deed, such as thrashing a child, or punching a woman, or pimping to the police about his mates in the underworld.

'There is a lot of good, boy,' he often said to me at that time, 'in all of us – even the most hardened criminals. I have known them to weep, boy, when they spoke about their mothers – but not about their wives, boy (you'll understand that later on, you mark my words). They're often very kind to children. When I was a chaplain at Long Bay, a man named Butler advertised in the papers for a companion to go prospecting for gold. At that time of the day when the man's shadow was as long as his height Butler took a measurement, dug a grave, shot his companion, and buried him. He despatched three, boy, before the police nabbed him. I tell you, boy, I have never met a gentler person than Butler in my life. He had a lovely smile.'

My mother was always ill at ease when my father spoke in a kind way about men or women who could not stop. She was not fascinated by the psychology of murderers, brutes, sodomites, or any of the great sinners. She thought they were all 'peculiar'. If I ever asked her why there were such people in God's world she would say, 'I wish you wouldn't ask such questions, Mann dear, you make me feel giddy.' My father was drawn to the dark side of the human heart like a moth to a light – that is, he not only lacked the power to resist the temptation, he never saw it as a temptation, even though he knew this taste of his would expose him to condemnation by the people whose goodwill he so desperately sought after from the time he became a chorister at St Andrew's Cathedral. He believed in human goodness. 'There is a great deal of goodness in all of us', he was fond of saying, but he was fascinated by evil. 'The heart', he was fond of quoting, 'is deceitful above all things and very wicked. Who can know it?'

My mother not only would not, but could not, quote such words. For her, the men and women attracted to such behaviour were unsavoury. For her, much of human life was what she called a 'right down cruel shame'. She never believed depravity was part of God's creation, and probably never asked herself why some men and women were fascinated by depravity. My mother could never have dreamed of being one of those souls in Byron's 'Cain' who 'dare look the omnipotent tyrant in His everlasting face,/and tell him that His evil is not good.' The thought probably often occurred to my father but he, I believe, would have dismissed it quick smart with his 'at least we can all have a good laugh' response to everything that pained him, everything that came between him and his belief that we should all be kind to each other.

My father once knew 'Squizzy' Taylor, a member of the underworld, through his chaplaincy work with criminals. My father never forgot one thing about him. 'Boy,' he said, 'Squizzy Taylor called me Mr Clark.' Squizzy Taylor was polite: Squizzy Taylor was not like the patricians of Sydney, or the members of Yarraside in Melbourne. And later when a man named Murray was hanged at Pentridge Gaol for murder, my father added Murray's last words to his long list of memorable remarks: 'I've been a bad man,' Murray said to the hangman and the chaplain, 'but I've never used firearms.' My father had an innate sympathy, a powerful attraction towards those who knew they were bad, those prepared to confess their faults and ask for forgiveness. My mother had sympathy with all those who suffered, but she did not feel the need to confess or beg for forgiveness: being no sinner herself, she was a stranger to my father's world.

For a boy it was all very puzzling. My father was a universal-embrace man, a man who loved Christ's words to the erring woman, 'I forgive you because you have loved much.' Yet my father was censorious of others, a judge who condemned. He never forgave those who hurt him. By contrast, my mother seemed the slave of her own moral code. Morality seemed to be the guiding star of her life. She was always talking about it. She was full of instructions on how to behave. One time she said, 'Envy, Mann dear, is a terrible thing.' If any of us transgressed against her moral code and said we were sorry, she would say with a warmth of love and understanding, 'Of course, I forgive you, Mann dear. You didn't know what you were doing.' She harboured no long-term grudges: she never ever mentioned revenge, nor did she ever betray pleasure when she heard that those who had done things which were not pleasing to her had suffered some misfortune. It was contrary to her generosity of heart to say, 'Serves them right.' She did not pass judgement. That belonged to God. Christ had commanded, 'Judge not', and she had no difficulty in heeding the divine command. My father and mother both lived on in me: I had inherited much of my father's temperament, but I was attracted to my mother's inner serenity. My father was rarely in a state of grace; my mother was always in a state of grace. The question was: Could anyone with my father's temperament ever find grace? How could any pilgrim for the means of grace shed the temperament which choked off such yearnings? Who could work that great marvel? That would be the quest of a lifetime.

At Belgrave, as at Cowes, I spent some of my time watching and puzzling over these two 'mighty opposites'. My father loved games. On those nights in the vicarage when there was no choir practice, no vestry meeting, no committee of the ladies' guild, there were family games. My mother rarely, if ever, played. 'Come on, Mum, we want you to play.' But my mother would generally ask to be excused because she was bottling some more jam for 'little Mrs Bleakley' and 'little Mrs Robins', as it seemed to mean so much to them. So my father, my brother, my sister, some visitors and I would sit down to a game of 'Up Jenkins' – that is, after those preliminary skirmishes which always preceded any move in our family, with my brother threatening not to play unless my father promised faithfully not to 'act the goat', my sister promised to concentrate on the game, and I did not try to be too clever for my boots. There would be crises. My father would play the role of difficult to get ('Well, if you'd prefer me not to play?') to which my brother would reply, exchanging one extravagance for another, 'Of course we want you to play, it wouldn't be a game without you.' My father would smile and say, 'There's one good thing about Russ, he always means what he says.' And all would be well – that is, until the game started. In 'Up Jenkins' the side which had the penny tried to prevent the opposition from guessing who was holding the penny. The opposition then would ask them to do one of many things – 'creepy crawlies', 'dancing elephants', 'slam', etc., hoping the holder of the penny would be so clumsy that the guessing would be a pushover. My father excelled at 'dancing elephants': he stole the show. Even my mother enjoyed his mixture of skill and clowning.

It was the same at cards. 'Five Hundred' was the family game. Later there would be 'Bridge'. But in those middle and late 1920s 'Five Hundred' and 'Euchre' were the *petit-bourgeois* games, and 'Bridge' the game for the members of Yarraside and postulants for a climb up the social ladder. A game of 'Five Hundred' provided my father with many openings to display his skill at ridicule: 'The little varmint', as he sometimes called my sister, 'doesn't know the difference between a left and a right bower.' A game also gave him a chance to make some observation about life, some wisdom or knowledge he had picked up during his years in the ministry: 'And I will tell you another thing, boy, I have learned. Beware of any woman who volunteers to help with the Girl Guides or Brownies.' I had no idea of what he was talking about at the time. But my mother knew; 'I wish you wouldn't speak like that, Charlie, in front of Manning. He's already far too interested in the dark side of things.'

My father also excelled at billiards. 'The wife's parents', he used to say to those unwise enough to accept his invitation to a game, 'gave me this three-quarter-size billiard table and a set of ivory balls as part of their wedding present.' My father loved the exotics of billiards, the 'kiss' canons, the shots where the player holds the cue behind his back and 'in-offs' the red or the white ball, and where the cue ball must only shave one side of the other ball if it is to lodge in one of the pockets. My father loved the challenge of the seemingly hopeless, the shot which could either end in disaster or be the beginning of a break of fifty or more.

That daring, teetering as it so often did between foolhardiness and the success which brought the applause and the fulsome compliments of the ladies, lived in me. When I was twelve, while the other boys were making serviceable bows and arrows I was always experimenting with a bow and an arrow which would do the equivalent of breaking the sound barrier by defying or overcoming the laws of nature. More often than not my monster bows and my monster arrows, both of which required patience in the making, ended either with the bow-wood cracking, or the arrow lodging in some inaccessible branch of a tree. I was either absurdly stubborn and vain about my powers, or driven never to accept defeat. No failure ever stopped me making an even bigger bow, or a more eccentric arrow.

I also began to make a boat. The vicarage in Belgrave was built on the edge of a steep hill, so there was plenty of space under one end of the house for a bench for carpentry and other hobbies. With my father's saws, hammer, brace and bit, chisels, screwdrivers and gimlets I started. First I had to earn the money to buy the rust-proof screws and the wood from O'Donohoe's timber yard. That name itself was anathema to my mother, though she always expressed her opposition obliquely. 'What do you want to build a boat for, Mann dear?' she asked; I said, ''Cos I do.' And that was that. I wonder now why we never really spoke except in the sentences which left out so much of what we wanted to say. I wonder now why our minds were so manacled, why we were so enslaved to the lore of our tribe.

One of the O'Donohoe boys taught me how to bend the slats for the frame of the boat: to put them in water, then use the uprights under the house as a frame for the curve between the bow and the stern. That all took time. So did the shaping of the keel, the bow and the stern – a year in all. No sooner had I put the canvas around the frame and had the boat ready for the trial on the placid waters of the front beach at Cowes that I had been dreaming of for the whole year, than my mother gave the boat to Les Robins, a local builder. I was there when Les Robins and his brother Alf carried it away. I was beyond speech, beyond tears. Why had she done this? It could not be to hurt or punish me because she was never either a hurter or a punisher. 'Mann dear,' she said, 'you know you have trouble in the water. I couldn't bear it, Mann dear, if anything happened

161

to you.' My mother had prescience – though I did not realise it at the time. All I knew was loss, inexplicable loss, the feeling that something had happened which was unfair – something not explicable in terms of that order in the universe to which my mother so often referred. I guessed then, I know now, deep down that my father feared there was no moral order in the universe – that no man or God had ever imposed an order on the chaos. To add to my wound, Les Robins later complimented me on the boat!

The boat saga occurred at a time when the frontiers of our world were expanding. The vestry in Belgrave decided to give my father money to buy and run a car. His first choice was a bull-nose Morris Cowley, a single-seater, with a dicky seat behind the cabin for those prepared to brave the open air. Those were the heroic years for owners of small cars. There were many challenges to drivers and passengers. There was the crank start, and all its menace to body and mind; the cranker must not grip with his thumb in case the engine backfired. Our family was one of those families which never blamed the car if it failed to start – we blamed each other: 'I told you not to flood the carburettor', 'Of course we all know Manning knows best', 'Don't laugh, boy, or I'll knock your block off.' But when, after sundry splutters, choking sounds and silences, the engine not only started but kept going there were handshakes and words of praise, 'Good on you, Mann, I knew you'd do it. I've got great faith in you.' We always lived close to breaking point.

The car meant we could travel each January to Phillip Island without all those train and boat changes. Reggy Justice had begun to run a punt for cars from San Remo to New Haven. My mother and sister travelled by train and steamer (the *Alvina* had replaced the *Genista*); my brother, Marge, my father and I crammed into the Morris Cowley. My brother had a strong arm for cranking the car, and I was handy at unscrewing the fuel pipe into the carburettor and sucking out the petrol so that the dross no longer blocked the entrance to the 'carbie'. 'Good on you, Mann, I always knew you could do it', my brother would say as I tried to clean my mouth, and dreamed of the huge waves rolling in from the south when we finally made it to the Pyramid.

The Island was still my Swanee River, the place where my heart was turning ever. The magic never faded; familiarity never staled its charms. There were reunions with my old school friends. There was a Plugger Bennell hand-shake, a Plugger Bennell smile, a Plugger

Bennell dancing eye when I looked him up in his father's butcher's shop. There was the shy hope – a hope I did not risk putting to the test – that Jean Davie, one of W. Dawson Davie's daughters, would remember the boy who had looked at her with such longing earlier in the playgound of the Cowes school. There was Mrs Archie Finlay, with her heaving bosom and her voice like the screech of a cockatoo, but, underneath, such oceans of goodwill. There was the sight of Bing Edgar standing at the entrance to the bar of the Phillip Island hotel, polishing a beer glass with the reverence and love of a priest cleaning the communion cup at the end of the service. There was May Sambell ('She's still not well, Mann dear') silhouetted against the sky, her face still peering out west, as she stood there, rod in hand, 'charmed to be' – but doomed. There was the rattle of the small rocks at the Pyramid and the Nobbies when the waters of a wave rushed desperately back to join again that ever-restless, ever-complaining sea. There was the roar and the boom, the one big smash and boom, when the sea raced into the blow-hole at the Nobbies.

There were those moments like an epiphany when my father told one of his stories after lunch, as we sat around the fire planted in the rocks at one of the bays on the east side of the Pyramid, and Marge laughed in a way I had never seen a woman laugh before, and my father looked so very happy and turned around to face us all again and said, 'Did I ever tell you about the time . . .', and Marge looked very wise and very knowing and we all laughed: no Greek chorus were we to my father's yarns, no soothsayers or doom-sayers. For brief moments we were acting out the words of the Prayer Book. We were all in love and fellowship with each other – though not necessarily committed to leading a new life. We had a bond, the bond of those who have been refreshed by that very vast sea. Sometimes my father would look sad and quote those words from Shakespeare – that not even these multitudinous seas could wash a man clean. A shadow would fall across his face; the crinkles of laughter flattened out, and the light in his eyes faded.

During our stay on the Island in the New Year of 1927 my brother (then thirteen) began to take an interest in the girls who sunbathed on the white stretch of sand in front of the Clergy Rest House. At that time if my father and my brother had been asked the question Rogozhin put to Prince Myshkin in Dostoevsky's work, *The Idiot* – 'And women, prince, are you very keen on them?' – my father would either have given a tortuous answer, the answer of a man flayed on

163

one of his raw spots, or he would have turned the question against the questioner – 'You like women yourself, do you?' My brother's 'Yes, I do' would have been as unqualified as Molly Bloom's 'Yes, I will'. But at that time I would have said 'No', and meant it. Women, for me, were often moral police persons, people standing between me and what I wanted to do, or they were the ones who said the wounding words, the ones who wanted to bring out into the open what I was trying to conceal, probers of the things of which I was ashamed, and not offering anything in exchange for probing into my secret world. Later, I would give a very different answer. But not then, then women turned nasty if I came near. So I stayed more than 'a pace or two apart'.

I felt the same about the members of my mother's family on the few times I met them during visits to Sydney. My father saw himself as Tom Jones: he was a man of 'heroic ingredients'. He was always setting himself tasks he could not possibly achieve. Perhaps he was still hoping for my mother's approval, perhaps he was hoping to think well of himself, or perhaps he was just showing off, looking for things to say about himself. He was like a high jumper: he no sooner leaped one height than he asked for the bar to be raised. So, for the Sydney trip he announced, 'The car will rev. at 9 p.m. on Sunday, after evensong. We'll all have a cup of tea first. I'm a beggar for time you know. I'll drive all night and all the next day [Monday] and arrive in Sydney in time for dinner.' My father, mother and sister sat in the front, my brother and I sat in the dicky seat, fighting as usual, squabbling over the rug, the cushions, the 'extras', even before the engine began to 'rev', well after the appointed time, and my mother had appealed to us with one of her disturbing remarks, 'I don't know what I'm going to do with you boys. Sometimes I think I'll have to go right away.' My brother became very contrite and loving to my mother, and begged her, 'Don't talk like that, Mum. I can't stand it.' My mother said, 'No living person would stand it.' My father exploded, 'God spare my days, woman, what do you think you're saying?'

The engine at last 'revved', the head-lights came on, and the car, with suitcases roped onto the running boards and to the rear of the dicky-seat, climbed slowly up the vicarage drive, and turned towards Melbourne and the road to Sydney. At that time the bitumen ended at Seymour. There my father needed a spell. He left the car, saying he would not be long, and walked towards a two-storey building where there was one light only, and that in a room behind the front wall on which the word 'Bar' was printed. My mother urged us to be nice to our father, as he was tired after taking three services; he would not be long. When he returned we set off along the dirt road for Euroa, the car going bumpty-bumpty-bump over the corrugations. Ten miles out of Seymour we stopped again at Tubb's Hill, my mother assuring us that Miss Tubb's mother would be sure to give us a nice hot cup of tea before we fell asleep. So she did.

I remember my father said to us in the dark, 'The engine will rev. at crack of dawn. You know I'm a beggar for time.' The journey seemed to go on forever, with stops outside the buildings where we were told 'Reschs Refreshes', my mother's pleas to call on some member of the country gentry who belonged to the cousinhood of the Marsdens, the Hassalls and the Hopes, and my father's grudging acknowledgement of how much he owed to 'your mother's family'. There was much talk from my father about what the corrugations in the road were doing to his tyres, and how one day we would all learn he was not a millionaire. How talkative my father always was after a 'mood improver' or two at his favourite stopping places! Then there was the descent into what was then the forlorn town of Tarcutta, and the exhilaration on first seeing those noble hills and those deep cuttings on either side of the road between Tarcutta and Gundagai.

We were in the country of the 'vision spendid', but that did not touch either my father or my mother. They were, in their different ways, both 'spiritual exiles', Australian versions of 'Englishmanism'. My father never commented on the fragile beauty of the ancient continent, and it was to take me time to notice such things, before I accepted the 'haggard continent', and stopped yearning for another country 'far, far away'. From Tarcutta on, my mother concentrated on calling on Miriam and Ernie, her sister and brother-in-law, at Goulburn. We were given to understand that she and Miriam had once been close. That reminded me that my mother's one love in life was for the members of her own family. She was on the way back to her father. Her other father, her Father in Heaven, in His infinite goodness and grace had once again poured down His blessings on her. She was returning to where she belonged, to the life-style she could never shed.

I, too, was attracted to that life-style. My grandfather was an imposing figure at the breakfast table, with the *Sydney Morning Herald* in front of him on a silver stand, and a bowl of porridge, which he sprinkled with salt. He took a spoonful, and dipped it in a basin of milk before swallowing. 'That's how the Scots ate their porridge', he said. My mother, I noticed, laughed much more than at home. My father was not there: he was staying with his father and mother at Florence Street, St Peters. My mother loved talking to her two unmarried sisters, Gladys and Edith – they were unmarried not because of the errors or jests of nature, but because 'Father', as they reverently called him, had dismissed all suitors as being unworthy of them and their position in society. So instead of going to bed with a lover they studied the birth and death notices in the daily papers for news of their contemporaries, and took up hobbies such as needlework, dressmaking, reading, playing golf and playing the card games which were *comme il faut* in the drawing rooms of the gentry.

It was all so different from our life in the vicarage. My grandfather was an agnostic: he did not scoff at religious belief, but never betrayed any thirst to believe, or any discomfort at the thought of annihilation. Their house was a model of 'conspicuous waste'. For coffee there were delicate tiny china cups, and a maid asked whether you would take cream. The silver sugar bowl was filled with brown crystals I had never seen before. Even the white sugar sparkled. The drawing room was cluttered with so many *objets d'art* that I was afraid to move lest I knock over some precious vase or disturb some occasional table on which a bowl of multi-coloured flowers was standing. My grandmother loved playing 'huff patience' with me. Between her favourite exclamations of 'Goodness!' and many wheezes (maybe because her maid had tied her corsets too tightly – bearing children had played havoc with her figure, and certainly something made breathing difficult for her), she always paid me extravagant compliments, such as 'Manning is the brains of the family', to which my grandfather would reply through his tobacco-and tea-stained moustache, 'Don't flatter the boy, my dear, he's conceited enough as it is.' My grandfather was the lord of the household. Even the cup from which he drank his tea was double the size of the cups served to us by a maid in uniform. 'Father' was the one they all delighted to honour.

Perhaps that was why I sometimes took the risk of being cheeky and irreverent to him – to my mother's alarm and consternation. I could never abide grovellers or the object of their servility. The former must be punished, the latter mocked and ridiculed. With my grandfather I knew I had to be discreet and careful: there had been that episode in childhood when, enraged by my lapses from the ranks of the worshippers, he had threatened to give me a good thrashing. But I could never resist the temptation to be 'clever' at someone else's expense. I thought they would enjoy my wit as much as I did, never thinking that such wit might pain another person. So as I caddied for my grandfather when he played against Colonel Arnott (of Arnott's Biscuits) on the Croydon golf links, I could not resist the temptation to have a go at those two lords of creation in their plus-fours, their golf-hose, their Niblick shoes, their hand-knitted Scottish cardigans, and their cloth caps which sat on their heads with the air of distinction which separated them from the caddies and the green-keepers. So I said, 'You're not playing very well today, grandpa. Your putting is like you say, "Never up, never in".' There was silence on the green. I was never asked to carry his clubs again. My brother Russell was the one who always said the right thing. My Aunt Gladys never forgot my remark. She was still taking about it when she was close to eighty. Perhaps that was what she had wanted to say for years, but had never dared to. Who can tell? All I know is that she was as warm to me as she believed the lore of her tribe would permit.

After a week or so of life with the patricians my father took me to stay with his sister Alice and her family in Porter Street, Marrickville. My Aunt Alice had a slight stutter, her eyes flickered nervously, and she was always fidgeting with a cloth with which she rubbed the dust off a table-top, or the arm of a chair. But she was warm. My grandmother Hope and my mother's sisters gave me a peck on the cheek with their dry lips; Aunt Alice kissed me on the mouth and gave me a bear hug, and told me there would always be a warm welcome for me at Porter Street. There were other pleasing surprises. My father did not wear his clerical collar. He was adored by his mother, his three sisters, and his nieces, Millie, Ruby, Gwen and Gloria. In the glow of such adoration my father probably again knew heart's ease. He told the stories which were frowned on by the Moore College miserables and the desiccated country gentry, who now survived in the suburbs.

'Charlie,' he said to Aunt Alice's eldest son, who was then twenty, 'when I was your age you only needed a bob to take a girl out for the night: threepence each to get into the music hall, threepence for peanuts and lollies – you needed the peanuts, boy [turning to me] to throw at the performers if they gave you a belly-ache – and threepence for a bucket of prawns if you did not do any good for yourself at the end of the evening.' We all laughed. I thought at the time Aunt Alice wore an anxious look on her face when my father loosened up. Perhaps she knew why things had not gone well for him in the church, why his vast talents as preacher, pastor and musician had been ignored, and he had seen his contemporaries at Moore College nominated for all the fat livings by His Grace the lord Archbishop of Sydney.

Aunt Alice had married a German, Herman Heesch. She had celebrated her twenty-first birthday in the labour ward of the Petersham Hospital giving birth to her third child; 'Your Aunt Alice, Mann dear,' my mother often said, 'has had a hard life.' But my mother never drew close to her. Uncle Herman was the problem. Uncle Herman expected a wife to be a packhorse by day, and a partner in his lust late at night; women were not just different from men, they were inferior in body, mind and soul. Uncle Herman also used coarse language in front of ladies. When he needed to go to the lavatory he asked in a loud voice, 'Where's the place in this house where you splash your boots?' No gentleman would speak like that to a lady. I was always afraid of Uncle Herman because of the stories 'Joe' (Albert) Heesch told me, when we were in bed at night, about the hidings his father administered to him with the razor strap for any 'lip', or lapse from the draconian code of laws he had drafted for his children. 'Mind you, Mannin, he never lays a hand on my sisters but he'll belt me till I'm black and blue.' So when Uncle Herman uttered the command, 'Joe, quick smart off to the shops', Joe shot off like a hare frightened in its lair.

I liked all my father's nephews and nieces, even though at first they eyed me with suspicion as someone in their family who had gone over to the other side and now fraternised with the class enemy. The blazer my mother made me wear was, I learned later, a badge of division. My expectations were different from theirs. My mother always assumed her second son would enter one of the professions – law, medicine, the church or teaching. My girl cousins all expected to be married young and spend their lives at the kitchen sink, the wash-tub, the clothes-line, the mangle, the ironing board and the sewing machine. The boys expected to become apprentices to some trade. They belonged to the skilled working class, the respectable working class, members of which attended Sunday school and church each Sunday and sat down to a baked dinner after church, even on one of those stifling, steamy summer days in Sydney. My grandmother Clark spoke very little, though I remember once she told me I was like my mother to look at but had a lot of my father's temperament, a mixture, she added, which would not be easy to carry through the world.

My grandfather Clark was also tongue-tied when I was around, though I remember at a family picnic at Newport Beach he puzzled me by saying, out of the blue, that I belonged to my mother's class. He could tell, he said: he always knew. Well, I was tempted by what I saw in Sydney, just as I had been tempted on Phillip Island when I saw Guy Boughton and his friends wearing their Geelong Grammar School blazers. My mother's class had luxury; they had elegance; they behaved as though they were not only different but also superior to all other people. I remember during one visit to Sydney hearing a Sydney patrician say to my grandfather, 'The mistake we made was giving the workers the vote.' My grandfather nodded and smiled, and wore on his face an expression I had never seen before. Now I would identify it as the delight of a man who believed he was entitled always to be on the winning side.

Class, like nature, was very strong. My mother's brother Syd had also married out of his class. I felt a bond with his three sons, Bryan (known as Bill), Robert Marsden (later a judge of the Supreme Court of New South Wales) and Jeffrey Denbigh (later a dentist) – they having the cheek, the bounce, and the warmth of my father's nieces and nephews, without the impudent deference, and the remarks about how class kept us apart. The youngest, Jeffrey, was already a superb mimic and mocker of those who put on airs. Later my cousins were to be the source of information on the wayward members of my mother's family.

I was also told later by the members of Syd Hope's family that my mother was always fearful of what I would say to powerful, pretentious people, people to whom, later, I always wanted to say, 'What knowest thou which is not in us?' There had been an episode at the home of W. M. Hughes, the war-time Prime Minister, when I had made a joke about the latter's poor style as a batsman. Mr Hughes had not been amused. I do not remember that episode; all I remember now is my mother's frequent whispers to my father, 'Do you think it would be safe to take Manning?', and her anxious look as she said to me after yet another unfortunate incident, 'You spoil yourself, Mann dear.'

There was an incident at the house of my Aunt Bobbie (Roberta) in David Street, Croydon, New South Wales. She was one of my mother's younger sisters and had married Norman Howe, a director of the Colonial Sugar Refining Company. They had four children – Rhona, Patricia, Donald and Malcolm. All was not well with Norman Howe. By the time we arrived in Sydney he had been in bed in his home for some months. We were never told how many. I knew there was something terribly wrong with him. There was a smell of bodily decay in his room, a smell which no deodorants ever hid. His cheeks which had once worn the bloom of a lawn-tennis player and a surfer were deathly pale, and the bones of his fore-arms were almost visible beneath the dry scaly skin, which looked as though something inside him was shrivelling it. No one would tell me what was wrong with Uncle Norman, why his flesh was wasting away so rapidly that even his lips no longer covered his teeth. My father was not there (he always kept out of the way of Aunt Bobbie). My grandfather had dropped a cryptic remark ('Your Uncle Norman is far from well'), but then put on one of his looks which told a young boy there were to be no further questions. I had overheard my mother whisper to her sister Gladys, 'Bobbie's being very brave' and then look startled when she feared I had heard and might clamour to know what was wrong with Uncle Norman, and implore her, 'Please, Mum, tell me what's going on.' But that, I realise now, would have meant mentioning the unmentionable – DEATH. There were two unmentionables in my childhood and boyhood: one was sex, and the other was death.

The tyranny of silence was too much for me. Again, there was an incident, this time so shameful, so painful, that I quickly wiped the details off the screen of my memory. There are many picture shows from the past for which there can never be a repeat performance in the mind. All I remember now are the chilling words of rebuke by my Aunt Bobbie: that I was 'low and common', and that my behaviour had not surprised her, because, after all, that was to be expected seeing where I came from and almost certainly belonged. I remember, too, my mother's loving concern for what might happen in the future if I did not mend my ways. 'Don't spoil yourself, Mann dear,' she implored me, 'you're really a very special person.' I remember my grandmother Hope wheezing over me, and, after much use of her signature word on such occasions, her 'Goodness', which seemed to come up from somewhere deep inside her, she assured me that they all really loved me, but I was a very peculiar little boy, and perhaps not everyone would always understand me, and I would be much better after a long sleep.

I lay awake for hours, feverishly sampling words which would enable me to get my own back on Aunt Bobbie, and shaping questions which my mother must answer, questions she could not evade. But the following morning over breakfast with my grandfather dipping spoonfuls of porridge into his own special bowl of milk, and adjusting his copy of the *Sydney Morning Herald* on his reading stand, and my mother offering to say grace (her father not being a man for that sort of thing at the dining-table), those words I had carefully composed the previous night were blown out of my mind like a sea-mist in the morning when the wind gets up. I had added to my reputation of being 'difficult' and 'unmanageable'. There was a warning from my mother not to spoil myself, because she knew I was a very special person, and understood much for my years. So I never risked putting the question: Why don't we speak about what is happening to Uncle Norman?

By then there was another cause of friction between me and my grandfather. That year, 1926, I had started to go to Mont Albert Central School. For some reason I do not understand I tried to convince him it was as good a school as any church or private school, even though it was a State school. I tried to convince him Mont Albert was something special. He would not listen to me, so my praise became more and more extravagant. I do not know now why I should have provided further evidence for his harsh judgement of me. In life one is often one's own Judas, the one who provides the incriminating evidence for those whose approval one desperately desires, but can never attain.

That was a minor madness and folly. But that was not all. I was not only defending the indefensible, I was in a false position, speaking warmly of a school where I was afraid of both the masters and the other boys. There were girls at the school, but we boys were not really aware of them. Those were the days of segregation, the days when the boys sat on one side of a classroom and the girls on the other, when there were separate playgrounds and shelter sheds for boys and girls, separate lavatories. In their buildings the State schools of Australia had their own quaint ways of illustrating the verse in the book of Genesis: 'Male and female created he them.' Boys walked with boys and girls with girls to the railway station or tram stop.

171

The teachers terrified me. Once a week the boys were taken to Box Hill for 'sloyd' (woodwork). This was Melbourne, and Melbourne was a citadel for moral improvers and character builders; in learning mastery over wood we boys, being close to those years when the storms of adolescence would burst inside us, were supposed to be learning to control ourselves. The instructor at Box Hill had an extraordinary way of imparting the precious gift of self-discipline and sleight of hand to young boys. We were shown a small piece of oregon wood, a plane, and a set-square, followed by a demonstration on how to plane the length of wood into a perfect square. We were then ordered to do likewise. When we had finished, the instructor ran a square along the four sides of the wood. If any light appeared between the arm of the square and the wood the instructor picked up an ebony ruler and struck the boy quite hard on the head, after which he delivered an unfavourable character sketch of the pupil who had failed. The other boys laughed, not because they thought it was funny, or from pleasure in seeing another human being humiliated, but rather because laughter was a temporary relief from the fear that it might be their turn next. Our sloyd instructor was yet another in what was becoming quite a long list of those who taught me, that not being their intention, to beware of all moral improvers. They generally wielded a whip, a cane, a belt or an ebony ruler on all who broke their laws or failed in their standards laboratory.

I did not know then that while I was telling fibs to avoid facing the dreaded sloyd instructor, the girl I was going to marry, Hilma Dymphna Lodewyckx, had been at Mont Albert Central School. She had sung about 'the school that's on the hill, sir'. We had both sung, 'We love our school and keep her rule'. We did not know each other then.

The headmaster, Mr Harley, or 'Boss' Harley, as we called him, was a formidable man. He wore grey suits, with a waistcoat, watch chain and silver watch. His hair was grey and wiry, as was his moustache, which was not stained by either tobacco or tea. Mr Harley was remote. He spoke at us rather than to us from the verandah on the first floor overlooking an asphalt quadrangle on which we were all lined up. Mr Harley did not use the language of persuasion: he told us what we were to do, there being terrifying rumours of what Boss Harley would do to you if you did not obey his commandments – beware of rousing Boss Harley's temper, he was slow to anger, but when the storm broke, we were told, there was all hell to pay. So, look out for

Boss Harley. Say nothing, do nothing, look at the ground when he comes near. Boys whispered to each other the tales of terror. Remember what Boss Harley did to Joyce Gittis? Boss Harley belonged to those generations of men who believed girls could not handle mathematics, well, maybe arithmetic, but not algebra, or geometry. Girls belonged to the weaker sex. Not even Boss Harley could make girls mistresses of quadratic equations: that was far beyond their reach. But Boss Harley would terrify them into understanding. Yes, we were told, once Boss Harley had grabbed a girl by the scruff of the neck, held her over the banisters, and yelled at her, 'Give me the answer, or I'll drop you.'

I doubt if this ever happened. But at the time I believed it, and sat in the classrooms waiting for the volcano to erupt again. At the end of my two years at Mont Albert Central School, Mr Harley spoke words of encouragement to me. I was so grateful, so surprised to discover this kindly and loving Boss that I had difficulty in not weeping. That would have been quite wrong; those classes in sloyd were there to teach us self-control. Besides boys never cried. Girls cried: they were snivellers – that was why they always kept a handkerchief in the pockets of their blazers or their tunics.

Boss Harley's school of terror was a mere kindergarten in comparison with that of 'Poppa' Holmes, deputy headmaster and science master. Like Hamlet's devil, Poppa Holmes always wore black, a jet-black alpaca coat which matched his black hair, and contrasted with the perpetual red flush on his cheeks, which I took to mean there was always a fire of anger inside him. He was a hunter, and we were his quarry. There was a song about him as a hunter of delinquent or erring boys: 'Poppa's coming, Poppa's coming,/Look out, look out!' One was wise to heed the advice in the Book of Common Prayer about the devil, for Poppa was a roaring lion seeking not so much whom he could devour but whom he could strap. Poppa carried his strap with him, a piece of leather horse-harness, double thickness of course. Rumour had it that Poppa did not remove the brass studs; but that was just an example of how we terrified children exaggerated the doings of a bully. The boys got a lashing with the strap, the girls with the tongue. I never heard anyone complain that such discrimination between the genders was unfair. We were all too preoccupied with keeping out of Poppa's way to have any time for questions about justice.

I remember one day in the science room spilling ink over a

well-scrubbed tabletop, Poppa's special source of pride. There was no opportunity to deny I was to blame, for Poppa caught me in the very act. But Poppa did not reach for his strap. He put his arm around me and told me not to be afraid, he was not going to hurt me. Poppa had a heart: Poppa understood. Years later I heard more about Poppa, and the price he paid for having a passionate heart; I remembered this encounter in the science room, and saw us all, teachers, boys and girls, as playthings or victims of the world to which we belonged. Boss Harley and Poppa Holmes probably believed the strap sharpened the mind, that the cowed and terrified were empty vessels waiting to be filled with knowledge and wisdom. They were doing it all for our good.

I remember one other incident in a classroom at Mont Albert. There was a teacher we called 'Scaramouche' because of the temper he displayed whenever he was displeased with us. One day in 1927 Scaramouche blew up with a boy named Knox Jamieson, and threatened to flay the skin off his hide. I am not sure now of the words, except that I got the impression that Knox Jamieson would be lucky to escape with his life, I as usual allowing my unruly passions to overheat my mind. As was to happen many times in my life, I borrowed from the Bible the words which would express for me this sense of terror. Knox Jamieson's 'last state', I said to myself, would be 'worse than his first'. But no, it was not so. Knox Jamieson defiantly said, 'I appeal to the Headmaster!' Scaramouche himself looked scared. Scaramouche agreed. A boy with courage had won a victory over a man with power. Right *could* sometimes triumph over might, and that was something which no previous event had prepared me for. I had heard my father assure the members of his congregation that the good would have their reward, that it was not true in God's world that the wicked flourished, and the good were of no account. In church I had joined in singing lustily the words: 'We have Christ's own promise/And that cannot fail', but outside the church all I had seen had convinced me that the world belonged to the strong and the cunning. I did not want that to be true: I hungered after another dispensation. Now here was Knox Jamieson showing me and all who had eyes to see and ears to hear that a boy with courage and a conviction about his own righteousness could topple a tyrant. Knox Jamieson won his appeal, and Scaramouche controlled himself for the rest of the year.

For me there was one other memorable scene from these days at

Mont Albert. In 1927 the Victorian Cricket Association picked thirty or forty boys (I forget the exact number) from the Melbourne State Schools as promising cricketers, and organised an afternoon at the Hawthorn Cricket Club ground where those chosen would receive special coaching by Bill Ponsford, the Victorian and Australian Eleven batsman. I was surprised to be chosen. The sports master at Mont Albert said he was surprised too, but thought he knew what the V.C.A. was getting at. So one afternoon in the early summer of 1927-28, dressed in white shorts, white shirts, white socks and white sandshoes, we gathered round Bill Ponsford. He was shy, and he spoke very little. He told the bowlers length was the principal thing. The groundsman had painted a white line across the pitch at a good length. Bill Ponsford trundled up to the wicket and bowled a ball which lobbed on the white line. He decided not to bowl another ball. He told us there were only two strokes in cricket: playing forward and playing back. He demonstrated both of these with the grace of a ballet dancer. In between each demonstration stroke he gripped the handle of his bat lightly with his left hand and spun it like a top with his right hand. For me, on that sunny day at the Hawthorn cricket ground everything about him was perfect. In my young eyes he could do no wrong. So when, a few years later, Don Bradman overshadowed him I felt hurt. Once again life mocked my idea of the fitness of things. In cricket, as in other walks of life, the world belonged to the tough, not to the ones with the grace and beauty of a Ponsford.

By then, for those leaving the school at the end of 1927 it was scholarship time. I decided to sit for the Melbourne Grammar School scholarship examinations in English, Arithmetic and French. All I remember now is the sense of freedom in writing the essay. I was not inhibited by what the master I knew would think, or what he had told me about how to write. For the first time in my life I could 'have a go'. In the Arithmetic exam I was erratic: in the French I was out of my depth. All the candidates were interviewed by the Melbourne Grammar School headmaster, Richard Penrose Franklin. To my surprise and delight I found I was talking to someone to whom I could tell anything.

One night two weeks later the phone rang in the vicarage. My father took the call. It was from Mr Franklin offering me a share in the Charles Hebden scholarship for 1928, my share, as a boarder, to be £70. My father was so moved he was not able to speak. My mother, at first, was very proud of me, and kissed me, and said, 'Being a boarder will make a man of you, Mann dear.' I was not sure I wanted to be a man, if that meant leaving the world of the known and plunging into the world of the unknown. Then my mother looked quite sad, and said, 'I will ask the Father [her God] and He will tell me if it is the right thing to do.' I was young and foolish – no use to talk to me about what I could and what I could not manage.

The Ordeal

In February 1928, just before I turned thirteen, my brother and I became boarders at Melbourne Grammar School, and to me it was like surfing a dumper, or facing an express bowler in cricket. It frightened me: it exhilarated me. I was ill-equipped to survive the ordeal unscarred. Within eighteen months it created what I call that 'wound of mine' of which few knew, that wound which took at least thirty years to heal. Perhaps that was my fault, my weakness. Who can tell? Judge not, judge not! We have been told 'none doth offend'; we have been told, 'No one . . . was to blame. (Blame if you like the human situation.)' Perhaps the beginning of wisdom is to blame oneself and not others, to find the fault inside oneself, and not to seek comfort in any faltering by 'the hand of the potter'.

I do not remember now, sixty years after the event, what I was expecting. My mother had said it would make a man of me, but, not being then quite a man, I did not know what that meant. Perhaps I was tempted again as I had been tempted as a child on Phillip Island by the thought that now I would wear one of those blazers with the school badge on the top left pocket. Perhaps in time I could misquote Adam and say to my Creator after falling for the temptation, 'The blazer, it tempted me.' Perhaps I believed I was about to pass through the rites of initiation into a richer life than I had known so far. Well, there was to be an initiation, but not to prepare me for a journey of discovery of all the wonder and beauty of the world, but rather to make me conform to the lore of Yarraside. Perhaps I believed that my teachers would talk to me about all those things which had puzzled me in childhood: now there would be answers. Perhaps I was grabbing at the chance to be liberated from the tyranny of vicarage life. I found instead moments of terror which made the terrors of childhood fade into insignificance.

There were the humiliations of belonging to the genteel poor in a school where most of the boys came from the homes of the rich in South Yarra, Toorak, Brighton, and the western district of Victoria. The tone and values of the school, I was to find, were set by the rich. These humiliations started the moment my father parked his car outside Creswick House in Domain Road, South Yarra. Creswick House was opened that year as one of the houses accommodating boarders; the others were School House and Wadhurst. My brother, my mother, my father and I stood on the footpath beside the single-seater Morris Oxford, watching the Buicks, the Packards, the Hispano-Suizas, the Rovers, the fluted Vauxhalls and the Lancias, some chauffeur-driven, some with vases of flowers on the inner wall of the back seats, all dripping with wealth, oozing luxury, glide effortlessly close to the kerb. Boys jumped out in their expensive suits, so different from the bargain-price outfits my mother, by great determination, had managed to squeeze out of the warehouses in Flinders Lane. The others were all so jolly, so free of the fuss and fret which never left us wherever we went.

Elegantly dressed mothers farewelled their sons with a light-hearted 'I'm going to miss you, darling', delivered in a stage voice as distinct from a real-life voice, while my mother took me aside and with the eyes of someone foreseeing disaster, shook me and asked me, through tears, 'Are you sure you're going to be all right, Mann dear?', adding, 'And promise me faithfully, Mann dear, you won't forget to say your prayers every night. Ask the Father, Mann dear, and He will give it to you.' (Alas, I had already found asking the Father to make runs in cricket always ended in being out for a duck – and I already doubted whether God was interested in 'promising' cricketers.) I found myself saying to myself, 'Please God, don't let me cry in front of all these people', only to find to my dismay that try as I would and did to hide my fears about the impending loss, tears were streaming down my cheeks, and my brother told me not to be such a bloody baby, and asked me, 'What do you think the others will think of you?' My father, as ever, pasted over anything embarrassing or painful by saying we would all laugh about it one day.

There was worse to come on that fateful day. The acting house-master of Creswick House was Mr McCrae. With that lack of charity which distinguishes adolescents he was known to us as 'Dill', or what adult Australians now sardonically label a 'fucking no-hoper'. But that was not part of our vocabulary at the time. Mr McCrae was a most kindly man, but he too, like all of us, was a slave to the conventions of the school. He was too timid a man to stand up to those who inscribed the tablets of the law for us. Perhaps he had his own private reason for not attracting the attention of those in power – the self-appointed vigilantes of what Barry Humphries brilliantly identified as 'Grammar and that sort of thing'.

Amongst others, my mother, my brother and I were ushered into a large room where Mr McCrae was seated at a huge desk. On the desk were an ink-stand, with two pens dipped in glass vessels, one containing red, the other black ink, a round ebony ruler, a blotting pad, and a leather-bound notebook. Mr McCrae opened the book and told my mother he wanted to enter what he called 'certain particulars' about 'your two boys'. Was there, for example, anything he, as their guardian, should know about their health? My mother said Russell was a very healthy boy. 'And Manning?', Mr McCrae asked. My mother hesitated. Mr McCrae asked whether there was something she wanted to add. My mother said yes, there was. 'Manning', she said, 'is rather nervy. He's the one in the family with the brains – he's highly strung – he worries too much.' I wanted her to stop.

Mr McCrae gave me a kindly reassuring smile, as though to say he would hold me if I should fall, and comfort me according to my special needs. Then he asked my mother how much pocket money we were to receive each week. I had overheard the other mothers answer this question with five shillings (that being the maximum the school allowed), half-a-crown, or two shillings, but not this stingy ninepence. It was as though my brother and I were to start with the scarlet letter of 'P' for Pauper (I had remembered my father's sermon) on the lapels of our jackets. I raged inwardly, trying not to give Mr McCrae his first piece of evidence that I was 'nervy'. At the time I thought it was another example of my father's 'tightness' with money, or, maybe, my mother's fear we may lose our immortal souls by indulging in too many milk-shakes at the school tuck-shop. Now, when it's too late, I realise it was all, or possibly even more, than they could afford. Being the two ninepence-a-week pocket-money boys was only part of the price we had to pay for the great benefits we were told we were about to receive at the hands of the school. I was going to be made into a man.

My brother, being more than two years older than I, was allotted to a different dormitory. I remember the next torment was whether or not to kneel down beside the bed and say my prayers, as I had promised my mother faithfully I would do. All the other boys took off their clothes, put on their pyjamas and hopped straight into bed. I knelt down, but, like the King in *Hamlet*, while praying my words went up, but my thoughts, or more accurately my fears, remained below. On that first night I realised that a school boarding-house was like a vicarage. The question was the same: What will the others think? We were all under the tyranny of opinion; we all must learn to conform; we were now under the straiteners, or rather we were all straitening each other. But what if you either could not or would not be straitened?

There was perhaps a hint of what the answer was on the first morning. One of the boys in our dormitory was Phil Harris, the son of a Beaufort farmer and merchant. He had never worn a shirt with a detachable collar in his life before his mother dressed him to go to Melbourne Grammar. I found later he had considerable gifts as a boxer, a swimmer and an oarsman – and also gifts of the heart, but no one dared to show the latter gift at Creswick House in the late summer and autumn of 1928. That was simply not done, not *comme il faut* behaviour. Phil, I remember, got up at 6.30 a.m. on that first morning. At five minutes to eight, with only five minutes to go before the breakfast bell went, he was still struggling with both back and front studs. He was too proud to ask for help, and we were all so obsessed with making ourselves neat and tidy that we took no notice of him until he became desperate. Then, if I remember rightly, we all laughed at him, relieved probably to find there was someone who could not manage, someone whose state was worse than ours. That comedy went on every morning for quite a while, because Phil was slow to learn.

There was one other singularity. The four boys with what at the time were deemed to be strange names – Thonemann, Zimmermann, Busch and another – slept in a dormitory of their own. I had no idea at the time why they were separated from their contemporaries. I noticed that all four of them played the fool when talking with boys from other dormitories, and that their humour seemed to be a compensation for what they were suffering. I noticed, too, that they did not attend chapel either on week-days or on

Sundays. They were not the only ones excused from attendance. There were others with recognisable Anglo-Celtic names. Later I was told the latter were Roman Catholics, sent by their parents to Melbourne Grammar School because of the school's reputation for scholarship and learning.

That was what the school was there for. Every Sunday morning and every Sunday evening in chapel we went down on our knees while a man dressed in a robe of white linen, with a hood hanging down his back as evidence of his learning and wisdom, petitioned God graciously to pour down his blessings on the school so that the paths of true learning may 'ever flourish and abound'. He asked God to pour down His blessings on all bishops and curates, on our sovereign Lord the King, the Queen, and all other members of the royal family. Wisdom was the principal thing. Then there was being British and therefore members of the British Empire. I had the impression that God had some special relationship with the British, that they were His chosen people, charged with responsibility for rescuing the heathen, who in their blindness bowed down to wood and stone, and that in return for performing their duty as God's chosen servants, the British people were entitled to rewards. There were special things for special people. In the chapel I never heard of Australia, or its people. I heard about the British, the King, the Governor-General and all who were placed in authority under him. We all sang with gusto the words of the Psalm: 'O Lord, our Governor, how excellent is thy name in all the world?' In my childhood I had sung to a penny:

Hurry penny quickly,
Though you are so small,
Help to tell the heathen
Jesus loves them all . . .

Now here I was, on the edge of manhood, joining with a hundred boys each Sunday in thanks to Almighty God for being British. I had the impression that, when we sang the words, 'The Lord of Hosts is with us', it meant God was on our side and all was well.

We were all like film extras in a Hollywood extravaganza. The school was the stage and we were the players. There were set pieces in the hall in which school assemblies were then held – upstairs on the south side of the quadrangle. I remember the special assembly

181

to commemorate Anzac Day, 25 April 1928. The speaker that day was J. Henning Thompson. I saw a very old man with a white beard, a bowed back, shaky hands. I heard a squeaky voice battling to interest boys (whose minds were as ever on 'other things') in the heroic deeds of the Australian soldiers who waded ashore at Anzac Cove on the first 'sad Anzac morn'. Perhaps if I had known then that this frail octogenarian had earlier taught Alfred Deakin I might have mended my ways and stopped muttering to myself, 'When is he going to stop?'

There was an assembly once a week. There were also special assemblies. The masters, all wearing academic gowns, sat on the dais. There was the solemn moment when the headmaster, R. P. Franklin, entered the hall, head bowed, hands joined in front of his waistcoat, eyes cast down in sorrow as though he had just been called in to witness yet another act of human madness and folly. He always looked as though he were about to cry out in anguish the words of Sophocles: 'Call no man happy that is of human kind.' I had no idea at the time why he often wore such a sad expression on his face. I had no idea of the strains under which he lived. I only knew I had adored him ever since first meeting him in the interview for the scholarship. We called him 'Lofty' because he was so tall, being at least six feet three inches. That meant we young boys always looked up to him when we risked letting him see our eyes, and for a worshipper and an adorer this seemed just right.

One Saturday evening in the autumn, one of those clear evenings in Melbourne when moon, stars and sky merge gently into the darkness of earth, he came through the door leading to the head-master's study, and rested his left hand on one of the verandah posts. We, his adorers, gathered around him. He spoke to us in his musical voice, that voice which conveyed the same message as the face, a message of how he had found to his everlasting pain that what happened in life mocked his idea of the fitness of things, and that we human beings could do nothing about it, or if we tried we would only make things worse. Neither then nor later did I 'pluck out the heart of his mystery'. All I knew were these magical moments, such as that Saturday evening when he said, 'I've been hunting today, boys – [Long pause, and much nervous movement of the head] I hope one day you will find that life can be very beautiful.' But before any one of us could say a word, he had disappeared through that stained-glass door, leaving me gazing with awe and wonder at that vast sky and feeling for a moment tender towards everyone, and wanting the moment to go on forever.

He should have been the hero in a Greek tragedy. He believed with the ancient Greeks that transgressors against the moral law would and should be punished. But he had the eye of pity for the transgressors. Towards the end of the first or the second year I remember we were all summoned to a special assembly. The headmaster began to speak to a hushed six or seven hundred boys, telling us that it was his melancholy task to let us know that –, giving first the surname in a soft voice, then the two Christian names in the loud voice of a town crier, would, as he put it, 'have to go'. He has crossed the line between the pardonable and the unpardonable: he had altered the date on his birth certificate to enable him to run in the under-sixteen events at the Combined Sports, and, as we all would know, had won all three events. Thanks in part to —, Grammar had won; but now Grammar had been disqualified, the cup of victory had been taken out of our hands. We must not judge or condemn —. He was the victim of human weakness, the victim of human folly. He was not to blame; we were all to blame for his fall. Prizes enjoyed too much prestige. We were all responsible for the disgrace to the School. Then he swept out of the hall, leaving in my mind the idea that we were all the playthings of some larger power, that the power of evil, the power of ambition in this case, was greater than the power of good. I felt both terror and awe. I did not know then that the Greeks believed the role of tragedy was to excite pity and terror in our hearts.

Not long after the expulsion of the boy who altered the date on his birth certificate, we were all summoned again to a special assembly. Again there was the hum of expectancy, as we asked each other and asked ourselves, 'What's this, what's this?' One's very presence in the hall gave one both the sense of relief and the sense of virtue that 'it can't be me'. But there was the excitement – who is it this time? Again I felt both the terror and, let it be confessed, a secret pleasure. We did not have long to wait. Heads turned. Boys whispered to each other, 'Lofty's coming'. The knight with the sorrowful countenance strode on to the platform, wrapped his gown around him, lowered his chin on to his chest, raised it and cried out to us, as though he were almost sobbing, 'Boys, it is my melancholy duty to tell you that — [again giving the surname first in hushed tones], —— [again the two Christian names in a crescendo] has had to go.' He had been found stealing money from the clothes in the lockers in the day-boys' changing-room. 'Lofty' told us the boy had stolen the money to enable him to dress and pursue the pleasures his widowed mother could not afford to provide. We must not blame him. We must pity him as a young man who had been corrupted by false values, a young man who had worshipped the god of Mammon. The School was arranging for him to have a fresh start in New Zealand.

Three things interested me in the life of the young man who would have represented the School in the Combined Sports if — had not fiddled with his birth certificate; he would have had that glory. Both boys had beauty of body and beauty of movement. There was nothing in their faces or their behaviour which hinted that all was not well within. Both had achieved a triumph, both had done what we were told in the school song we should all strive to do – 'bear the dark blue flag to glory'. They had both obeyed the other command in that song, 'Grammar to the fore!' Yet they had fallen: they had been expelled. The school would know them no more.

Years later there was a sequel. The papers in Melbourne reported that the Melbourne Grammar thief had been sentenced to a term of imprisonment for stealing. By then I was not surprised. By then I had shed Lofty's high-minded teaching that we were all responsible for each other. I had come round to Shakespeare's view that the fault lay in ourselves. As on so many questions in life, he put into his own words the point made by the Galilean fisherman that it was what came up from inside a man which led him on to his destruction. Life would lead me back to all the remarks He made about life, but never to the claims the gospels attributed to Him after He had met the frowners and the straiteners in Jerusalem on that fatal last journey – the journey He need not have made. By then life had tempted me to play with the idea that even in that most perfect being there was madness and folly.

In 1929 we boys were again in the audience for yet another theatrical drama, this time in the school chapel. On 9 November three boys from the school, Lindsay Gordon Cuming, Andrew Philip Joshua and Richard Henry Lewis, members of Bromby House, lost their lives in a boating accident in Canadian Bay near Frankston. A fourth member of the party, John Grayton Brown, swam ashore to safety. A few days later we were all gathered in the chapel for a memorial service. There were three coffins in the aisle just below the altar. Hymns were sung, prayers were offered to Almighty God, the mothers of the dead could be heard sobbing. Then Lofty stood beside the coffin closest to the altar. In a voice which belonged not to this world, he told us that there were two views about death: one was the Christian hope of resurrection: the other was the Greek view that death was final, death meant annihilation. He hoped these three deaths would turn our minds towards thinking about the things that matter in life. But he did not give us the answer. I wanted an answer then, and I want it now. I remember then the pain and the shock of discovering that Lofty did not know the answer to death, and if he did not know, he, the man I worshipped and adored, maybe no one knew. Alas, there was no one at the school, neither master, matron nor boy, to whom I could risk uncovering what was going on in my mind.

Once again, years later there was a sequel. In the Melbourne *Herald* one evening I read a headline announcing that a Melbourne doctor wanted all drunks in Australia to be kept off the roads. The doctor was Grayton Brown, the one who had swum ashore in November 1929. I thought then, as I think now, that Grammar under Lofty gave us all a morality, but not a faith. When we were confronted with the sharpness of death we were told there were no answers. We were given a beautiful demonstration of resignation and acceptance and were encouraged to behave with dignity and courage; we were exhorted to cultivate the will to endure. But by the time Grayton Brown was wagging a reproving finger at Melbourne drunks, Australian society had moved into an era in which people had neither a faith nor a morality, and I was asking myself: Is it true that a society without a faith ends by believing everything is allowable? If so, perhaps there was a case for 'Grammar and that sort of thing' – a case for dignity and discipline, provided that was not the privilege of the few.

I suspect now that Lofty believed in élites, in the role of the gifted, in the aristocracy of talent but certainly not the aristocracy of birth: that the one prayer he would have uttered with fervour, or rather the one prayer to which he would have given a loud, approving 'Amen' was the one which conveyed to God the hope that 'there never may be wanting [Lofty would have muttered under his breath 'my boys'] to serve Thee whether in Church or State'. I suspect that as an Englishman he often despaired of his capacity to interest the sons of the squatters, the stockbrokers, the doctors, the lawyers, the teachers, the engineers, and even the parsons of Australia, in his vision of life.

He knew every boy in his school. He had a close personal relationship with nearly everyone, he not being a man for the universal embrace, or a man who loved everyone. He asked the unanswerable questions. He would loom up out of the Melbourne winter murk, on one of those days when the mind can see no point in all those promises that seem to comfort cruel men. He would rub his hands gently, smile, and look down at me and ask, 'Have you noticed anything different about yourself lately?' I did not know then what he was getting at, but I do now. While I was stammering out, I hoped, a confident 'Oh no, sir', he was already starting to say, 'Well, others have', and I wondered what that could be, whether someone had guessed those thoughts of mine about which I told no one. So I started to say again, 'No sir, I haven't', but by then he was gone, and I wondered what this 'something different' could possibly be.

Another day he asked me, 'What's this I've heard about you?' For a moment I wondered whether he was burrowing down into that secret life about which I told no one, because I had not by then found that other person with whom I would dare to exchange minds and swap ideas, all my previous tentative moves being crushed by my mother's plea, 'Don't talk like that, Mann dear. You make me feel giddy', or my father's flamboyant 'That's my great subject, boy. You wait till you're older', or my brother's promising we would have a long talk one day and promptly falling asleep, leaving me to face the tempest of chaos and annihilation in the dark. My fears were groundless: Lofty was not about to make me confess to that. He wanted to know why I mixed with boys who had few, if any, intellectual interests. Well, it was not possible to answer that, because then I did not know why. But now, looking back, I believe that in seeking out the company of boys like Jack Thomson, the son of a horse-breeder in Kyneton, Phil Harris and others, I was living again the days with Plugger Bennell, Noel Cleeland, Harry Williams and others. I was living again in the lost Eden of Phillip Island, the place where at times I felt safe and knew some liberty. I was frequenting the ones with whom I could be myself, the ones who accepted, who did not judge or set standards no one could attain and then punish me for not observing those standards.

Another day Lofty put to me another one of his unanswerable

questions: 'You know you're doing wrong. Why do you do it?' Why indeed? Again there was the moment of panic: has my secret life been betrayed? But no, Lofty did not have that in mind. He was probably putting the question to which neither he nor anyone knew the answer. Later at the school I found Lofty was fond of the tag from Ovid:

Video meliora, proboque;
Deteriora sequor
[I see and approve better things,
but follow worse].

By then I realised Lofty was a profound pessimist about human behaviour, that, in the words an American Negro used to me in 1963, 'Man, there ain't nothin' you can do about it.' Lofty wanted to keep the show going. All he knew for certain was that anyone who let the side down 'had to go'. That was an essential condition for the survival of his world.

I owe him so much. By his example he taught me about the majesty of life, he taught me the importance of what he called 'getting things straight'. He was always asking me, just one amongst the seven hundred in his pastoral care, 'Are you getting things straight?' I doubt if I ever did, whether I ever could. I realise now that he did not mean the Christian answer as summed up in the Lord's Prayer and the Beatitudes. He meant the Greek ideal of harmony, of moderation in all things, of balance between the Dionysian frenzy and Apollonian restraint, between passion and reason, heart and mind, the Greek advice to 'Know thyself', to call no man happy that belongs to the human race; the Greek teaching to balance resignation and acceptance with the desire to find out what holds the world together in its innermost parts.

Lofty believed in a classical education. Those with intellectual ability studied Latin, Greek, mathematics, English, history, French and elementary science. When they reached the Leaving Certificate year they dropped the science. In Leaving Honours they dropped either English or French. Lofty believed anyone who could master Latin and Greek could master anything: Latin and Greek were the foundation for professional courses at the university in law, medicine, dentistry, science and theology. Latin and Greek trained the mind. Latin and Greek sifted the chaff from the wheat.

It was an education for an élite. It was an education designed for a governing class in that country which ruled over a large portion of the world, the Empire on which the sun never set – but Australia had neither a governing class nor an Empire. It was an education for an aristocracy: Australia was a democracy. For those who could master Latin and Greek it was a key which opened a door into a palace of riches, to Homer, Aeschylus, Sophocles, Thucydides, Aristophanes, Plutarch, Herodotus, Xenophon, Livy, Virgil, Horace and Catullus. It was also, as I found later to my delight, one way of finding out for oneself what Christ probably said, and not what the standard translators said he said, or what St Paul wrote. I suspect that Lofty was not interested in those who could not manage the Latin and Greek. He did care for his Latin and Greek boys: they were the ones who won renown and glory for the school at the public examinations; they were the ones who went on to serve either in church or state or the professions – judges, Collins Street doctors, Harley Street specialists, professors, bishops, leaders of political parties – an Old Melburnian, Stanley Melbourne Bruce, was then Prime Minister of Australia, though he was beginning to have a rocky time. Lofty's Melbourne Grammar was a preparatory school for leaders. The finishing school was Oxford or Cambridge, or, if that was not possible, Trinity College and the University of Melbourne. There was, however, another part of the School – the guardians of another meaning to be placed on that Barry Humphries phrase, 'Grammar and that sort of thing'.

I was fortunate to be placed in the Latin and Greek group. In 1928 boys entering the school after finishing the eighth grade at a State primary school or E form at a State central school were placed in a form called Specials. We needed special tuition to prepare us to enter the top classes above us. I was to discover also we needed special treatment to mould us into believers in the 'dark blue flag'. In Specials, Latin was the principal thing, and we were encouraged with all our might to 'get Latin'. ▪

We were lucky. Our teacher was Harold Kinross Hunt, a Sydney graduate in Classics, a Cambridge graduate in the classical Tripos, and later Professor of Classics at the University of Melbourne. Within a month we were all chanting together '*amo, amas, amat, amamus, amatis, amant*, and *mensa, mensa, mensam, mensae, mensae, mensa, mensae, mensae, mensas, mensarum, mensis, mensis*', with the same enthusiasm as Eric Hatfield when he led us in the chanting of 'r-a-t spells rat, c-a-t spells cat, b-a-t spells bat' in the State school at Cowes.

Every week or so Lofty came into the room, clasped his hands together over his stomach, and asked Mr Hunt whether his boys were 'getting things straight' and whether his boys were 'coming on'. He would then ask to see our work. It was a magical moment when his eyes met mine after he had said encouraging words about the value of Latin for those with a lively imagination. It was a black day when I carelessly forgot the 'i' was dropped in the past participle of *tenere* and Lofty warned me of the terrible price a boy with my sort of mind might pay one day for not being meticulous about details. Harold Hunt defended me, saying Clark only lapsed into error when he was feeling 'nervy'. Lofty, putting on one of his grave looks, seemed to send me a message with his eyes, a message that he understood, and that in time all would be well.

Lofty had astonishing insights into what I was really thinking about and what I could manage. There were the illuminating and memorable remarks he dropped while teaching history, or Latin or Greek. A few years later when he was teaching Greek and Roman history he paused in the middle of dictating notes to us about Pompey and, as it were, spoke to himself while speaking aloud to us, 'Let me see, did Pompey come after Sulla or Sulla after Pompey?' – a confession that he did not claim to be omniscient, a confession which promoted him still higher on the short list of people I adored. Then he added hastily, as though he were ashamed to allow us to share one of his failings, that we would find the Roman civil service in the first century BC enjoyed the same reputation for freedom from corruption as the British in the nineteenth and twentieth centuries – quite different from the behaviour of the Russian civil service, as we would see when we read the works of Dostoevsky. There was a pause, after which he looked at me and said, 'Clark, you will be interested one day in the novels of Dostoevsky for quite different reasons.'

I was. Two years after Lofty dropped his enigmatic remark about Dostoevsky, as a university student I began to read his novels in the reading room of the Melbourne Public Library. At the time I was supposed to be reading about Bates's case, the Petition of Right and John Hampden's case. I had the impression from my lecturer, Jessie Webb, at the University of Melbourne, that I should want to say 'Thou fool' when I read such words of James the First as 'the king is such a mighty subject that he will not have a sovereign' and 'a subject and a sovereign are clean different things'. I also had the impression that anyone of any natural decency whatsoever would choke with horror when they read what happened to Prynne, Burton and Bastwick. But I wanted to know *why* men made such mad remarks, and behaved so abominably to each other. My teacher always wore a startled look if I risked letting her know what interested me.

Dostoevsky was an oasis in my early years at the University of Melbourne. It was as though he drew the curtain aside and showed me what was on the other side, or led me round a corner where I could see the dark side of the human heart. He discussed what I had noticed about the human situation, but had never been encouraged to mention, for if I did I became the victim of a character sketch, identified as someone with an unhealthy mind, someone perverse and unnatural. Here was someone who called himself 'a child of the age of unbelief', someone who confessed as I had often wanted to confess to a 'thirst to believe', someone who put into memorable words the creed to which I was moving during the Belgrave years: 'I believe in Christ . . . one day I will believe in God.' Here was a man whose words told me much of what he had endured: 'God knows, brother, what goes on in the heart of a woman . . . and I'll come back to that one day.' But, and this intrigued me, as far as I could find out, he never did.

So I wondered then in the Public Library, whether he did not know what goes on in the heart of a woman; maybe no man has ever known it, maybe no one has ever answered the question in Isaiah, 'Who can know it?' I remember rushing down the marble steps in the Public Library in a state of wild ecstasy, not because I had understood why the English and some Australians revered John Hampden's stand on ship money but because I had just read this passage in *The Possessed* (as we called it then) by Dostoevsky:

Listen to a great idea: there was a day on earth, and in the midst of the earth there stood three crosses. One on the Cross had such faith that he said to another, 'Today, thou shalt be with me in Paradise.' The day ended; both died and passed away and found neither Paradise nor resurrection. His words did not come true. Listen: that Man was the loftiest of all on earth, He was that which gave meaning to life. The whole planet, with everything on it, is mere madness without that Man. There never has been any like Him before or since, never, up to a miracle. For that is the miracle, that there never was or never will be another like Him. And if that is so, if the laws of nature did not spare even Him, have not spared even their miracle and made even Him live in a lie and die for a lie, then all the planet is a lie and rests on a lie and on mockery. So then, the very laws of the planet are a lie and the vaudeville of devils. What is there to live for? Answer, if you are a man.

I remember it was like all the other moments in life after a revelation: there was no one with whom I could share it. The tram conductor did not look as though he wanted to be told about that 'day on earth'. Nor did any of the passengers. Back at Trinity College my fellow students, as ever, had their minds on 'other things'. But for me those afternoons in the Public Library were golden; there had been someone else who knew 'what's what'.

There had been someone else who wanted to be forgiven, some-one, incidentally, who could be quite witty about my great hunger – Grushenka, in *The Brothers Karamazov*, tossed off this remark in the middle of a wild carousal at a road-house: 'If I were God I would forgive everyone.' In *The Possessed* Stavrogin expressed one of my never-to-be-satisfied hungers: 'Listen to me, Father Tihon, I want to forgive myself.' In *Crime and Punishment* Marmaledov put it more picturesquely. He was a drunkard: I had my own reasons for being pleased that a drunkard saw into the heart of the matter:

And He will judge and will forgive all, the good and the evil, the wise and the meek . . . And when He has done with all of them, then He will summon us, 'You too come forth.' He will say, 'Come forth, ye drunkards, come forth, ye weak ones, come forth, ye children of shame!' And we shall all come forth, without shame, and stand before Him. And He will say unto us: 'You are swine, made in the Image of the Beast and with his mark; but come ye also!' And the wise ones and those of understanding will say: 'Oh Lord, why dost Thou receive these men?' And He will say: 'This is why I receive them, oh ye wise, this is why I receive them, oh ye of understanding, that not one of them believed himself to be worthy of this.' And He will hold out His hands to us and we shall fall down before Him . . . and we shall weep . . . and we shall understand all things! Then we shall understand all . . . and all will understand, Katerina Ivanovna even [i.e. Marmaledov's wife] . . . she will understand . . . Lord, Thy kingdom come.

Yes – and for me there was the moment of moments, the moment when the world stood still when I read the words of Ivan Karamazov in *The Brothers Karamazov*. Ivan cannot understand why the world is arranged as it is – just as I could not understand what was happening at Melbourne Grammar School. Ivan knows a great truth: 'There is no sin, no crime, only hunger.' Ivan has the great longing:

I want to be there when everyone suddenly understands what it has all been for. All the religions of the world are built on this longing, and I am a believer.

Maybe it is now possible for me to write about what had gone on under the mask behind which I shielded, behind which I had a life I did not dare to share with anyone. The question, then, was: How would these thoughts be expressed? Poetry was not open to me. I had never written a line of poetry in my life, only hundreds of verses of doggerel composed at night in bed to settle scores with those who had despitefully used me, or the pompous, and all who put on airs, or saw themselves as far greater than others saw them. But poetry never came to me – even in the dark days of pain and despair at Melbourne Grammar School. Fiction had its appeal. My father was a novelist who never wrote a line in his life. He had two of the essential gifts of the story-teller – the power to entertain, and the desire to instruct and increase the store of human wisdom – but not the will, or the strength to start, let alone endure to the end.

Lofty planted an idea in my mind. 'Clark,' he said to me one afternoon when he was handing back our essays in Greek history, 'you can manage history. You can tell a story – only those who can tell a story should write history.' What he did not know and I did not know at the time was that the early years at Melbourne Grammar School had given me something to say later as a historian, cushioned and deadened though it was to be during the years when I wasted my life searching for salvation 'in the muck', when I sampled one after another the remedies of those who claimed to have the answer – the Newman Society, the Student Christian Movement, the Communist Party, the psychologists, the meditators, the Buddhists, tobacco, alcohol, women, love, diet, exercise, back-to-nature – and found it was all folly, that these people peddling their wares in things of the body and things of the soul were like confidence tricksters. Well before I went to Melbourne Grammar I wanted to be there when everyone suddenly understood what it had all been for.

Melbourne Grammar School taught me a lesson about life, or rather to whom the world belongs. Years later I read the remark by a German author (was it Goethe?): *'Dem Mutigen gehört die Welt'* [The world belongs to the brave]. I was to have jokes about that later with my wife. I told her that Goethe must have meant 'the tough', even possibly 'the cunning' or 'the bullies'. I need a man of Goethe's stature to say that, but I cannot even tell my wife why this is so. There are still some things too painful to talk about to anyone.

Even now, sixty years afterwards, I stumble in my search for words in which to tell about the discovery. There were rumours of a coming ordeal: there were rumours about initiations. They would not be as savage as in previous years, rumour had it, because last year (1927) the son of a prominent Melbourne man suffered concussion when THEY, the members of the Long Dorm ('What's the Long Dorm?' I ask in alarm. 'You'll find out soon', was the reply, and so I did) rolled him down the stairs from the dormitory floor to the ground floor. The School, Lofty had said, would not stand for that sort of thing. There were stories of what it would be like when our house-master, 'Dingo' Clarke, returned from a trip to India with a party of Grammar boys. Dingo, I gathered, had terrible rages: some said it was all because he had a silver plate in his head, and some said he was just like that. I wondered if Lofty knew how Dingo terrified and tormented young boys – the more a boy was terrified, rumour had it, the greater Dingo's pleasure.

I wondered if Lofty knew initiations were still going on. I wondered if those men who wore a surplice of white linen every Sunday morning and every Sunday evening in the chapel, and read out those words about the 'lilies of the field' and having compassion on the 'least of the little ones', knew what was going on. I was even foolish enough to believe that those least able to endure the ordeal would be exempted, classified as unfit for initiations just as some men were declared unfit for military service. I soon learned they were the choicest morsels for the initiation rites conducted by the boys of the Long Dorm. What gave them pleasure, what tickled their lust, was a terrified boy. What I did not know then, but I do now, was that a sensitive, vulnerable boy who did not crack under their blows fed their madness and their frenzy. It was like snatching meat away from hungry dogs: they bared their teeth, growled, and tore into their prey.

On the night when it first happened there was only terror. I remember we were told at tea one Friday night that we were to attend a meeting in a room where boarders sat and talked on rainy days. Eighty boys crowded into a room plunged in darkness except for one light over a table at the far end of the room. The members of the Long Dorm were standing around three sides of the table, their coats and ties off and their sleeves rolled up. Some of them were soaping the table to make the surface slippery, some of them were dipping pages of newspaper into a bucket of water and rolling the wet paper into balls the size of a croquet ball. At their end of the room, among the Long Dormers and the initiated from previous years, there was laughter. At our end, where the uninitiated were huddled together there was silence, as frightened eyes watched the preparations, or looked to each other for comfort and reassurance, only to discover that in such moments there is no solidarity, no fellowship between the victims, each victim being concerned with protecting his own skin. The members of the Long Dorm were the boys from whom the next batch of house prefects were chosen; they were on the first rung of the ladder of success in the school. I did not realise then the role of these young men as guardians of bourgeois society in Victoria. I saw them as bullies, as young men of whom I was scared. I had been scared before, but this, I discovered, was a super scare, like those early scares about annihilation, the scare on first confronting the men with the qualities, temperament and character of those who come to the top in every human society.

It was like a stage show in which we, the young, were both the audience and the players. The Long Dorm were organised like any hierarchy, and numbered off in order of seniority from one to twelve. Number twelve, I gathered later, had to carry the 'piss pot' each morning from the dormitory to the lavatory – a ceremonial walk through the other dormitories where the young cowered before his person and his chamber, fearing a summons into the Long Dorm for some 'unders and overs' – under one bed and over the next, while the members of the Long Dorm belted him with knotted towels. They would throw him out at the end with the threat of much more if he offended again, that is, broke the lore of the tribe. That was a follow-up to the initiations.

That night they began with the head of the Long Dorm calling out, 'I want all you young fellers to show how well you can sing the school song.' So we start, the voices of many of us not having broken, but so terrified are we of what is about to happen that we, the very young, sing with the irregularity of pitch of a voice that is breaking, some of us being so terror-struck that the saliva dries up in our mouths so that no sound comes out. That was what THEY wanted. Members of the Long Dorm threaded their way through us, poking an ear next to a mouth. A cry goes up: 'Here's a boy who does not know the School song.' Those round the table shout gleefully, 'Bring him up.' I am led forward, a path opening for us as though we are Moses and the chosen people crossing the Red Sea.

At the table they dance around me shouting 'Up, up, up' as I climb onto the table and duck to avoid the wet paper pellets thrown at me and the swishes with a roll of wet paper at my face. 'What's your name?' 'Clark', I reply, as they shout, 'He's scared, he's scared.' 'Yes, but what's your other name?' 'Manning', I reply in a shaky whisper. One of my tormentors – I can still see his face, and remember his name, and remember how he jerks his head like a golliwog, though 'Nuer', as he is called, is no clown – turns to the chorus of boys, and, miming an effeminate voice and making effeminate gestures with his hands, says, 'Our ickle Mann's quite a poet.' Gales of nervous laughter erupt from the spectators. When bullies hold the floor no one among the onlookers displays sympathy with their victim, no one dares call out, or may even want to call out 'Stop'. They want more, provided they are safe – and loud laughter is part of their insurance premium. The bully, not the victim, is what human beings are interested in.

I do not give them the satisfaction for which they hunger. I do not put on a counter show, like so many others, or treat it as a joke. I sing, and then lapse into sullen silence, while the paper cannon-palls burst on my face. Nuer sneers at me, 'See how you like this, "ickle Mann"', and he knocks my legs from under me, and I fall hard on the table, and have difficulty in standing up again because the soap has made it as slippery as ice; Nuer aborts all my efforts, as the others laugh at my impotence. The audience, too, find it funny. I wonder how long it will be possible to endure without giving them the satisfaction they crave. Insecurity from whatever cause is one of the states I cannot handle then and never will be able to handle. One among the pack of my tormentors takes pity on me, or maybe he is bored and wants to get on with the next act in the show – who can tell? He calls out, 'Break it up.' I am told to stand up, shake hands with Nuer just to show there is no intention to ostracise me from the pack.

I am now an initiated member of the pack. I step down from the table, and feverishly look into the eyes of those of my age, hoping for some sympathy, but they all look the other way. No one says 'sorry'. Perhaps their laughter was genuine; perhaps for them it was very amusing; perhaps the humiliation of one of their own was a pleasure like all spectator sport – very pleasing if you suppress sympathy and pity.

Some treat it as a joke. 'Where's Nigger?', Nuer calls out. He means Alex Tartakover. 'Come on Nigs. Give us one of the songs you sing when we're all in chapel.' Nigs steps up onto the table. He smiles. He cracks jokes with them. He asks them what they would like him to sing. There is a discussion. There is much laughter. Nuer trips him up, and Nigs falls flat on his face. Nigs rises gracefully, bows deeply to Nuer and thanks him. Nuer winks at his confrères, and says, 'Roy Rene ['Mo', a stage comic] has become a boarder at Melbourne Grammar.' Everyone laughs, and Nigs laughs too, and asks them whether that will be enough for now. Nuer calls for an encore, to which Nigs replies cheekily, 'The price of living is going up.' They all like that. The outsider knows how to humour the standards men. Nigs bows deeply, and jumps down off the table, his whole face elated, his eyes exalted. Nigs has become one of them: he has won an entry permit to the world of which he wants to be a member.

Others do not fare so well. Poor Jimmy Stephen, I remember, was deeply shaken. He was the son of a doctor in Albury. Jimmy Stephen could not be a clown: he did not have any inner strength, any of that will to endure which can save the sensitive from the assaults of the straiteners. I can still see the look of terror in his eyes as they marched him up to the table. Perhaps we should have spoken to each other, but that was not to be: the lore of Melbourne Grammar was to keep people apart. Jimmy Stephen had no faith; he did not believe the Lord would uphold all that fall, certainly not those who fell on the Long Dorm's slippery table, or that Christ would not allow him to suffer more than he could endure, or that painting, music and poetry could atone for all he had to put up with. Jimmy Stephen was frightened of everyone and everything. I was not surprised to hear that after he left school he turned to alcohol as a shield and comforter.

Years later in Canberra I heard he had destroyed himself. That night I took down the photo of the school boarders in 1928, and looked for a long time at the face of poor Jimmy Stephen, and asked myself the question why such things were fated to be, whether a boy of his temperament would have rushed on to his destruction no matter what society he lived in. I remembered then that all those who 'cracked' during the initiations had difficulty settling down. I wondered whether that was what my mother meant by her enigmatic remark that being a boarder 'will make a man of you, Mann dear'. Maybe – but what a price, what life-long wounds? And what of those who fell by the wayside, those who could not be made into men by this rite of initiation?

There were other moments of terror. In 1929 I began to study Greek. Our teacher was Carl Keppel. Learning the language presented no immediate problems to me, as my memory stood up to the daily test of reciting the principal parts of such irregular verbs as *didomi*, *histimi*, and *tithimi*. Carl Keppel would hand out a cyclostyled sheet for each irregular verb and say 'By tomowwow, Wads', and, by God, tomorrow it was, or there might be a thrashing. I sat there day after day wondering when I would arouse his wrath. I was young at the time, and had no idea of what triggered off the rages of Carl Keppel; I do now.

One of the members of our class was George Slutzkin. Carl Keppel turned all his fury on to him. I could not understand it. George was a gifted boy, as gifted as any other member of that class of the boys of promise, one worthy of being a 'Gweek Waddie'. George had a beautiful face, and beautiful melancholic eyes, eyes which were a picture-show of human suffering, and human gaiety. George did not go to chapel. In George's presence Carl Keppel became like a wild animal. He thrashed George for every error he made, but overlooked the mistakes of the rest of the class. After four or six weeks Carl Keppel walked into the classroom rubbing his hands with glee, his eyes betraying how much he was enjoying some subterranean satisfaction. 'Wads', he said, 'I have some wonderful news for you. Slutzkin has given up the long unequal stwuggle.' Then he added with contempt, 'Slutzkin will take extwa classes in Fwench.' It was not until I read later about the aims of a party in Germany, called the National Socialist Party, that I understood why Carl Keppel had persecuted poor George Slutzkin. Nor did I understand at the time why the other members of the class had no reason to fear they might one day be the targets of one of his rages. We were his 'Gweek Waddies'. We were the objects of his affection. But I was never at ease in his presence. Even later when he stroked my hair, as he did with all his 'Gweek Waddies', and praised my somewhat unusual translations of the passages about death in the tragedy *Ajax* by Sophocles, I was not reassured: I always remembered the roaring lion who had reduced George Slutzkin to a frightened animal.

I do remember one other episode with Carl Keppel. In 1930, I being then fifteen, he taught Latin to our class, Intermediate A. I remember one afternoon Don Sandy dared to ask a question: 'Sir,' he said, 'how can you tell whether an adjective is declined like *niger* or like *pauper*?' Carl Keppel did not answer the question. Instead he said, 'Sandy, go round to the book room and fetch me a cane.' When Don Sandy returned Carl Keppel ordered him to bend over, and then gave him six strokes with the cane. At the time I could not understand the motive. Don Sandy was a chapel-goer; Don Sandy was not a George Slutzkin, not a natural target for a bully; Don Sandy was one of those tough men to whom later in dark moments I believed Australia belonged. Now I do begin to understand. Don Sandy was not from Yarraside, not a *comme il faut* Melbourne Grammar boy. In the boxing ring, I remember, and on the running track, Grammar boys wore white shorts, and their house singlet – the shorts made of purest white cotton. Don Sandy wore silk shorts; Don Sandy sometimes wore green, sometimes red, and sometimes yellow shorts. Don Sandy seemed anxious to let observers know that while some may have the 'head-piece clever', he, Don Sandy, had the 'cod-piece large'. No one else ever spoke about any part of a woman except her face. Don Sandy, I remember, boasted each Monday of the liberties he had taken with a girl in the dress circle of the Palais Picture Theatre the previous Saturday afternoon and what liberties the girl had taken with him. In the dark, I gathered, they had allowed each other much. Don Sandy boasted of how if you really knew what was what, you could 'shoot the bishop' in one of the tunnels at Luna Park. Don Sandy was all we were supposed not to be. Yet we listened fascinated, we the boys who were being dragooned into membership of the vast army of timidity perverts in the Australian suburbs during those years when sex was a 'dirty little secret'.

All those who believed in 'Grammar and that sort of thing' despised Don Sandy. I did not know to which camp I belonged – those who waited for Monday morning for another instalment in the Sandy saga, or those who dismissed him as a 'lousy swine' and the possessor of a 'filthy mind'. The latter wanted me to believe that those who were not *comme il faut* in their dress, were not 'gentlemen' with women. Cads put their hands up ladies' dresses: gentlemen did not do that sort of thing, gentlemen did not even *want* to do that sort of thing.

E. D. Scott, I remember, was the paragon of all those virtues which Don Sandy most obviously lacked. E. D. Scott rowed in the crew. E. D. Scott did not run out of wind in the 880 or the mile: E. D. Scott had not wasted his substance in the darkness of the Palais Picture Theatre, or any tunnel at Luna Park. E. D. Scott wrote poetry, beautiful poetry about a country far away, or the pleasures of discipline and self-denial, not the filthy doggerel Don Sandy recited while we wondered whether Carl Keppel would turn up for the lesson that day. (There was always the chance that he would not make it – one had to cling to such hopes in those days. That would mean more boasting by Don Sandy, or delightful fantasies by the lovable Doug Reed on why Essendon would win the flag in 1932 – they being then at the bottom of the premiership ladder.) E. D. Scott was a boxer who used his brains in the ring. That enabled him as a light heavyweight to put the heavyweight Kenneth Francis Cole on the canvas for the count of ten in the final of the boxing championship. I remember Carl Keppel always took a ringside seat for the boxing contests. I can see him now, in my mind's eye, chewing the back of his hand with his teeth as the two boxers exchanged blows. E. D. Scott did not need to be told that the Lord would uphold those that fall. E. D. Scott was not a faller, or a stumbler, or one of those who could not stop. I looked at him with awe. I wondered that the man within could be so quiet. I was puzzled by the difference between Don Sandy and E. D. Scott.

There was a bizarre coda to this story. Not long after the end of the Second World War, Charlie Howlett visited us in our home at Croydon in Victoria. It was a hot north wind day, so hot that perspiration ran down Charlie Howlett's face as he spoke. I had always been fond of Charlie Howlett. As a young master at Melbourne Grammar School he had been very comforting to me when I could not manage. I had always put him on my list of those 'not of the marrying kind'. I was wrong: Charlie married very happily, and was as kind to his wife as he had been to all the outsiders at Grammar. Charlie, when he got going, was a non-stop talker. That day in Croydon he told us about the last days of E. D. Scott.

'You were always interested in E.D. [as we called him] weren't you, Manning?' I gave a shy 'Yes', I was. 'Well, did you ever hear of what happened to him during the war? You knew he was killed on one of the islands off the south coast of Java?' 'Yes. I knew that.' 'Well, did you hear how E.D. died? No one knew until recently, but it turns out that one of the boys he was at school with was there when it all happened. When a party of Japanese captured him, their officer slapped E.D. on the face. E.D. knocked him out. That was E.D.'s last punch. Another officer shot him dead.'

Charlie Howlett only paused for a moment. A shadow passed over his eyes. Within a minute those eyes were again full of light. 'But I haven't told you who the man was who watched it all? You'll never guess. It was Don Sandy.' So Don Sandy lived on, and E. D. Scott fell. By then I was interested in the problem of desert. I could not fit E. D. Scott's death into either the Greek or the Christian views about desert. I was glad Don Sandy survived. He had always been magnificently alive. Years later I opened the *Age* one morning and saw in its social page a photo of Don Sandy, top hat in his right hand, left hand holding the hand of his bride, standing on the steps of St Patrick's Cathedral in Melbourne. Don Sandy, in the eyes of those initiated into 'Grammar and that sort of thing' was at last wearing the right clothes, but he was outside the wrong church. By then the blinkers of childhood had fallen from my eyes, and I felt glad that Don Sandy also seemed to have stopped trying to obey the rules of Yarraside. Perhaps he never had.

By then I was also puzzled by what had happened to the boys I had known at the school, why two whom I remember with great affection, two to whom the gods had been generous with their gifts, had died in the war. I could not believe that any loving god would want to take Jock Ross and John Lander away from us. They should live on. Why should their beauty be consumed, snuffed out? I also could not understand the fate of Chester Wilmot. In 1930, the year when he was captain of the school, we talked briefly to each other outside the lavatory backing on to Domain Road. I had heard him debate, had sat there astounded that any human being could pour out words, long words, words which I had never heard before. Now here he was washing his hands and telling me, one of his adorers, that one day he would be the first Labor Prime Minister of Australia who had been at Melbourne Grammar. I believed him. Ten years after Charlie Howlett told me about the death of E. D. Scott, Chester Wilmot was killed when the Comet in which he was travelling from Rome to London exploded in the air. Once again I could not fit together the great jigsaw puzzle of what happens to human beings. By then I had started to write *A History of Australia*, and this question of desert was very much in my mind. Was what I had been told as a child true: there is one event unto all? By then I wanted to know why most human beings find it difficult to believe that what is happening to them is what they deserve; few accept that. They blame others, and make themselves more wretched. By then I was coming out of the fog of anger in which I thrashed around as a child. I was beginning to view all human beings with the eye of pity and the eye of love – but that is to anticipate.

All I knew at the time was that the masters stood over me in the classroom, as did the Long Dorm in the boarding house. The Long Dorm was in charge of those parts of behaviour which did not come under the masters or the prefects. The masters and the prefects administered the law, the Long Dorm the lore of the tribe. They were the guardians of the unwritten commandments:

Thou shalt attend and barrack at all school or house games.
Thou shalt not wear brown shoes with a blue suit.
Thou shalt not wear shoes with pointed toes.
Thou shalt not have a 'nana' hair cut, i.e., allow the barber to shave the
    back of the neck so that the bottom of the hair becomes a straight
    line, &c, &c, &c.

Penalty: a summons to appear in the Long Dorm, dressed in pyjamas, and be interrogated while standing on the cupboard containing the 'piss pot', and then to be told the number of 'unders and overs' to be performed while being belted with knotted towels – then the dismissal, after a confession of regret at the sin against the lore of the school and a promise not to sin again.

They succeeded. I do not remember any rebels, any martyrs, or anyone – either master, boy or parent – saying that this bullying on questions of behaviour was a disgrace, that it should stop immediately. I wondered at the time whether Lofty knew, and if he did why he did nothing about it. I wondered whether I should tell him, weaving as I did a picture of myself as the saviour of I knew not quite what against barbarians like Nuer. But I knew then that betrayal was the Long Dorm's sin against the Holy Ghost, the sin which they would never forgive, and maybe the sin for which one would never forgive oneself. Years later there was a whole sackful of thoughts and deeds for which I wanted to, but never could forgive myself. Thank God I never succumbed to the temptation to be the saviour. That would have meant being a Melbourne Grammar 'Flying Dutchman'.

I wondered if one of the chaplains knew about it – I remember there was one young assistant chaplain who looked as though he might understand. I knew that chaplains were forbidden to reveal sources of information given to them in confidence. But whenever I saw this young disciple of Christ talking in the quadrangle he was always laughing and joking with the principal bullies. I could not understand why he seemed so anxious to ingratiate himself with the agents of terror, why their approval seemed to mean so much to him. He always bubbled over with delight when swapping jokes with the boys who wore the expensive suits and high quality shirts. I can see him even now, tossing brand-new tennis balls into the air, and cracking his racquet against his cream trousers, and releasing a high-pitched giggle of ecstasy as he said to his fellow-player, 'Let's go', as they swept off together towards the tennis courts. I decided then that it was no good speaking to him: his mind was on other things. Anyhow, what would I say? How would I start? Whenever I had tried to get words out about my pain, the masters and the chaplains interrupted me, or soft-soaped me by changing the subject, or threw out hints that the 'nervy' were unreliable, unsteady, even potential traitors to what the School stood for. Judas Iscariot, I gathered, was not a good member of the team. Judas never got things quite straight.

I remember one Sunday evening the organ was played by William McKie, an old boy of the School and soon to be organist for the city of Melbourne. After evensong, for the procession led by the choristers, the headmaster, the masters, the prefects and the chaplains, he played a solo. It sounded like the music for a triumphal procession, the music appropriate for the wisest and the best, for boys who were reaching for the stars. On such occasions I rarely heard the music: my mind was generally on the much more worldly problem of how to get to the supper table before the other boys so that I would get at least one and possibly even two biscuits to fill some of the empty spaces in my stomach.

This night the music was stronger than hunger. I stood on the top step outside the chapel, one voice inside me clamouring for food, the other hypnotised by the music. Soul wanted one thing, body another. That night soul won. I waited until the organist, gowned and hooded and capped, walked down the chapel aisle, the sound of the leather soles of his shoes on the tiled floor letting me know he was near. When the door opened I asked him what he had just played. He said it was the 'Passacaglia in C minor' by Bach. He might as well have spoken in a foreign tongue. But, perceiving my embarrassment at my ignorance, my sense of being an intruder in the gardens of Paradise, he tried to put me at my ease by adding, 'At least you know what you like.' I could not speak. I wanted to ask him why there could be such beauty, such exaltation in a place where there was also a Long Dorm. We stood there in a shaft of light edged out against the surrounding darkness. I wanted to speak to him about many things. Why then did we not speak?

Years later the memory of the scene teased out a question in my mind: What did it matter if there was so little light in which a man could stand up? That was during the years when life had persuaded me that some prefer the darkness to the light. Now I think of the scene as one of many experiences where two human beings should have said something, but the lore and conventions of Melbourne Grammar, of Yarraside, kept us apart. It was many years since William McKie had been baptised with soap and water and sundry flicks of the towel into the one true Church of Yarraside, outside which there is no salvation for those who are reaching for the top. The world of Yarraside belongs to them. Hell belongs to the damned, Heaven to the angels with a vision of God's throne, and Melbourne to those who conform to the lore of the bourgeoisie. They have decreed: thou shalt have no other lore but ours. Those of the Long Dorm were the guardians of the lore of the tribe at Melbourne Grammar. They enforced the tyranny of opinion, the tyranny of behaviour. They held no formal position, held no legitimate power. Lofty, the masters, the Council, and the prefects hold power *de jure*, but *de facto* the members of the Long Dorm were the standards laboratory, and the enforcers of those standards.

I am bewildered. I try to conform, try to be accepted by doing those things which are pleasing in their sight. But I am ill at ease in their presence. I can never belong to them. Yet there is a temptation to conform, and win the glittering prizes of success. In the chapel we sing the words about looking upwards to the skies where 'such a light affliction shall win you such a prize'. This is an affliction I can never endure. Other outsiders at the School discover how to survive. Nigs Tartakover clowns his way into acceptance. Nigs is lucky. He is an elusive half-forward flanker at football. Nigs can make them laugh, and later can put a torpedo punt through the big sticks from fifty to sixty yards out. Nigs can 'bear the dark blue flag to glory'. So – Grammar to the fore, and Nigs to the fore.

Nature also has been kind to me. THEY are astonished. The 'ickle man' who is 'quite a poet' can hit a cricket ball out of the ground. THEY are astonished. THEY do not know what I know, that the 'ickle man' has told a lie. He has told the captain of the under-fifteen team, Mervyn Austin, later a Rhodes Scholar and a Professor of Classics at the University of Western Australia, that he opened the batting for the First Eleven at Mont Albert Central School. In truth I was their wicket-keeper, and always sent in last. But during the summer holidays I had read a book by H. Sutcliffe, M. Tate and H. Strudwick on how to play cricket. Sutcliffe repeated what Bill Ponsford has told us at the Hawthorn cricket ground: there are only two strokes in cricket, playing forward and playing back, both of which must be performed with a straight bat. So that summer I practised the straight bat in front of the tall mirror in my mother's wardrobe. 'What are you doing, Mann dear?' she asked. 'Why can't you go outside?' I also rehearse the late-cut, the square-cut, the cover-drive, the leg-glance, the hook and the pull, like a ballet dancer at the barre. I reminded myself that it was not physical strength, it was all in the timing, bat, wrists, arms, trunk, hips and legs working in harmony. I taught myself the 'flick of the wrists', keeping the left eye above the ball at that moment when bat strikes ball, keeping the head down – and discipline, discipline, discipline, restraint, self-control, knowing oneself. I was applying the teaching of the Greeks on life to the game of cricket.

The hours spent in front of the mirror, and the lie, brought their reward. Luck also played a part. In the third term of that year the coach of the First Eleven, 'Tickle' Turner, happened to walk around the ground where the under-fifteens were playing just as I hit a medium-pace bowler straight back over his head for six. Tickle stayed on to watch. I played up to him: I showed off all I had learned. At the end of the innings he asked me, 'Where did you learn to play like that, son?' I did not risk telling him it all started with a lie about past performances. Tickle was an old Digger – one did not own up to lies to an old Digger. By the end of the year I found myself in the House Third Eleven, batting with boys three or four years older than myself – batting with some members of the Long Dorm, playing on their side, secretly hoping that playing with a straight bat, cutting, glancing, driving, pulling and hooking, will make me one of them, that there will be no more of those rites with the soap and water.

That was all make-believe. The expressions on their faces did not go away. They were everywhere. Even on the cricket field they set themselves up as my judges. They all wore 'creams'; I wore 'whites'. They chided me for my habit of spinning the bat in my left hand just before facing up to the bowler. They ridiculed my graceful movements. Nuer said, 'Our "ickle man" thinks he is a poet with a bat.' They all laughed. They were everywhere. The captain, Peter Dawson, one of the school prefects, was kind to me. He asked me why I was so 'nervy', saying he wished he had half my talent. I did not dare to look pleased, because I knew by then that anyone puffed up with pride would have that knocked out of them quick smart on the soapy table, or running the gauntlet through the wet-towel men in the Long Dorm.

The faces of the Long Dorm boys will never go away. They become long-term members of my nightmare world. I think of them as the ones to whom Australia belongs, the types who rule Australia. I never know heart's ease in their presence. For me they are everywhere. It does not matter which group or which society – capitalist, communist, or fascist – they are the self-appointed standards men. They wield the wet towel. I recognise them in many parts of the world. I see them walking round the corridors of Congress in Washington in the late fall of 1963. I see them in a painting of the Boers as I walked on the pavement outside Parliament House in Cape Town in 1978. Five years earlier in Novosibirsk, I had seen them in the faces of the young men attending a school for the training of party officials. I see them in King's Hall in Canberra. I see them in the faces of the men who make the successful takeover bid for the government of Australian universities.

I also know, but this, alas, very rarely, as it does not happen very often, that moment of moments when my eyes meet another pair of eyes, and there is instant recognition: that mystery of mysteries why those who have suffered from the Long Dorm are always attracted to each other, why they always recognise each other, why that bond transcends all offences the one may commit against the other. Yet I, one of their victims, sang with gusto the boarders' song, and looked at the boys around me as though we had all been in love with each other:

> You ought to be a boarder
> For a week or two.
> You work all day,
> You get no pay,
> You're fed on Irish stew.
> The potatoes they are rotten,
> And the meat it walks to you.
> You ought to be a boarder
> For a week or two.

I, too, saved up enough money to buy peaches and cream and ice-cream, and join other boys of my age for that treat at the end of tea on Saturday night. I ran down the stairs with them, and out into the quadrangle, and looked for a moment at the stars, and thought everything was really all right: there was order and justice in the world, and one day there might be love, and wisdom and understanding.

In 1928, at the age of thirteen, I heard an American musical comedy star sing about love in the musical comedy *Good News*, at the Princess Theatre in Melbourne. She looked very tiny to a young boy looking down from 'the gods'. She cast her eyes down, raised them suddenly, to the row where we boarders were sitting (yes, I was silly enough then to think, or at least to hope, that she was singing to me). A man on stage said, 'Those who are lucky at cards are never lucky in love', to which she replied by singing:

> Lucky in love,
> Lucky in love,
> What else matters if you're lucky in love?

I knew nothing of that longing at the time. I sensed she knew about a different kind of suffering, of loving someone who only liked you, or felt about you like a sister to a brother. But her melancholy and my melancholy were blown away by a pop song about 'Good News':

Good news is welcome to me.
Bad news is Hell come truly.

The whole atmosphere of Melbourne Grammar, the Church of England world, the ethos of the times, was all to direct our hearts and minds towards the 'good news'. We were British, we had a King who cared about us, we had a Prime Minister, Stanley Bruce, who was looking after us. He was an O.M. (Old Melburnian) and therefore knew 'what's what'. All the popular music was about being happy. At the talking pictures I heard an American sing:

Don't bring a frown to old Broadway
For you must clown on Broadway.
Your troubles there are out of style,
For Broadway always wears a smile.
A million lights they flicker there,
A million hearts beat quicker there.
No skies are grey on that great white way.
That's the Broadway melody.

On the wireless and on the gramophone I heard the songs which summed up the spirit of the decade:

I want some mon-n-n-ey.
Give me some, give me some do.

It all sounded so simple:

I want to be happy,
But I can't be happy
Till I make you happy too.

Fun was the thing. Luna Park was there 'Just for Fun'. One song reflected the frantic search for a thrill:

I still get a thrill
Thinking of you.

For those who failed, those who did not arouse any response
in what was called

The object of my affection
Can change my complexion
From white to rosy red,
Any time she holds my hand,
And tells me that she's mine.

there was an easy escape:

Let's do the shakeaway,
Get hot and breakaway.
. . .
Write a little note with your toes,
Don't forget to dot the I.
Look at what you wrote,
Goodness knows,
It's easy as pie.

There was a theatre night each term. In second term in 1928
we hopped on to the tram again, then walked up to Her Majesty's
in Exhibition Street, and climbed up to 'the gods', this time to see
The Desert Song. That night I heard a man dressed in the robes
of a sheikh sing with passion the words: 'One love alone/Is *not*
for men.'

That puzzled me, because the Prayer Book, I knew, asked the
bridegroom to take the vow to forsake all others. But I could not
ask anyone at Melbourne Grammar to solve the puzzle for me. Our
housemaster, 'Spuddo' Giles, was not the marrying kind. One master
I quite liked was said to be very bitter about women. We had
explanations for everything except what I wanted to know.

After the theatre I imitated the principal actor and the principal
actress to a circle of boys, who giggled and called for more until
one of the Long Dorm, maybe it was my tormentor Nuer, interrupted
my act and told them to gales of laughter that I really should have
been a girl. For me, that meant another night tossing on the bed,

savouring what I should say to Nuer next time he held me up to ridicule. By then I was used to such nights.

Life at the school was often a free theatre show. A shell-shocked clergyman at the school gulped down alcohol to shield him against an attack of the horrors. One morning in the chapel the clergyman, in a rather unsteady voice, got as far as the phrase 'for Jesus Christ's sake'. He paused, then said, 'Christ Jesus', then more hurriedly, 'Jesus Christ', until he let out an hysterical laugh and was led away from the altar by the other officiating clergyman. We were all delighted by this comedy in front of the altar. Boys have no sympathy with the tormented: they take vicarious pleasure in the sport of the tormentors.

We were pleased when Lofty told us the unsteady clergyman needed a rest, and that he would be back with us very soon. We did not have to wait for long. One evening there were sounds of an axe striking a 'reproduction' oak door (Melbourne Grammar was never the genuine article, it being in most ways imitation English) and a drunken voice, which we all recognised as that of the clergyman who had had trouble with the words 'Jesus Christ', could be heard shouting somewhat incoherently, 'I'm going to chop down this door before I leave the place.' We scampered to the place from which the noises were coming, and saw the clergyman's huge bulbous eyes, the eyes of a frightened horse, the sunken cheeks – a pitiable figure making a pitiable protest against a system which had no sympathy with and little understanding of misfits and weaklings. The clergyman did not belong to 'Grammar and that sort of thing': the clergyman was an outsider. He had to go.

Not long after this bizarre event I was sitting near an Old Boy who was standing close to the boxing ring. His two hands were holding firmly on to the two arms of a hunting stick to steady him. He was swaying gently from side to side. His clothes, especially the handkerchief tucked into his top left-hand coat-pocket in the shape of a fluffy pyramid, snowy white, and looking as though it were there for display rather than for use, and the stick with its highly polished fittings, established him immediately as a member of Yarraside. Another man, also dressed by Henry Buck, or some Collins Street tailor, greeted him, 'Hello old chap, how are you?' To which 'old chap' replied, 'Shickered as an owl.' Everyone around us laughed that unmistakable laughter of the approvers. There was no suggestion that 'old chap' would 'have to go', or, at the least, be asked to keep out of the school grounds. 'Old chap' belonged. Besides, 'old chap' was so amusing: even in his cups he was the perfect gentleman. I was fascinated by his elegance, the aristocratic cast of his face, and the confidence with which he confronted the world.

It was all becoming too much for me. I remember later reading a remark by Dostoevsky: 'God sets us nothing but riddles and we must solve them as best we can.' There was so much I did not understand. Later I believed that we were all pitifully equipped to handle the problems of life, but that was just another ducking away from the truth. The test is whether a man can face the truth about himself, who he is, and what made him that manner of man. Years later I was also tempted to believe the remark about the hand of the potter, 'The hand of the potter faltered', or the variant, 'Thou, Lord, art the potter and we are thy clay.'

I began to falter. One day in 1929 in a Latin class conducted by Harold Hunt, I was asked to report to the headmaster. But I did not get as far as the door of the classroom. My arms and my legs did not move, my mouth opened wide and would not shut. Petrified, not having any idea what it was, I asked Harold Hunt to hold me up. But before he could reach me I fell to the floor. Dear, kind Harold Hunt put his arm around me, and lifted me up, and whispered to me I would be all right, I was just becoming too 'nervy'. Some boys laughed. Harold Hunt, his brow furrowed, told them to shut up, that this was serious.

Harold Hunt took me to see Lofty, he of the kindly eyes, the man to whom I always believed you could tell everything. But that was the whole point. I either could not or would not speak about the tempest in my soul. He asked me whether there was anything I was worried about. I said no, there wasn't. He asked me, 'Have you noticed anything different about yourself lately?' I assume now he was referring to adolescence. Again I said no, I hadn't; that was true too. Lofty was kind. Lofty did not pin me down. He was not acting as counsel for the prosecution. Lofty did not say to me what he was reported to say to other boys, 'Well, others have.' As I left his room he put his arm around me, and said the best thing was to wait and see what happened. It may not happen again.

It did. It would not go away. Nothing I did seemed to make the slightest difference. I had no control over when and where it revisited me. I prayed. I had been told, 'The Lord shall uphold all that fall.'

But, alas, He did not seem to be interested in doing that for me. It continued. I thought there must be something wrong with a part of my body, that it was like toothache or a headache, or a boil, something which would go away. But it would not go away. The episodes became more frequent. I remember falling down while filing out of the chapel one Sunday morning.

I was sent to dentists, and doctors. They all looked very grave. They said very little to me. They talked about a fat-free diet. One in Spring Street whispered to my father and my mother that there would be no improvement unless I spent a year away. But they would not tell me anything about it – why this was not like any disease or frailty of the body. They all looked so wise – but perhaps they did not know. One of them, Dr Adey, told us, my father, my mother and me, we ought to be relieved to know one thing: it was not *grand mal*, it was *petit mal*, a form of epilepsy which was a common affliction for those with extraordinary imaginations, stormy temperaments, and strange insights into human behaviour. I should think of it not as a badge of infamy, or a handicap, but as a gift which I must treasure, and turn to advantage. He spoke to me very much as my mother had spoken to me on that day in December 1919 when I made the remark about the aeroplane in which Keith and Ross Smith had flown from England to Australia.

That comforted me little at the time. I wanted them to fix me up, to do a quick repair job so that I could play cricket properly without fear of falling down. Again I was like John Bunyan's Mr Passion: I wanted it all now. That was not to be. It took me many years to accept my lot. There were to be wild years in which I nourished the terrible delusion that others may be dirtied in the gutter, but not me. That innocent one who had been wounded by the world, he could never be besmirched. There would be many years in the fog, in which I would hurt many people and be hurt in turn by many others. There was the pleasure, if indeed it was a pleasure, of finding that many distinguished people had been members of the club to which I was to belong till I was well over fifty. There was the need for a mask to protect me against the world, and the world against me, to make sure that only those who understood, only those who would not laugh, ever came near. There was the gradual, the very reluctant acceptance of this flaw in my being – tearing out of my heart the idea that it was all unfair that it should happen to me, or asking why this should happen to me, and punishing everyone for what had happened, for the cross (as it seemed to me) I had to bear. It was many years before I convinced myself that a weakness could be converted into a strength, that a weakness may be the means of getting wisdom and understanding, that a boy's descent into Hell – into what the mystics identify as the 'dark night of the soul' – can nourish the eye of pity, the understanding of all those others who cannot stop. That came very slowly. In the interval there was much doing of what ought not to be done – and I had to find the strength to live with that, to live in the knowledge that one day one must forgive oneself.

At the time my father says not a word. My mother expresses her great grief in another remark which would live with me forever. In childhood she had puzzled me by saying in moments of anguish, 'There are things in my life, Mann dear, I hope you will never know anything about'; now she tells me she is going to pray, she is going to ask the Father, and He will not fail her in her hour of need. But months pass, years pass, and the Father does not come to her aid. The Father does not uphold me when I fall: the Father, who alone worked great marvels, does nothing. My mother begins to cry whenever it happens. Tears stream down her cheeks. She says to me, 'Mann dear, perhaps God is punishing me for what I have done. Perhaps I should not have let you go to Melbourne Grammar.' I do not know what to say. I am in the presence of something I do not understand. My brother tells my mother, 'Don't cry, Mum dear. I can't stand it when you cry.' My father is silent. What, after all, could be said?

Epilogue

My mother died on 31 March 1943. At the two funeral services, one in the church at Mentone and the other at Box Hill cemetery, an archdeacon and an archbishop spoke eloquently of her goodness and her Christian virtues. They were right. But no one spoke of why her beauty had been consumed, like a moth fretting a garment. I heard her saying, 'There are things in my life, Mann dear . . .' I could tell no one of my great grief. My brother asked me to make a demonstration of the Christian faith, to be of good cheer: 'You do believe, Mann, we will see her again.' I was silent. I could not say a word.

My father died on 16 January 1951. Neither in the church nor at the graveside did anyone refer to the huge fire which had once kindled within him. For years afterwards I often dreamed I was standing on the shores of the Styx waiting to be ferried across to the other shore. My father rowed over from that shore, and started to collect bait for fishing. I asked him to help me cross over to the other shore. He replied, 'Boy, that is the one journey you must make by yourself.' The teaching in Melbourne, Canberra and Harvard, the books on the history of Australia, the book on Henry Lawson, and the short stories, are all interim reports on that journey.

A Short History of Australia   Manning Clark

In this lively, very readable book, the eminent and controversial historian Manning Clark portrays the evolution of Australia with remarkable breadth of vision.

He begins with the Aborigines and the coming of white men, then traces the progress of the First Fleet to Botany Bay, the unfurling of the British flag in January 1788 to the accompaniment of a regimental band, and Governor Arthur Phillip's harangue to the convicts in his charge.

With a provocative style the author describes convicts and settlers, architecture, exploration, immigrants and squatters, politics and culture, the gold rushes, radicals and nationalists, the world wars. The incisive concluding chapter deals with the years from 1969 to 1986 – Manning Clark's 'age of ruins'.

This elegantly written and well illustrated book brings to life the people and events that have shaped Australia's history.

Collected Short Stories   Manning Clark

Growing up at Phillip Island, solemn moments in church, memories of school, confrontations in academe, fishing with a son – this is the stuff of the short stories of the historian Manning Clark.

This collection contains those stories originally published as *Disquiet and Other Stories* together with the later 'A Footnote to the Kododa Story' and 'A Diet of Bananas and Nietzsche'.

Stirring the Possum   James McClelland

From his days as a young Trotskyist in the 1940s – secretly in love with an enemy Stalinist – to his role in the 1980s as commissioner in an inquiry into the Maralinga nuclear tests, Jim McClelland has been known as a stirrer.

In his autobiography he offers us a perspective on Australian politics spanning fifty years. His critical assessment of public figures and events is both humourous and acerbic; his account of a distinguished and varied career reflects his energy, his sharp mind and his unfailing capacity to 'liven things up'.

Solid Bluestone Foundations   Kathleen Fitzpatrick

This 'magnificent book of memories', as Manning Clark has called it, represents the life of Melbourne historian Kathleeen Fitzpatrick. Growing up in Australia in the 1920s, in a world fragmented by religion and class differences, Kathleen came to associate the bluestone foundations of her grandparents' home with the security and abundance she needed. Later Melbourne University with its bluestone foundations became her source of 'constant enrichment'. Kathleen Fitzpatrick's delightful autobiography is itself a rich source of wisdom and wit.

Autobiography of My Mother   Meg Stewart

This unusual biography of Australian artist Margaret Coen is not only an intimate portrait of a woman determined to be a painter at a difficult time for women, but also a fascinating portrayal of Australia's lively literary and artistic world from the 1930s onwards.

Accidental Chords   Patricia Thompson

In a style both earthy and urbane, Patricia Thompson tells a simple story; her childhood in staid Auckland; her youth in 'jazz age' Sydney; the adventures of young womanhood in brilliant London; the grey world of maddeningly complacent Perth, and, finally, her discovery of Paddington, Sydney, which she and her poet husband John set about rescuing from the urban dumps. Through the book runs a vein of outrageous fun, especially in the figure of her zany mother Grace, and her four husbands. But there is a darker side to Patricia's life, the shadow cast by her dominating mother, the shadow she never quite managed to overcome.

PENGUIN – THE BEST AUSTRALIAN READING

The Penguin Book of Australian Autobiography   John and Dorothy Colmer

A lively and stimulating introduction to more than forty Australians who write of their own lives. They include Kylie Tennant, Patrick White, Joan Lindsay, David Malouf, Henry Lawson, Judah Waten, Charles Perkins, Donald Horne, Albert Facey, Clive James, George Johnston and Mary Gilmore.

Katherine Mansfield   Gillian Boddy

Katherine Mansfield was not only an extraordinary writer, devoted to her work, she was also a woman of great vivacity and strength, who led a brief but fascinating life from her birth in New Zealand to the literary circles of England and Europe. The leading writers of her age, people like Virginia Woolf and D. H. Lawrence, were a constant part of her life.

Gillian Boddy has drawn on her years of research to introduce to us a new Katherine Mansfield, not ethereal as has been the myth, but substantial, alive.

George Johnston   Garry Kinnane

George Johnston is perhaps best known as the author of the best-selling *My Brother Jack*, the classic novel of Australian life that has captured the imagination and affection of thousands of readers. A key aspect of this fascination is with its autobiographical nature: how closely does the novel and its sequels, *Clean Straw for Nothing* and *A Cartload of Clay*, reflect the author's own life-story?

Garry Kinnane's award-winning biography traces the often complex connection between Johnston's art and his life, and shows the process by which Johnston transformed the people, places and events of his experience into literature. The result is a fascinating account of the development of a creative mind, set against the wider backdrop of the Australian post-war cultural establishment.

PENGUIN – THE BEST AUSTRALIAN READING

The Education of Young Donald   Donald Horne

This is the classic autobiography of Donald Horne, the famous Australian who coined the term 'the lucky country'. It is both the personal story of one man in the 1920s and 30s and that of an entire generation.

First published twenty years ago, this edition, revised by the author, is now volume one of an autobiographical trilogy. It provides a perspective on the man who became best-selling writer, innovative editor, university professor, Chairman of the Australia Council, and trenchant social critic.

Confessions of a New Boy   Donald Horne

In this second volume Donald Horne gives a vivid portrait of Australia in the 1940s and his life as an *enfant terrible* at Sydney University; in the brutalising environment of the army; in Canberra where bleak 'provincial inferiorities' dictated things; and finally in the lively world of Sydney journalism, with its myths, legends and heroic figures. Young Donald falls in love, learns how to make mayonnaise, and what shoes to wear with a dark suit; friendships form and fall apart. At the same time we follow his journeyings through the world's greatest novels as he tries to make sense of his life through literature.

He is sometimes foolish, often pretentious or difficult to get along with, but always deeply committed to the priorities of the mind.

Portrait of an Optimist   Donald Horne

This third volume of Donald Horne's memoirs portrays a young man of the 1940s and 50s whose many enthusiasms are awkwardly counterbalanced by an instinct for self-parody. He shifts readily from novelist and Tory activist in an English village to tough and rumbustious Sydney newspaperman. He sees his life as 'a dream where you think you are running but your legs don't work'.

In presenting the uncertainties and triumphs of his younger self, Horne's 'saga of pratfalls' traces the onset of maturity with a sharp eye for the period.